Becoming an Outstanding M

Becoming an Outstanding Music Teacher shows how music teachers can provide a curricular and co-curricular experience to inspire and engage students, deliver memorable music lessons, and give every child access to great music. Drawing on a decade of education research, this book focusses on the three facets of music teaching: performance, composition, and how to listen, understand, and explain.

This practical book argues that the future of music teaching is best assured by filling classrooms with knowledge and with passion, by informing teaching through the intentional use of good research, and by building effective relationships. Exploring what makes music teachers stand out, as well as that which links them with all other teachers, this book covers a vital and diverse range of lesson ideas and practical guidance, including:

- Teaching music through composition

- Making the most of the rehearsal room and directing an ensemble

- How to make the best use of classroom time

- Setting goals, assessment, deliberate practice, and feedback

- Mastery in music

Encouraging all music teachers to reflect upon and develop their craft, this text is essential reading for both newly qualified and experienced music teachers alike.

Martin Leigh is Director of Music at King Edward's School in Birmingham. He has written for *TES*, *Impact*, *Hortus*, and *The Spectator*.

Becoming an Outstanding Teacher
Series Editor: Jayne Bartlett

For a full list of titles see: https://www.routledge.com/Becoming-an-Outstanding-Teacher/book-series/BARTLETT

Becoming an Outstanding Music Teacher

Martin Leigh

Routledge
Taylor & Francis Group

LONDON AND NEW YORK

Designed cover image: © Getty Images

First published 2023
by Routledge
4 Park Square, Milton Park, Abingdon, Oxon, OX14 4RN

and by Routledge
605 Third Avenue, New York, NY 10158

Routledge is an imprint of the Taylor & Francis Group, an informa business

© 2023 Martin Leigh

British Library Cataloguing-in-Publication Data
A catalogue record for this book is available from the British Library

Library of Congress Cataloging-in-Publication Data
Names: Leigh, Martin, 1973- author.
Title: Becoming an outstanding music teacher/Martin Leigh.
Description: First edition. | Abingdon, Oxon; New York: Routledge, 2023. |
    Series: Becoming an outstanding teacher | Includes bibliographical
    references and index.
Identifiers: LCCN 2022042029 (print) | LCCN 2022042030 (ebook) |
    ISBN 9780367631741 (paperback) | ISBN 9780367631734 (hardback) |
    ISBN 9781003112402 (ebook)
Subjects: LCSH: Music teachers–Training of. | Music–Instruction and study.
Classification: LCC MT1.L55 B43 2023 (print) | LCC MT1.L55 (ebook) |
    DDC 780.71–dc23/eng/20220902
LC record available at https://lccn.loc.gov/2022042029
LC ebook record available at https://lccn.loc.gov/2022042030

ISBN: 978-0-367-63173-4 (hbk)
ISBN: 978-0-367-63174-1 (pbk)
ISBN: 978-1-003-11240-2 (ebk)

DOI: 10.4324/9781003112402

Typeset in Melior
by KnowledgeWorks Global Ltd.

For Louise, without whom nothing would be possible.

Contents

Chapter 1

The best job in the world?

Music teachers are different

Music teachers like to think that we are different, and, to a point, we are. As an academic subject, music has a storied history, but an uncertain present; its future is best assured by filling our classrooms with knowledge and with passion, by informing our teaching through intentional use of good research, and by building relationships based on the highest of expectations for all.

But we are also practical musicians. Teachers need to be ready to provide a co-curricular experience which develops character, lays down memories, and affords every child access to great music. This requires of us not only considerable musical skill but also mastery of logistics, as well as a profound sense of social justice and of our societal obligation.

When our practices in the classroom, in the rehearsal room, and in the concert hall inform each other, great things happen: this is the magic you can release as a music teacher.

This book explores what makes music teachers different, as well as that which we have in common with other teachers. Rich deposits of ideas have accumulated in the last few decades: ideas about the craft of teaching and the properties of learning, about how we might help all young people to become the best versions of themselves. The first aim of this book is to explore how those ideas can work in music.

A second intention is to share some practical experiences of how to be a successful music teacher, how to manage the classroom, and how to make the most of the rehearsal room. There are ideas about managing our time, and our colleagues; about how to direct an ensemble, and what to prepare; and about one of the hardest things we have to do – to teach music through composition.

Finally, this book encourages every music teacher momentarily to reflect, to remember, for all its vicissitudes and demands, this is probably the best job in the world.

DOI: 10.4324/9781003112402-1

The best job in the world?

Pablo Casals (1876–1973) is one of the great heroes of twentieth-century music. His was the sort of life out of which myth is made: son of a disciplinarian organist, who taught the young Pablo the violin, flute, and the piano; the chance encounter with an itinerant musician who played something like a rudimentary 'cello made from a broom handle'; the gourd-cello made by his father (Kirk, 1974: 1); the discovery of the Bach 'cello suites', and his 13-year-long study of them before he was willing to play them publicly; the Spanish Court; Queen Victoria and the Crystal Palace; those Bach recordings which still resound; the trio with Cortot and Thibaud; the humanitarian work and support for Spanish republicanism; the Bach Festival at Prades; the Casals Festival in Puerto Rico; concerts in the great chamber of the United Nations and the Presidential Medal of Freedom. The lasting memory of a great musician and a great man is, as Thomas Mann put it, a legacy of 'proud, utterly incorruptible integrity' (Kirk, 1974: 557).

It's probably because of Casals that 'cellists today play the Bach suites, the Haydn and Dvořák Concertos, too; yet I'm not quite sure that even this is his greatest legacy. For his life was centred on teaching, learning, and performing, and he saw no distinction between the three. He worked hard throughout his life, rising early to play Bach, to practise and study; worked hard – 'I practise as if I am going to live a thousand years' – because he loved what he did, 'the steady, unrelenting steps to further refinement, towards the perfection that is always just a step beyond' (Kirk, 1974: 524). This love of subject, and the constant possibility of improvement, can make a job seem like no job at all, the best in the world.

One of the problems with writing about Casals is that he was also skilled with words, often repeating and refining the same aphorisms and tales: people listened when he spoke because there was in them both profound wisdom and great entertainment. People listened, and people tended (and still tend) to invent things that he should have said (Kirk, 1974; Baldock, 1992). Some of the quotations here are used without scholarly apparatus, attributed to Casals, simply because to the author they have the ring of truth about them, because their veracity is in tune with the honesty and insight of his playing. Listen to the Bach recordings, and you will understand.

Casals was capable of the most disarming, hopeful belief in the potential of humanity, in particular in the limitless capacity of children:

> Each second we live is a new and unique moment of the universe, a moment that will never be again. And what do we teach our children? We teach them that two and two make four, and that Paris is the capital of France. When will we also teach them what they are? We should say to each of them: Do you

know what you are? You are a marvel. You are unique. In all the years that have passed, there has never been another child like you. Your legs, your arms, your clever fingers, the way you move. You may become a Shakespeare, a Michelangelo, a Beethoven. You have the capacity for anything. Yes, you are a marvel. And when you grow up, can you then harm another who is, like you, a marvel? You must work, we must all work, to make the world worthy of its children.

(Kirk, 1974: 551–2)

At the end of his life, this great music teacher, whose influence still echoes today, begins with a near-naïve belief in the possibility of children, and in what they might achieve. This altruistic optimism, this desire to better the world, is one of the essences of teaching. We are altruists because we seek to give to others, and we know that, although there are limits to what an individual teacher – even Casals – can achieve, there are no limits, none whatsoever, on what our pupils might go on to do.

And there's growing support for our optimism, for our belief that habits, dispositions, and knowledge do make a difference. That our habits form moral character is an idea which comes directly from Aristotle – every morning Casals practised both humility and Bach, what he might have called a benediction on the house – and it's becoming more and more established as an essential part of what great teachers do (Bernacer & Murillo, 2014; Dweck, 2017). There's growing support, too, for the idea that musical knowledge, properly sequenced and practised, is a really powerful and transformative thing – that the pernicious old myths of creative talent serve merely to suppress children's potential rather than release it (Gladwell, 2002; Hirsch, 2019); that, when we teachers get it right, knowledge might even, just possibly, effect a permanent change for the better in the brains of our pupils (Huttenlocher, 2009).

Casals's playing technique was an extraordinary thing. He might have said that the most perfect technique is that which is not noticed at all, but his method is not at all like otherworldly perfection of that other great cellist Daniil Shafran. You can hear on Casals's recordings the strength of his finger finding its place just before he plays, the portamentos used perfectly to illuminate the musical line, the habit of tuning a note according to its harmonic function, his 'expressive tuning' (Cherniavsky, 1952). These are fascinating insights, but not the whole:

Technique, wonderful sounds ... all of this is sometimes astonishing – but it is not enough.

(Blum, 1980: 1)

The best job in the world?

When you watch a master at work, the effect can be overwhelming. To be in the classroom with a master teacher can be too much for many of us, the sense that we can never achieve anything even close. The lesson from Casals is that greatness comes from the painstaking attention to the tiny details of a craft, from analysis and thinking hard, from 'splitting every note to the infinite' (Cherniavsky, 1952: 400). The best job in the world is one which absorbs the one who holds it, absorbs because inherent in it is the relationship between effort and reward. Music teachers work hard, yes, but in our everyday work, in the cycle of rehearsal, performance, teaching, and our own study, we see improvement and development, perhaps more so than any teacher of any subject. When we remember to take a moment to look back on what we've helped children to achieve, then we remember why this is a great job.

Technique, the craft of teaching, like any other skill, can be practised, honed, and developed; and, for Casals, it's astonishing – but it is not enough. The most skilful teaching is not quite enough without a real understanding of the subject and a sense of the wonder of it all. We can none of us know it all, but there needs to be something about which we can speak to our pupils with authority and passion, whether the symphonies of Shostakovich, or the qualities and methods of great ensemble-playing, or the oeuvre of Taylor Swift. And we should have, more generally, a clear understanding of what to teach, when to teach it, and in what order.

But even that's not the final word. Casals again gets us closer, when he says, don't play the notes, play the meaning of the notes. The meaning of it all. We became musicians because of the wonder of music, the unknowable mysteries of the way sound-in-time can move us, can make us feel as others do, can transport us to distant times and distant places (Nettl, 2000). The ideas behind music – about what it means to be human, how we think and what we think about – are ultimately unknowable; but trying to find out is a pretty good way for a teacher to live.

This wonder of music, the wonderful ways in which it works, is the subject of the next chapter.

References

Baldock, R., 1992. *Pablo Casals*. London, Victor Gollancz.

Bernacer, J. & Murillo, J.I., 2014. The Aristotelian Conception of Habit and Its Contribution to Human Neuroscience. *Frontiers in Human Neuroscience*, 8, 883.

Blum, D., 1980. *Casals and the Art of Interpretation*. London, University of California Press.

Cherniavsky, D., 1952. Casals's Teaching of the Cello. *The Musical Times*, 93(1315), 398.

Dweck, C., 2017. *Mindset: Changing the Way You Think to Fulfil Your Potential*. London, Hachette.

Gladwell, M., 2002. The Talent Myth. The New Yorker, 22(2002), 28–33.

Hirsch, E.D., 2019. *Why Knowledge Matters: Rescuing Our Children from Failed Educational Theories*. Harvard, Harvard Education Press.

Huttenlocher, P.R., 2009. *Neural Plasticity*. Harvard, Harvard University Press.

Kirk, H.L., 1974. *Pablo Casals*. London, Hutchinson.

Nettl, B., 2000. An Ethnomusicologist Contemplates Universals in Musical Sound and Musical Culture. *The Origins of Music*, 3(2), 463–472.

Chapter 2

How music works

When a pupil comes into my classroom for the very first time, a year 7 with an outsized uniform and unlimited hopes, there stands before him a world of musical possibility. It's my job as a teacher to show him that nothing in that world is beyond him.

Music is a mysterious thing, its power veiled from view; an art-form which seems constantly to hover, just beyond our comprehension. If you compare it with the other arts, with visual arts in particular, then the mystery is immense. A painting hangs in the gallery, available to its audience at a single glance; you walk around a sculpture, its presence physical and tangible. In literature, even a novel or a poem allows, it seems, direct contact between writer and reader. A piece of music, however, is immanent in us, yet paradoxically, constantly beyond our reach.

Whether that year 7 is destined to be a great composer, or musical *refusenik*, whether to roam (or bestride) the musical world, or by choice to shun it entirely, the duty of a music teacher is first to educate listeners.

In his remarkable little book, *What to listen for in Music*, Aaron Copland seeks to 'put down as clearly as possible the fundamentals of intelligent music listening' (Copland, 1957: vii). The listener, he says, has laid upon them a serious responsibility to understand the composer, to collaborate with and correct the interpreter, and to nurture and propagate 'the future of music' (Copland, 1957: 163). A healthy musical future involves listeners of cultured and catholic experience, who listen, without preconception, to music from every place and of every time, who seek to understand more about the origin of each work, and the intentions of its creators.

From his own perspective as a master-composer, Copland tells us that the sole resource of any composer, their only message, is their own self. 'He [the composer] gives us, without relation to exterior "events," the quintessential part of himself – that part which embodies the fullest and deepest expression of himself as a man and of his experience as a fellow being' (Copland, 1957: 158). In language and intellectual concept, this is a message of its time (written in 1937), and I'm not

DOI: 10.4324/9781003112402-2

sure that I completely agree with either its expression or its metaphysics, but it's still a truly valuable idea for every teacher in every time.

We need our charges, thus, to understand the 'deepest expression' of the best of musicians: the faithful mastery of Bach, the profundity and playfulness of Mozart, Beethoven's rugged insistence on mankind's freedom, the peerless *Innigkeit* of Brahms, the chimerical disguises of Stravinsky, the epoch defining energy of four lads from Liverpool, or Ziggy Stardust, or just plain Mr. Jones. And not just to music of the West does our duty as listeners extend; it spreads 'a girdle round about the earth/In forty minutes', from the great kora masters of Mali and Senegal, the limitless bounds of the *rāga*, the community of the Gamelan, to the *Gagaku* of the Imperial Palace.

We need our charges to understand these things as markers of their and of our humanity, as well to understand our passions for music and for the ideas of music. Note that there's not one word of technique in that last paragraph, neither notation nor theory – just ideas and enthusiasms about individual instances of music, ideas of the composers, their places, their times.

A combination of humanity and passion to start then; a little information comes next. A composer writes, a musician creates, as part of a given epoch, within a given geography (literal or metaphoric); Copland asks us next to understand the notion of musical style. For Copland, this goes rather beyond that useful-but-staid continuum, Renaissance – Baroque – Classical – Romantic – Twentieth-Century, beyond those diligently-studied lists of characteristics and features required by GCSE or by ABRSM examinations. For Copland, it means a sense of what it means to be an individual musician at a particular time, in a particular place, subject to particular ideas.

Copland's example of musical style is Beethoven. He cites the difference between the 1801 composer of the first symphony, a composer steeped in the music of the eighteenth-century, that of Haydn and Mozart and Enlightenment Vienna; to that of the appreciably nineteenth-century heaven-storming wonder of the Ninth. To this example, we might add Bach's phase of instrumental composition at Köthen, his church-music in Leipzig, or the difference between The Beatles's *Please Please Me* and the *White Album*. These are single musical characters, individuals or groups, writing music according to 'whatever is fine in him as a man' and according to the period and geography in which they find themselves (Copland, 1957: 159).

The reason that an understanding of style is important is because music always flows through an interpreter, a performer. The ideas of the composer, half-recorded in musical notation or collective memory, are always filtered by the physical action, personality, and imagination of the player or singer.

There is an immense power in this. How many times do our pupils come to despise a piece, or the work of a composer, or an entire genre, because their first encounter with it is disappointing or dull? In a world where immense riches are available at the merest click of a mouse, how often does an on-line video reflect poorly on the joy, the true power, and the immensity of music's possibilities. The price of these riches is the loss of a presiding authority, the curation of quality by a record company, by the best of A&R, by the BBC. Because most music is immensely hard to perform well, some – opera an instance – nearly impossible. And the vast majority of performances, live and recorded, fall well short of the quality needed to hook a pupil for life.

The solution to this is partly in the hands of the teacher – to become the authority, and curate carefully the listening of their pupils – and partly through an education in style. Copland describes how a composition is neither static nor fixed; how the gaps left in the information provided by any score are sufficient that it can mean quite different things at different times. He suggests that the performer's fidelity is owed simultaneously to the composer and to herself, and this truthful heart is where the life-blood of music flows. Think of the difference between a perfectly-synthesised computer rendition of any composition, accurate and pristine in every regard, and the fallible but feeling performance by any human, let alone by a master at the very apogee of their (re-)creative life.

The ideal listener will have sufficient knowledge of the composer's character, of the times in which the music originated, and of interpretative possibilities. The act of listening – Copland's 'future of music' – becomes then a living three-way interchange between composer, performer, and listener.

To distinguish, to have the confidence to think and judge, to become an attentive and informed listener should be our highest goal and aspiration for every one of those hopeful year 7 pupils. And it's very hard to achieve.

Perhaps the most proven way is to divide the musical arena into six dimensions, consider and teach each separately. And the first of them is rhythm.

Rhythm has your two hips moving

We are rhythmic beings in a rhythmic world. Our hearts beat, the sun and moon rise and set, the tides wash, and the seasons turn. The earliest music must have been – and some of the most modern music is – purely rhythmic. Sound leaves no fossilised record, of course, but we can imagine what those first humans heard. Making patterns in time is one of the ways in which music is music, and this must have been true from the very start of humanity. Ethnomusicology has made an extraordinary world of music available to us, a bewildering richness of traditions:

essential to many of them is a complexity of rhythm Western listeners find hard to comprehend. By a process of induction we can take these findings of richness, sophistication, and unfamiliarity, and travel back in time, begin to imagine what those beginnings might have been.

Rhythm is closely related with the acquisition of the most basic and mysterious of human skills, too. In young children, rhythm has a special relationship with reading, especially with the growing awareness of and discrimination between phonemes; a skill which is at the heart of learning to read. Moritz *et al.* (2013) found that daily music training in pre-school children, especially in rhythm, had a strong correlation with enhanced reading achievement.

Rhythm is, then, universal. It is there at the start of the Western classical tradition. One of the most significant moments in the development of this tradition was when music was first segmented into regularly-repeating metrical units of a specified length – when what we call the bar became widespread. That moment, that invention, somewhere in the twelfth century, made it possible for music to become more-and-more autonomous from words, for rhythm to have its own composed structure, for composers more-precisely to prescribe and communicate their intentions; in short, for musical history to travel as it has. Because of the bar-line and the rhythmic notation it made possible, we can re-create music of the past – a re-creation not without significant limits, but plausible nonetheless; because of rhythmic notation, composers can create contrapuntal or polyphonic music of great complexity; because of rhythmic notation, it's possible for 1,028 players and singers, adults and children to make music together in the 1910 first performance of Mahler's Eighth Symphony (Johnson, 2020).

It makes much possible, but rhythmic notation is not without its compromises and confinements. It fails to capture the subtle shifts in emphasis, the tiny never-to-be-repeated inflections which are at the heart of all great performance – although one might argue that its very lack of precision is the generating possibility which makes such nuance possible in the first place. But bars also serve to lock-in the imagination, and the confinement imposed by rhythmic notation is equally a danger.

In the classroom it also causes a problem of definition and understanding; because tempo, metre, and rhythm are so fundamental to us, so ingrained in who are as musicians, the trio can be very hard to teach. Tempo is the easiest of them; it's a matter of drilling, pupils need instantly to recall that tempo means speed. But metre and rhythm are much more difficult.

Metre, as represented by a time signature, is both the measurement into regularly-repeating units of the music's pulse (beat), and the pattern of stresses and accents associated with those beats. It's the heart-beat of music. Generations of us have been taught that in a 3/4 metre, there is an accent on the first beat of the bar:

| ONE — two — three | ONE — two — three |

This has immense power, whether in the characteristic accompaniment-pattern of the waltz, or, when repeated, in the relentless hypnotic machine of a Bruckner scherzo – a power generated by the limitless repetition of stressed metrical units. It's the power of organised dancing, which itself is made possible by patterns of repetition.

The difference between metre and rhythm is the difference between the left- and right-hand parts of, say, a waltz by Chopin. The left-hand part is outwardly simple, unchanging, ONE — two — three; the right hand sings a melody of long-breathed and exquisite subtlety, related but seeming-independent.

Rhythm, then, is the way a composer groups music in time, the way duration and accent is controlled. It is contained within the metre (possibly circumscribed by it) but it has the capacity to move beyond it. An analogy might help here, a little poetic literacy-programme:

Spellink by Dr. Leigh

Staccato has two Cs,
But clef has just one F;
A chord has but one H,
But harpsichord has two.

Please don't mention rhythm …

You can read the first stanza here as the iambic doggerel it is:

stac-Cato Has two Cs,
but Clef has Just one F;
a Chord has But one H,
but HarpsiChord has Two.

Or you can read it much more as prose, reflecting the nuanced rhythms of speech and meaning (even if the verse is slightly lacking):

Staccato has two Cs, but clef has just one F; a chord has but one H, but harpsi-chord has two.

The rigid doggerel reflects the unthinking confinement of metre; the nuanced speech is rhythm. The two are quite inextricably related, but different.

Asking pupils to define rhythm is one of the hardest questions in the classroom, it's nearly unkind so to do. Part of its unkindness lies in the way we teach rhythm.

There are two quavers in each crotchet, two semi-quavers in each quaver. In schools the world over, the branches of the rhythm-tree are drawn on the board and in pupils' books. We test whether or not they understand that there are, thus, four semi-quavers in each crotchet (and that they remember to spell the word with the letter t both in the middle as well as at the end). This suggests that a bar can be divided in rather limited ways; a bar in 4/4 metre divided most-probably into quavers grouped 2 + 2 + 2 + 2.

This is the two-fold confinement of metre: that pupils need to be exposed to enough music to grasp that the rhythmic outline of a great deal of Western classical music is very simple indeed, with the bar at its heart; at the same time, they need to be taught that the expressive possibilities of rhythm are limitless. The problem in the curriculum is that internalised knowledge of the first is necessary to lead directly to the second. To suggest that the eight quavers of a 4/4 metre might be divided 3 + 2 + 3 without the context of three hundred years of glorious music renders it meaningless – you need to understand the rule, know the convention, before you can break or transcend it.

This is the case still more when one comes to polyrhythm – playing two-against-three in a piece of nineteenth-century piano music, or the immense complexity of African drummers or Chinese or Indian percussionists or of the great jazz players (John Coltrane, anyone?).

Our ideal listener will be know the historical inheritance of rhythm, be comfortable with the familiar; will, at the same time, be open to the new and the different, be confident enough to find, especially in the unfamiliar, boundless interest, engrossing wonder.

We are rhythmic beings in a rhythmic world, but there are other worlds to explore, worlds of emotion and meaning (Copland, 1957: 40).

Melody

Daniel Barenboim talks of the magic of juxtaposition (Barenboim, 2009). A single note, he says, is meaningless, only becomes its true self when placed before or after another. The very act of placing one next to another is the generative moment in music, where melody, where all music begins. For one pair of notes, the relations and connotation between them, leads inevitably to a third, and a fourth, until vast structures and ideas have ramified from that simple moment. It's a musical big bang.

Because its moment of genesis is so individual and so personal, melody is the most emotive of the musical elements. The third note is added to the pair because a composer thinks, feels, and imagines. No sunrises, no tides here, nothing external; melody comes from an individual. Even its limits, where a melody begins and ends, is governed by perception. A melody finds its genesis in a composer's imagination, finds its identity in a listener's perception.

Which is not to say that melody is entirely free, that it is not governed by a system. There are the unwritten rules of length, proportion, internal repetition (coherence), internal contrast (variety), and contour. The greatest melodies, one might argue, tend towards the highest, most intense, most climactic moment at a similar place – at about two thirds of the way through. This seems true of structure, too, the same process operating on two different musical scales, one relatively small, the other quite large. This is a useful aphorism which can help more-experienced young composers to develop the quality of their work.

The properties of a good melody are not easily summarised or taught, rather more are built in pupils through experiment, hard listening, and in judicious and regular feedback from a teacher. If a teacher can help their pupils to know how their melody is good, and why – and what to do to improve it if it is not – then it's possible in time to learn those properties.

There's an important point to be made about the teaching of melody here. Which is if a pupil is to develop skills of critical discernment, to develop the instincts of a composer, then they need to write a great deal, with great freedom, and with regular feedback – feedback from a teacher, possibly from their peers, and eventually from within themselves, by developing an internal sense of perspective and self-evaluation. The blank page is an intimidating thing, and the reason composers write music down is to fill that space. And the reason composers write using pencil (no, an erasable pen will simply not do) is that the most egregious mistakes can be erased – although the most egregious mistakes are often the most creative moments, and should themselves be evaluated, their possibilities explored.

The best way to think about the properties of a great melody, then, is to look under the bonnet of one. This is the melody from the first movement of Mozart's piano sonata KV331, a melody so good that the composer takes it subsequently through a set of variations:

The first characteristic is that the phrase is eight-bars long, divided into two, four-bar halves. The first half finishes on the second degree of the scale (2), implying chord V (the dominant); the second half on the first degree of the scale (1), implying chord I (the tonic). Even if we aspire that our pupils move beyond four-bar periodicity in their music, there is something fundamental in the four-bar unit, something which speaks to us as embodied humans – most of us are lucky enough to have pairs of hands, arms, legs, eyes, and ears, and, after all, as Casals said, two-plus-two makes four.

The second characteristic is repetition, of which there are two types here. The first type of repetition is that which is immediate; the second bar repeats the first but this time down a step, forming a descending sequence:

The third bar begins to do the same, but seems to change its mind at the last minute.

The second type of repetition is that which occurs over a larger structural unit. Mozart's first and second bar are repeated exactly in his fifth and sixth:

It's relatively easy this way to demonstrate melodic balance and proportion, harmonic balance, and internal repetition; but there is a coherence we sense in the greatest of melodies which is much harder to grasp. It's possible to explain this coherence in two ways: first that the melody is working to a long-term scheme, one which goes beyond merely thinking in four-bar units, and; secondly, that it will consistently draw on very a simple, coherent, and limited set of materials. This second is more far-reaching than simple repetition or melodic development.

One way to show both is to strip the flesh of the piece away, and to reveal its skeleton. This is one attempt:

How music works

On the lower stave are the first four bars of Mozart's melody; on the upper is an adapted Schenkerian analysis. Schenker's method sounds very highfalutin, is complex in its particulars, but it's immensely revealing and really quite easy to understand. The upper stave shows that there is a long-term scheme for these first four bars, an initial ascent to the note E in the first bar (the fifth note of an A-major scale, hence E (5), which is then taken-up in the fourth bar – the descending scale from E (5), through D, C sharp, and onto B (2). We observed before that the first four bars end on B (2); this merely expands the observation to explain how we get there.

This is interesting, but not as compelling as the other finding here: that the music draws consistently on the interval of a third. The upper-auxiliary in the melody of the first bar fills-out an ascending third (marked *x* on the example); the second bar elaborates in the same way the interval from B to D (*x*). From the third bar into the fourth the music moves from A, through B, to C sharp – the major third from A to C sharp, filled with the passing-note B (*x'*). The first notes of the first three bars move through a descending major third – C sharp, B, A (*x'*). (As an aside, the third is more-important still, because the bass-line moves in parallel tenths (compound thirds) with this melody.) This coherence is what great music looks like.

The long-term scheme continues in the second four bars, the descent from 5 this time ending on 1 in bar 8. Incidentally, this long-term scheme explains the very odd seemingly-misplaced *sf* accent in bar 7 – Mozart draws the listeners' attention this way to the moment to where the 5 moves to the 4:

Implicit in the foregoing is the knowledge that melodies work within the context of a scale. The first teaching of melody uses either an anhemitonic pentatonic scale (a five-note scale without semi-tones), or the first five notes of a major key (invariably C major). But the sooner pupils begin to understand and make use of the major/minor system of scales, the sooner they can move beyond its limitations.

Scales are contained between a starting note, a tonic, and the same note one octave higher. The Western tuning system divides that octave by semi-tone into twelve, and from the twelve available notes we choose seven for the major scale, distributed in the pattern: tone — tone — semi-tone — tone — tone — tone — semi-tone.

There are properties in this major-key pattern which are essential in the understanding and composition of melodies, and it's important that pupils learn them as soon as possible. The most important property is a pattern of stability and instability within the scale; that the tonic (which appears at both its beginning and its end) is the most important, with the third and the fifth degrees of the scale coming next. The notes in between are pulled up or back down to those three stable notes; in C major, thus:

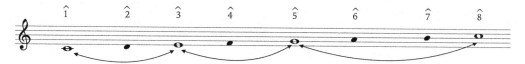

The three stable tones tend to move to the other stable tones: C will move either to E or to G; E to C or to G and so on. The notes between the three stable tones are unstable: D will be part of a movement from C to E or from E to C; either way, it acts like an unstable passing note which tends either to rise or fall by step. Between G and C (or C and G) are two passing notes, A and B, which work in the same way. Being smaller, the movement by a semi-tone is more powerful than the movement by a tone – the B is more likely to rise by semi-tone step to C than it is to fall to A, and the F is more likely to fall by semi-tone step to the E.

It's hard to read about this, but it's easy to explain this in the classroom, particularly to younger pupils: play the tritone from F to B in the context of a C major scale, and the power of the outward-stretching movement is inescapable.

It's important to note that there are different levels of stability and instability, levels which shift in accordance with the prevailing harmony. The stability shown previously applies to the tonic triad – which is the most important, powerful, and ubiquitous chord in any key. But there are different stabilities associated with the dominant triad (the second most important), and the sub-dominant triad (the third).

This system of stability and instability, of hierarchies, sits behind every melody written from the time of the ancient Greeks until the beginning of the twentieth century.

Working through the details of melody is important, because melody itself is important. It's the golden thread we follow through a piece, the way in which a composer helps us in sound to divide and understand the passage of time – the very definition of music. The ideal listener needs to be confident enough to hold on to a melody – whether that melody is an irritating 'ear-worm' implanted on the daily commute or the glistening endlessness of a *Lied* by Richard Strauss – should have made hundreds of melodies their own, and should have enough understanding of their mechanisms and conventions to find in melody a helpmeet and a consolation.

If rhythm is the inescapable core of all music, and melody its emotional and human heart, harmony, then, is its intellect.

Harmony

Our ideal listener will, by now, understand that there is something innate about rhythm, something about melody which is deeply rooted in the human experience: in harmony they will find the inventive genius of the human intellect. Harmony is a product of innovation, and, from its very earliest roots sometime in the ninth century, has continued to develop through deliberate experimentation, by means of imagination and calculation, and through trial, error, and luck. As teachers, we inherit this sum of human achievement, and have a duty to pass on what we can. We also need to understand that our pupils, particularly our pupils' experiments and adventures in composition, are part of this grand and living tradition.

The first harmony started from melody. In its earliest form, the organum voice was the second part added to an existing melody, either a fourth below or a fifth above. The voices move in fixed parallel motion, with just some oblique motion permitted at the end of a phrase. Only perfect intervals were used: thirds and sixths were forbidden. The music of the Notre-Dame school (the two composers' names we know are Léonin and Pérotin) sounds wondrous strange to us, but contains the seeds of everything which comes later – the importance of the perfect intervals, especially of the perfect fifth, the special treatment of the end of phrases.

This is music of the church, written to celebrate especial moments in the liturgical year, composed by master musicians. And it's in the nature of such masters to experiment and innovate. Over time, over several hundred years, the rules were altered; not broken but re-interpreted. Composers found that they could still use only the perfect intervals (fourth, fifth, and octave), but if the voices move in contrary rather than similar motion, a much greater range of effects can be obtained. Some call this discant, but the history is far too distant and murky for us to know this with any certainty. To the importance of perfect intervals (the fifth especially), and the special treatment of the end of phrases, as a result of this phase of musical development, we add the central role of contrary motion in good part-writing.

The final innovation might just have been English, or perhaps not. It's the moment when the forbidden intervals are tasted and found to be good. This involves adding a 'false bass' to a melody, a line which runs in parallel sixths beneath. A third part is customary, a parallel fourth beneath the melody – a third, then, above the 'false bass'. The effect, favoured, it is said, by the English in their improvised performances, is one we recognise, of parallel first-inversion chords. Thirds, and sixths are finally part of our harmonic repertoire.

Everything is now in place: the primacy of perfect intervals, the importance of the ends of phrases, the felicity of contrary motion, and the use of thirds (and their inversions, sixths). Part-writing, and chord progressions based on parallel thirds and sixths, especially parallel first-inversion chords, are now understood.

This should be taught in schools – because mediaeval music, that distant, us-but-not-us world, is a source of life-long fascination for some, and because it is a tremendous opportunity to teach some of the knowledge which is fundamental to harmony.

The basis of harmony

The most fundamental fact in harmony is that everything comes from the bass. Chords are built from the bass upwards, the strength of their relationship one to another derives from the bass, and, when trying to understand someone else's harmony you invariably start from the bass.

Using a scale, chords are built on a bass note (1) using intervals of a third, odd-numbers only: 1 — 3 — 5 — 7 — 9 — 11 — 13 (15=1).

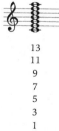

This shows the way in which the horizontal scale becomes the vertical chord; it's also the way in which figured bass works (how to teach it, and why we should).

The upper reaches of this pile of thirds totter somewhat, and, until the last decades of the nineteenth century, composers were mostly content to confine themselves to 1 — 3 — 5, with sometimes use of 7, and of 9, more rarely. But this 1 — 3 — 5 is a conceit of immense power, especially when re-arranged.

In its original, root position, the note upon which the three-note chord is built is in the bass (1 — 3 — 5), but in inversion any of the three notes can appear bottom, middle, or top (1 — 3 — 5; 3 — 5 — 1; 5 — 3 — 1). The lowest note in the configuration determines the inversion (whether the chord is in the root position, the first inversion, or the second inversion), but the chord is still identified by the note upon which it is based (1).

Of course, there are seven different notes in these scales, each of which can become the 1 of a new 1 — 3 — 5. And here is an important source of confusion in the classroom. Each of the seven triads has its own 1 — 3 — 5, and the 1 of chord I is not the same as the 1 of chord II, and so on, up the scale. That roman numerals are used to denote chords, and the Arabic numbers which generate the notes of those chords need constantly to be stressed and re-taught. It helps each time unfailingly to include the word 'chord'.

A hierarchy orders them: that chord I on the first degree of the scale (the tonic) is the most important, the chord V on the fifth (the dominant) the next, and then the sub-dominant (chord IV). This is a hierarchy of importance and function, and, as well, one of ubiquity. In any given composition there are likely to be more tonic chords than there are dominant; more dominant than there are subdominant; and on and on, until, at least in a major key, you reach the poor, unlovely mediant.

Seven three-note chords use twenty-one notes, but there are only seven notes in the major scale. This means that each of the seven notes are used more-than once, and that chords have notes in common. Chord VI, for instance, shares two notes with chord I, immediately suggesting a relationship between the two – one as an alternative to the other. This is the basis of Hugo Riemann's theories of harmonic function – that every chord functions as either a tonic, dominant, or sub-dominant function. It's a concept useful in the classroom when explaining interrupted cadence (VI as an alternative to I, the interrupted cadence as a perfect cadence gone to the dark side), as well as when working out which chords precede a perfect cadence.

We will return to cadences, to parallel movement in thirds and sixths, too; but the importance of the interval of a perfect fifth in generating harmony needs constantly to be stressed. It's the basis of a perfect cadence, of course, but also the source of all strength and goodness in harmony. When you put one chord after another, if their fundamental roots are a perfect fifth apart (the root of the second chord is a perfect fifth below that of the first). If the roots are a step apart, then the harmony has the potential to be both weak and ugly.

Harmonic misconceptions

There are two more misconceptions in harmony; both involve inversion. The first is the word itself, which has three uses in music. Their meanings are actually quite similar, and this similarity constitutes immense danger for the unwary. They are:

i. Chords and their inversions

Chords are built on a bass note, with piles of thirds above. But each three-note chord can be inverted, so that the tonic chord in C major, consisting in the notes C — E — G, is re-arranged in two other ways, thus:

This is what we write on the board when we teach this; it's been this way for generations of pupils and teachers. And it can be misleading, because, in the real world, a first inversion chord can look like so many different things. Having seen this diagram, pupils need to practise looking for the lowest note in any texture, and identifying whether the chord is in root position, first or second inversion. At the same time they need not to make the other common mistake, which is to believe that the three possible answers are first, second, or third, rather than <u>root</u>, first, and second.

ii. Inversions of intervals

Intervals measure the distance between two notes, but they also measure position: which of the two notes is above another. If those positions are reversed – maintaining the pitches unchanged and altering only the octave of one – then an inversion is produced. Simple intervals alter their positions within the octave, with seconds becoming sevenths, thirds sixths and so on. This is why invertible counterpoint works.

iii. Inversion of melodies

There are two types of inversion within this category, one used in tonal music, the other when composing using the twelve-tone method. A diatonic inversion of a melody is a mirror image of the original, which sticks rigidly to the notes of the scale. This means that the intervals are not exactly reproduced. In the original of *Polly put the kettle on*, for instance, there is a semi-tone between the fourth and the fifth notes (B and C); in its inversion, the interval in the same place is a tone (E to F sharp):

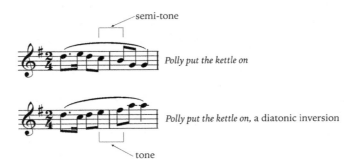

When composing using the twelve-tone method, as we shall see, an inversion of the melody (the row) reproduces exactly the same interval patterns: if the original interval is an ascending minor third, then its inversion is a descending minor third. Owing to the rules of the twelve-tone method, an inversion need not invert the contour of the melody, just the pitches used.

The second misconception returns to the inversion of chords, it's partly about the identification of chords and their inversions and partly about how composers use chords to plan their music.

The harmonic plan

Even the simplest melody, a nursery-rhyme for instance, is based on a harmonic plan. Restored to its proper shape, *Polly put the kettle on* uses the simplest of harmonic outlines:

This shows a two-stave piano arrangement of *Polly*, with a third stave showing the chords on which it is based. It starts and finishes on the tonic chord (I), and ends with a perfect cadence (V — I). Between beginning and end, the harmonic pattern is a simple alternation between tonic and dominant, changing every-other bar. This leisurely harmonic rhythm speeds-up at the cadence, and a new chord is used (the sub-dominant, or, if Riemann is to be trusted, the supertonic in the first inversion (II7b)).

These principles – start and finish on the tonic, end with a perfect cadence, use mainly tonic and dominant chords, use a faster harmonic rhythm near cadences – apply in almost every tonal piece. And it's fascinating that they apply equally, and with equal power irrespective of length: whether eight bars of a nursery rhyme, or in the 298 bars of the first movement of Beethoven's First Symphony, or in the vast edifices constructed by later composers.

This simplicity is hard to explain, because it seems impossible to go from a simple pair of root position triads to a movement of a Tchaikovsky symphony. If misconceptions are to be avoided, then this essential simplicity, that all harmony stems from the bass, needs to be stressed time and time again in our classrooms.

If the generative movement of music is the juxtaposition of one note with another, then how much more power is to be found in two chords, one after another. The ideas, inventions, and innovations we have just discussed have provided, and are providing one of the richest seams of human creativity – a world we should open for all our pupils.

Tone-Colour

Tone-colour in music is a difficult thing to pin down; even its name oscillates in confusion between tone-colour and timbre. In its definition, one possibility is to say what it is not: it's the way we tell sounds apart which is not pitch, or duration, or loudness. Viable and logical this explanation may be, but it's not terribly useful.

Acousticians tell us that there are two factors in a sound which determine its timbre: first, the interrelationship and spread of fundamental and its overtones (both harmonics and partials); and, second, the way in which it begins, lives, and eventually fades. Absent the characteristic attack, the piano or trumpet are very different instruments. This is interesting, and can be itself a starting-point for musical creativity, but is not helpful.

Those studying the cognition of music tell us that perception of tone-colour is rather mysterious. Perception starts from acoustics, but very quickly it becomes entangled with questions of colour and meaning, in the differences between music, speech, and noise, indeed in the way we respond to each other as humans, or as babies to our mothers' voices.

As teachers, tone-colour is often inextricably linked with learning about instruments – how to recognise the differences between instrumental families and their individual members, and as composers and performers how to understand their possibilities and limitations.

There's also a little history associated with this. In Western music, tone-colour first coalesces as an idea at about the time when instrumental music comes into its own: when it escapes the controlling influence of liturgy or poetry; when it is no longer the exclusive servant of words. It takes tone-colour a long time to achieve parity with the other musical dimensions. When one looks at the scores of Handel's operas, they are a remarkable mixture of specificity and ambiguity. In naming the singers for whom each part was written, specifying carefully which obbligato instrument is used, they are unnervingly precise; whether to double the violins' lines with oboe and the bass with bassoon is entirely up to the discretion of the players, left ambiguous, subject to some assumed conventions. There is a set of meanings in Handel's specifications: the obbligato horn plays the music of the hunter, King David plays the harp, trumpet for the Seraphin – these instruments are used according to their perceived nature, symbols which add rich texture to the story. J.S. Bach's approach is not dissimilar, but even more laced with pragmatism. He writes for the forces at his disposal (the Leipzig trumpeters are available for his Christmas Cantatas but not earlier in the year), and is willing to transfer music from one instrument to another, and to re-use material in entirely different instrumental contexts.

It can be argued, then, that melodies fall into three categories: Bach's flexibility is perhaps an example of the first. For some composers, the musical substance comes first, conceived in the abstract, without concern for the eventual instrumental resources. Singers describe the 'instrumental' difficulty of Bach's vocal lines; instrumentalists have to learn to make his lines breathe – often in a single piece, there is frequent and glorious melodic interchange between singer and instrumentalist. The second category of melody is one in which the melody seems inextricably linked with an instrument. The flute melody at the beginning of *L'après-midi d'un faune* seems inconceivable to us played on any other instrument (Copland, 1957). This seems true, although we can never be certain whether this truth is because the melody emerged fully-formed from Debussy's imagination as a melody for flute, or whether we believe it because Pan's flute is such a psychologically-perfect opening to the ballet, or whether we are unable to conceive an alternative owing to the paucity of our imaginations.

Examples of the third category of melody occur where the choice of instrument is deliberately provocative, either ironic, symbolic, or political. Stravinsky's unaccompanied bassoon hovering at the beginning of the *Le Sacre du printemps*, is one example; the neo-classicists' adoption of the harpsichord another; Mozart's co-option of the trombone in *Don Giovanni*, just maybe, another.

The emergence of tone-colour as a musical dimension of importance in its own right is linked with the technological development of instruments, itself the product also of increasing levels of sophistication in manufacture and design. The ability to cast the iron-frame of the nineteenth-century piano or to add the intricate Boehm key-work to a flute, and for different instruments of the same type reliably to sound (mostly) the same are all gifts of the industrial revolution.

What pupils need to take from this is a depth of learning about instruments. A single instrument can embody several characters at once. The character and acoustics of the clarinet are divided so much in three – into its lowest *chalumeau* register, its middle *clarion* register, and its upper *altissimo* – that it sometimes seems to embody three separate instruments. The bottom C-string of a viola is a special and unique place. The piano with the sustaining pedal is a very different creature, in both resonantly-expressive and practical terms, that without.

The piano is a very special case. It is an unnatural, technological instrument-machine. Its tone-colour is itself uninteresting, and it has significant musical limitations – it's incapable, for instance, of a playing a 'true' legato. But alongside its limitations, it is capable of miracles. The ability to create the illusion of legato is a mark of the great pianist, and the 'neutral' tone allows the piano to imitate other instruments, and other groups of instruments. The pianist should aim for a 'symphonic' tone, with each individual polyphonic line standing in clear definition – and when you listen attentively, you can hear this in the playing of the greats (Barenboim, 2009: 162).

The player can also make a huge difference when thinking about other instruments. George Pratt (1998: 73–5) suggests a listening exercise based on three different performances of Britten's *Six Metamorphoses after Ovid*, for unaccompanied oboe. In this he asks us to listen for three facets of tone-colour: first, the immediacy of attack and decay; second, the performer's use of vibrato, and; third, the 'density' of the tone. With three very different players (embodying the rather-different English and French schools of oboe playing) the tone-colour is strikingly different. An awareness of the possibilities of tone-colour, and imaginative deployment of them, is a central part of developing as a performer, the awareness which comes only from attentive and thoughtful listening.

But depth cannot come until the basic knowledge is in place; the best way to teach tone-colour and the recognition of instruments is through familiarity. Here, as in everything else, pupils need repeated explicit teaching, combined with practice, both guided and independent; meeting instruments is not done just once, it is a process which continues through time, with opportunities for repeated exposure and experience.

When teaching tone-colour, it's useful for the sounds of the instruments to be associated with rich verbal descriptions, with language which goes slightly beyond the perfect clichés of *Peter and the Wolf*. One highly-effective way to do this is to use Hector Berlioz's timeless treatise on orchestration (Berlioz & Macdonald, 2007). Berlioz is as skilled a writer as he is composer, and his distinctive prose is sufficiently memorable to adhere successfully to knowledge of the instruments' sounds and of what they look like, to provide hooks on which pupils' understanding can be hung.

Listening to different simultaneous tone-colours is also the start of thinking about texture.

Texture

Our ideal listener knows more now about the central place rhythm plays in our world, has felt the emotional tugs of melody, marvelled at the ingenuity of harmony, and felt the subtle play of overtones and their consequences in tone-colour. The combination of different voices, different instruments, and different lines comes next – the idea of musical texture. Our listener should start their explorations of this with some knowledge of three basic archetypes.

The earliest and most basic texture is a single voice or instrument playing alone. This can be as simple and lovely as a parent's lullaby to their daughter (*Polly put the kettle on*, for instance), or as complex, rich, and engrossing as Chinese opera. In the former, the accompaniment may be gurgles of happiness, in the latter, a percussive background of immense complexity and richness. We call this texture, a single unaccompanied line, monophonic. Monophony is relatively rare in Western classical music, and all-the-more potent as a result. Most GCSE examination boards muddy the water by making heterophony (simultaneous variation), properly a sub-category of monophony, a separate and emphasised element.

The second texture is where a single melody is given a chordal accompaniment. This can be as simple as the block chords which earlier formed the left hand of *Polly*, or can be as involved as the beginning of a 'cello sonata (with apologies to Brahms):

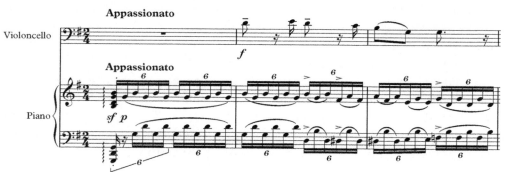

This is a homophonic texture – a melody with an accompaniment made mainly of chords. Its origin, as we have seen several times in other contexts in this chapter, is inextricably linked with the relationship between text and music. It's relatively easy to hear and understand words in a song when the melody is a single unaccompanied line – a monophonic texture. Add a little simultaneous variation (heterophony), perhaps a little percussion, and still the text comes through. But as soon as you start setting the melody with other lines, either with itself or variations of itself, the words become increasingly indistinct. This is a lesser difficulty when the text is simple, or part of the daily-repeated liturgy; but if it's important, say for the purposes of drama, for every word to be intelligible, then there is a problem.

But it's not just words, it's emotion too. The power of a single voice, with a simple chordal accompaniment is something you can experience from Caccini to *Cats*. And what a moment of invention must that first homophonic texture have been. (Even if innovation tends not to be a single moment but rather a series of related ideas, whose time was right, occurring to different people in different places.) For its dramatic possibility, homophony seems to have been adopted first in the seventeenth-century by the early Italian opera composers.

It represents a different way of thinking. Organum and discant were conceived as simultaneous melodies. Both are first horizontal objects, created with due respect to the vertical dimension, but are first and foremost melodies. Homophony, or at least the chords comprising the accompaniment of a homophonic piece, are conceived first vertically, as chords, and only then are considered horizontally, by checking that notes in successive chords move neatly from one to the next.

We've already met the third archetype, polyphony. The many voices of polyphony are independent and often equally-important melodic lines which weave and interrelate. In their interrelation they form chords, but the generated chords are a by-product, not the central artefact – polyphony combines a series of linear, horizontal musical units.

Polyphony and counterpoint are near-synonyms, certainly for the purposes of most examination syllabuses; but there is a difference between them. Polyphony is a texture consisting in many independent voices. (Here we use 'voices' to denote individual musical lines, either sung or played.) These voices might 'sing' the same thing, but it's best in the classroom to teach that they are independent in material, too. *Polly*, with a little alteration, can fit with many different melodies; in the following example, she combines with some near-Paganini, and a version of *God Save the Queen*:

How music works

These are three separate melodies which combine in a single polyphonic (*Polly-phonic?*) texture.

A contrapuntal texture also consists of many voices, is also polyphonic; but it's best in the classroom to reserve the term contrapuntal for textures in which both voices use the same material. Here's *Polly* in imitative counterpoint:

The imitating left hand in the second bar is not exactly the same as the right hand in the first, but it's clearly derived from it.

And here is *Polly* again as the beginning of the strictest form of counterpoint (of imitation, too), a canon at the octave:

The ideal listener should know about the three basic categories of texture – monophonic, homophonic, and polyphonic – but need not necessarily be able to name them. They do, however, provide three ways of attending to a piece. If you listen repeatedly and deeply to a monophonic work, you are more likely to pick out the design of the melody, how its contour is shaped through time and the pattern of repetition and development which shapes it. In a homophonic work, the intricate hierarchy of the chords will emerge. In a polyphonic work, you can try to follow each strand in the weave in turn. It's easier for the inex-perienced listener, perhaps, to listen repeatedly to polyphony than to the other textures (although the choice of which voice in, say, a fugue by J.S. Bach should subtly already have been made for you, at least if the performer is sufficiently skilful).

If you can add a dash of composition to attentive and directed listening, then you have a powerful mixture in the classroom. Pupils learn best when they have tried themselves to create at least the three different types of texture – rather in the way in which *Polly* might provide a set of music examples for a section on texture in a book. *Frère Jacques* is an ideal melody to use for this, and these might be the stages of a productive sequence of lessons in which pupils produce their own music examples:

1. doubling the melody in unison at the octave (teaching unison);

2. a homophonic texture with block chords (teaching both texture and the use of chords);

3. a homophonic texture with a broken-chord accompaniment (teaching Alberti bass and broken-chord accompaniments);

4. a heterophonic texture (teaching the use of passing-notes, auxiliary notes, and broken-chord elaboration);

5. a contrapuntal texture (teaching that canon is three things: first, an imitative texture; second, the strictest form of counterpoint; and third, a form of polyphony);

6. a polyphonic texture (in which *Frère Jacques* is combined with a new melody);

7. melody with a drone (a long-held root and fifth held as a double pedal);

8. melody with a pedal (teaching the difference between pedal and drone).

For our ideal listener, understanding polyphony is easier, too, if they have a little knowledge of polyphonic structures.

Structure

It's harder, perhaps, to understand structure than it is to grasp any other dimension of music. It's partly because structure operates not within the moment-to-moment experience of a musician, but rather at the scale of an entire piece. To grasp a structure at first listening is an act of attention and memory, as well as understanding. It's also an act of rather-sophisticated processing, which measures sense-data against knowledge, which, in turn, generates meaning.

The temptation is immediately to teach the formal moulds and archetypes which are so prevalent in music. The text-book suggests binary, or ternary, rondo, or sonata forms, and we diligently follow. There is here simultaneously immense strength and some little danger.

The strength is in the forms themselves. Over hundreds of years, these forms have been used, and with use, have themselves evolved. A new form is vanishingly rare, simply because composers have found the existing handful to be effective and practical, and rather have changed them – just a little bit – better to suit their needs and their temperaments. The evolved form is then passed on to the next generation. There is something in binary, ternary, rondo, and sonata which simply works, which is pleasing to and comprehensible for the human listener.

The danger is that it's possible to become trapped in a text-book. Every true work of art is different, and in each, the formal outline is determined by the 'musical content' (Copland, 1957: 75). The musical content – the ideas – if strong enough, will determine how and when the next structural division is reached, and how long that section is. If the musical substance determines it, the return, say, of an A section in a ternary form may well be considerably abridged or developed, an extended coda might be added to a sonata form (a coda which itself seems to become a second development), or a returning rondo might need to be the beginning of a development section, rather than a simple reprise. This is all a matter of degree and scale: a short and simple strophic song is more likely to exhibit a simple a formal archetype than a sprawling nineteenth-century symphony.

Great art is infinitely various, and a composer's treatment of form is different in every piece. Beethoven approaches first-movement form in 32 different ways in his piano sonatas, and it's hard to think of any of them which quite fits the text-book. But it's hugely useful for our ideal listener to understand the text-book sonata-principle, or some variant of it, because that magical invention will help them to comprehend a work, at least to some extent, on their first hearing of it. This last, 'at first hearing', is the key idea: the text-book articulations of sonata form give the new listener way-markers, help them to remember, to understand, and to follow the longer musical line. Those way-markers can be re-visited on a second hearing, and around them coalesce the knowledge which, with repeated hearings, will make possible a more-complete understanding of a work.

Form and genre

Structure works on different scales and different levels. Let's start with the largest scale, with the question of genre. There are musical forms which apply to individual movements; those movements often coalesce together to make multi-movement works; and those works can be of one genre or another.

Some examples might make this clearer:

> An aria for soprano and baroque orchestra might be in *da capo* form (ternary form, in effect); the aria belongs to a single larger work which itself contains recitatives, duets, orchestral pieces, and choruses; the work is generically an oratorio. A very-similar aria, combining with a very-similar collection of movements, might equally belong to a different genre, a baroque opera.

A movement for solo piano is in sonata form; it fits with two other movements, one slow, and one in sonata-rondo form; together these three movements form a piano sonata in the sonata genre.

It's important to be clear about the distinction between form, multi-movement works, and genre. It's especially important to be precise about the difference between the proper noun 'sonata' in its two related guises: as a formal archetype for an individual movement; and as a three- or four-movement work for solo instrument and piano, or for solo piano – a genre. This is an easy misconception which should be clarified very early.

Simple structural principles

Within a single movement, structure seems to adhere to similar principles, irrespective of scale. The most important principle of any form, of almost every form, is repetition. Repetition is everywhere in music, from the folk-song's refrain or the K-pop chorus, to the group's response to an individual's call in a Zulu choir. In the Western tradition, repetition is the mechanism by which composers achieve coherence and balance within both small- and large-scale structures.

The repetition of a musical unit can be immediate or it can be significantly delayed; the repetition might be exact or it might be significantly altered, varied, or developed.

This fundamental principle of structure makes possible strophic songs (A — A — A), binary (A — B), and ternary forms (A — B — A); enables rondo (A — B — A — C — A), 32-bar song form (A — A — B — A), and sonata. It is also there in variation forms of all types (A — A' — A") in theme-and-variation form as well as in ground bass, passacaglia, chaconne; the fugal and contrapuntal forms would also be impossible without repetition.

As an aside, a composer's decision not to repeat is also a principle. There are examples of this in folk-song, as well as in Bach's preludes to the '48'.

Binary or ternary?

Teachers like to use letters to represent formal sections, but seldom get beyond the first three or four letters of the alphabet. We use the letter A many, many times, because its repetition signifies repetition in the music we are discussing, and repetition is the most important principle of structure. But the letter B comes quite often, too.

This leads to a second fundamental of structure – repeating material after a contrasting section. Teachers represent this as A — B — A, but this is only the starting-point.

How music works

Let's deal with each section in turn. The first A section introduces the material. The section is very often repeated immediately. This repetition helps the listener to remember what's there. Assuming that the material has been made sufficiently memorable by the composer, and realised well by the performer, all three of the participants here have now completed their assigned roles.

The second section is the contrasting B. The degree of contrast here depends on the scale and length of the piece: in a very simple nursery-rhyme, the contrast might be minimal, using secondary material from the A section, a digression almost filling time; in a more-extended work, the contrast needs to be more pointed, in sharper focus.

The return of the A section may be exact (A), or it may be altered, developed, or varied in some way (A').

The second and third sections of this three-part form (the B — A) may well themselves be repeated. This means that teachers' A — B — A should properly have double bars and repeats included, thus:

A :|| : BA :||

A literal-minded pupil at this moment will inevitably point out that this should be expanded to:

A — A — B — A — B — A

Which sequence, when shown to them, demonstrates that the compressed version is both simpler and more meaningful.

If poor *Polly* were in this form, she might look a little like this:

The two A sections are identical, the B section is a diversion, repeating the motif of the second bar and then in bars 15 and 16 inverting the step-wise crotchets first heard in 7 and 8.

Here is one of the harder things to explain in the classroom. This structural principle, of repetition following contrast, is present in many forms. In many of these it is quite easy to understand – in ternary, rondo, and sonata for instance; but it's also there in binary, too, in a two-part, A — B form. *Polly* is in binary form, a two-part structure, clearly outlined by double bars and repeats. But it also adheres to the repetition-following-contrast principle, a three-part structure. A way to teach this which is both truthful and easy to understand is to call it rounded binary – which is a two-part form, with repetition at the end of the A section first heard at the beginning. It's not the whole truth (there are many different rounded binary forms), but it does work. It sometimes helps to represent it like this:

A :||: B(A) :||

One of the best ways to explain the difference between binary and ternary is to use a minuet and trio. These are sufficiently short to be useful in the classroom, of sufficient complexity to make possible the teaching of quite sophisticated ideas.

It's likely that both the minuet and trio will individually be in rounded binary form (A :||: B (A) :||), easily navigated by the pattern of double bars and repeat-signs. The return of the A section at about two-thirds through is often very clear indeed.

The trio follows the minuet, and is often contrasting in character. And after the trio comes a repeat of the minuet. Repetition and contrast, the essence of forms. A formal outline would look like this:

A. minuet:

A :||:B(A) :||

B. trio:

A :||:B(A) :||

A. minuet:

A :||:B(A) :||

It's clear from this that what we should properly call a minuet — trio — minuet structure is a ternary form (A — B — A). And it shows a property of many ternary forms: namely that its component parts each tend towards independence and autonomy. It's not invariably the case, but many times the B section could be performed as a separate piece of music, and, as such, would be completely satisfying.

Which leads us to the formal elephant in this particular room: that in Western music, form is less a property of patterning and disposition, less a collection of letters repeated and contrasted, than it is a musical function made possible by tonality and key. Where there is repetition, it's likely that the home key (the tonic) is going to be repeated; where there is contrast, the contrasting key is highly likely to be the dominant (or the relative major in a minor-key piece). The minuet will start and finish on the tonic; the succeeding trio will start and finish on the dominant; and the minuet's return will itself return home to the tonic.

The reason that the elephant is so visible, is that teaching structure and form, achieving a true understanding of it, requires a little understanding of harmony. And because great art is infinitely variable, because the form of each individual piece will tend to reflect its musical materials, the tonal layout of every piece is going to be slightly different. Even given a little understanding of harmony, there is no single simple explanatory formula which can be taught in the classroom.

That having been said, the propensity of Western music to treat the tonic key as its 'home' – start at home and return there at the end of the adventure – and the dominant key as a metaphorical 'away' (in a minor key, the relative major takes on the role of 'away') is the single most powerful explaining factor in tonal music. And, like the idea of repetition, it permeates different levels of the music, controls the structure of a melody as compellingly as it controls the form of a symphony movement.

Glance again at the rounded-binary *Polly* (example 15). The melody of the first eight bars is in the tonic key (G major). Underlying it are alternating tonic and dominant chords, and the melody is defined at the end by the perfect cadence (dominant to tonic). In this tonic-key melody, the tonic and dominant are related, both powerful, but exist in a defined and comprehensible hierarchy (the tonic has primacy over the dominant). At the smallest level is played out this drama – 'home' is settled and certain, but 'away' is an inherent part of it.

In the central eight bars, the first half of the B section, the dominant chord is more prominent. The melody returns again and again to the note D (a dominant pedal would be a plausible bass-line), and the harmony alternates dominant chords with tonic, dominant first, then tonic. This is the moment of 'away' in the piece, when the balance moves ever-so-slightly towards D major, in which the dominant chord is much more prevalent and significant.

Order is restored in bar 17, when the A section, returns 'home'.

This example of 'home' and 'away' is played-out at the very smallest scale, in a mere twenty-four bars; but it can scale up and ramify outwards, to the point when it makes comprehensible the longest movements. Some more practical ideas about teaching form are found in chapter six, but it's worth introducing a few ideas now about the teaching of large-scale form.

Repetition is the easy part to demonstrate. With short, well-chosen, and often-repeated audio examples, with scores projected at the same time, even quite-inexperienced musicians can hear and see relationships and similarities.

A composer repeats their A section in order to fix the idea in memory; a teacher needs to repeat the same audio example several times to achieve the same effect. Using notation to support this is tremendously useful. Even if the pupils have not yet mastered its intricacies, to see shapes at the same time as hearing them adds a second dimension, links our teaching to what we know about the limitations and opportunities of the human intellect, helps significantly in the building of usable knowledge. As part of this, if, whilst the music is playing, the teacher points to each bar in turn of a score projected to the whole class, then the pupils' attention is focussed, and all can follow or at least feel that they can follow. Even if that act proves to be illusory, every pupil should be given the opportunity to try.

Provided that they are simple, oft-repeated, and well-planned, teaching using visual and simultaneous audio examples is very powerful. It's powerful, too, if the teacher can pick out melodies on the piano. The whole can be played slowly and repeated often, and salient features can themselves be repeated and simultaneously explained. It's important that the teacher plays then talks – it's too easy to do both at once – otherwise the effect is lost and the pupils' faculties are overloaded with sound. A second hearing on a different instrument, using a different or a simpler timbre, often clarifies the moment and makes it more memorable. For younger pupils, there's also magic when you play to them – however unsteadily – which helps to link you to them, and them to the unreachably-perfect professional recording which you have just played for them.

Contrast, particular the contrast of keys, is harder to teach.

A certain amount can be achieved in the classroom by simple juxtaposition. This is valuable when the same material is repeated on different key-centres. The second subject in a sonata structure will most-often appear first on the dominant, and then later return in the tonic. In extracts of both, played alongside one another, contrast of keys is easy to hear, easier still to see in notation.

This is the first stage in the conscious development of pupils' harmonic instincts. The harmonic processes we seek to teach are common to many thousands of works, and composers tend to do the same things in the same places. If a pupil knows that a modulation onto the dominant or the relative major is most likely, then that is what they will look for. Even if, early in a piece, a composer embarks on a particularly complex ramble through a thicket of keys, the eventual destination will likely be the dominant, and the preceding material can be dis-counted as secondary or transitional.

A little knowledge first, but then some visual instincts, too. The importance of notation cannot be stressed too strongly here – in the culture we inhabit, for better or worse, modulation can be seen much more easily than it can be heard. An outbreak of accidentals in the score, the pattern of which becomes established over a few bars, will often indicate a momentary change of key. A stray sharp or natural will most likely be the leading-note of the new key, and the tonic note of that new key can be found one semi-tone higher than the accidental; a stray flat is often the flattened seventh of a dominant-seventh chord. The accidental sharp- or natural-sign will take the piece from the tonic onto the dominant, and are most common early in a piece; the flattened seventh will take the music from domi-nant back onto the tonic. These visual cues, and how they are evaluated, are very important. They provide highly-effective tools of musical understanding which should be part of regular classroom-drills.

Following the course of a larger-scale piece, its form and structure, really is much easier with the score, but it requires neither complete fluency in score-reading nor even in notation. Composers seek to make their works intelligible. Beethoven may delight in bamboozling his listeners, nudging and implying and laying false trails, but once the game's over, once the joke's been told, both coher-ence and comprehensibility are important to him. If art is about anything beyond craftsmanship, however elevated, then it's about the capture of attention and the communication of feeling – neither of which are possible if the listener perceives mere gibberish.

Composers use certain features of harmony to make their works intelligible, which are most-often to be found in the bass-line. In the classical period, there is regularly a moment of silence before a new section – a pupil should know to look in the preceding bass-line for the cadence and identify the new key established. Before the moment of recapitulation in a sonata-form (or in many rounded-binary forms, too) there will be a dominant pedal, an extended V of the delineating per-fect cadence. In a transition section, a fast-changing bass-line produces unsta-ble harmony, travelling from one moment of stability to another (in other words, a modulation); stability, the point of arrival will often be indicated by a more-consistent and unchanging bass, perhaps the repeated use of the dominant and tonic of the new key. Such signs are not infallible, but knowing what to look for and where to look for it are powerful tools for pupils – and understanding of the score helps them to become a listener whose abilities are slightly closer to those of our ideal.

Our ideal listener's journey

The six musical elements are the place to start our ideal listener's journey – next comes a map which shows where that journey might lead: a curriculum.

References

Barenboim, D., 2009. *Everything Is Connected: The Power of Music.* London, Phoenix.

Berlioz, H. & Macdonald, H., 2007. *Berlioz's Orchestration Treatise: A Translation and Commentary.* Cambridge, Cambridge University Press.

Copland, A., 1957. *What to Listen for in Music.* New York, New American Library.

Johnson, S., 2020. *The Eighth: Mahler and the World in 1910.* London, Faber & Faber.

Moritz, C., Yampolsky, S., Papadelis, G., Thomson, J., & Wolf, M., 2013. Links Between Early Rhythm Skills, Musical Training, and Phonological Awareness. *Reading and Writing*, 26(5), 739–69.

Pratt, G., 1998. *Aural Awareness: Principles and Practice.* Oxford, Oxford University Press.

Chapter 3

Musical curriculums

Yes, there are external constraints – things which universities or examination boards or school leaders deem it necessary for our pupils at a certain moment in their lives to know or to be able to do. But one of the most remarkable things about being a music teacher – one of the things which truly makes us different – is the autonomy we enjoy in the classroom, the freedom we have to choose what to teach and how we teach it. Through four very-different models of music teaching, this chapter is an invitation to explore.

What is taught in schools has been contested, sometimes fiercely, sometimes more judiciously, for at least 200 years, probably longer. It's easy to look back on the pre-Renaissance world with a little envy, especially in its contented and obedient relationship with the past. Roman ancestors provided revered examples of thought and action, and the act of ageing in an individual was the slow unveiling of 'his most characteristic form of being' (Arendt, 2006: 190). It is in different ways today that we hear talk of tradition, authority, and history; and the sense of estrangement from the past is, in many quarters, quite palpable. Yet the task of education – tightly-bound with teaching and here taken as the society-defined finite period of childhood – is essentially 'to teach children what the world is like ...' (Arendt, 2006: 192). Humanity is old, and this necessarily requires spending time in the past; 'the best which has been thought and said in the world' is in the perfect tense (Arnold, 2009).

But humanity is old and our ways of thinking and being wear out, generation-by-generation. Our profound hope is vested in, has always been vested in the young; in the revolutionary promise which every new birth brings to us. Teaching children what the world is like is an act of love, opening up the authority of the past in that special way which is near-impossible today save in education; we are seek 'to prepare them in advance for the task of renewing a common world' (Arendt, 2006: 193).

DOI: 10.4324/9781003112402-3

Defining the curriculum

Opening-up the musical world is the task of a lifetime's trial-and-error, some of which might readily be avoided by setting some parameters for success. Dylan Wiliam (2013) offers a seven-part model of whole-school curriculum design, which we might readily appropriate for our purposes.

Wiliam suggests, first, that a curriculum should be balanced. He reminds us that 'we are the first generation of educators who know we have no idea what we are doing' (Wiliam, 2013: 15), and that preparing children for an unknown future necessitates thinking hard about our inherited assumptions. The notion of a 'balanced and broadly-based education' (Education Act 2002, section 78) is to our advantage as musicians in the recognition for the arts we can infer from it; but it should also be at the heart of our thinking in our own curriculums. When deciding what music not to teach – the inevitable consequence of a world full of knowledge – the selected knowledge needs to reach as far as possible in geography and time, and should offer rich, satisfying, and balanced fare.

Second, what we teach needs to be rigorous, 'taught in a way that is faithful to the discipline or field from which it is drawn' (Wiliam, 2013: 20). Common ground is shared between musical thinking and thinking in almost every other subject, but our discipline, in common with all the other traditional school subjects, represents a 'powerful — and qualitatively different — way ... of thinking about the world' (Wiliam, 2013: 22).

Wiliam's third parameter is that the whole is coherent, 'that the totality of experiences reinforce each other' (Wiliam, 2013: 28). By this he means making explicit connections between ideas which pupils encounter in our musical classroom at different times and in different years. This is closely linked with the conscious building in our pupils of stores of knowledge in their long-term memories (so-called schemas), all-the-while attempting in individual lessons 'to make more effective use of what short-term working memory we have' (Wiliam, 2013: 28).

The fourth parameter for our curriculums is that they are 'vertically integrated' (Wiliam, 2013: 28). This builds on the idea of coherence, but goes further; it suggests that 'Every curriculum needs to have a clear model of what it is that gets better when someone "gets better" at a discipline or subject' (Wiliam, 2013: 28). Implicit here is the need to plan carefully – Wiliam suggests planning collectively – in order that musical progress is clearly defined, and that each necessary component of it comes in a proper sequence.

In a proper sequence, but also at the proper time; Wiliam's fifth parameter is that the material is presented at an appropriate time. The variation of musical experience in our classrooms is quite extraordinary, and this is one of the hardest curricular needles to thread. Wiliam suggests that 'stage, not age' (Wiliam, 2013: 34) is one solution, but acknowledges that, in practice, this is terrifically hard.

The sixth parameter is the curriculum's focus, that 'the good schoolmaster is known by the number of valuable subjects that he declines to teach' (Sir Richard Livingstone, quoted in Wiliam, 2013: 36). The musical curriculum needs to identify and focus on the subject's 'big ideas' (Wiliam, 2013: 36). Again, this is hard, and requires a great deal of knowledge and some little teaching experience; but it is a practical exercise which can help to make a curriculum manageable.

Wiliam's final parameter is that the work is relevant (Wiliam, 2013). In education, this is a word used often and thoughtlessly. There is little we teach in schools which is, at face value, relevant to our pupils' immediate interests; the curriculum exists to make possible 'the extraordinary way that good teachers get students interested in things they never knew they were interested in' (Hidi and Harackiewicz, quoted in Wiliam, 2013: 39).

Music teachers are different, and, within the limitations of institution and circumstance, each music teacher's curriculum is different. Each individual's musical world is unique, shaped in them by culture and experience, by education and disposition. That's the wonder of it, and why the musical curriculum is so often defined, perhaps more so than in any other subject, by the person teaching it. Jack Longstaff's curriculum was one such.

Lessons from Longstaff: Jack, Annie, and Roger

I had two years of the 'Prod' treatment, and it was not long enough, nothing like. Jack 'Prod' Longstaff's curriculum was an extra-ordinary thing, hinted at in his *Times* obituary:

> ... it was as the director of music for almost 20 years at Queen Elizabeth's Grammar School in Blackburn that he established a reputation as a music pedagogue throughout the north of England. The breadth and depth of the musical education he gave his pupils was remarkable: boys were expected to know all the Mozart and Beethoven string quartets and a good proportion of Haydn's, as well as the cornerstones of the symphonic repertoire.

> Jack's mastery of harmony and contrapuntal techniques was second to none, and he passed on his knowledge many times in individual sessions in which criticism was detailed not to say unsparing. Many pupils remarked that the training often surpassed the tuition they received at university.

… School holidays were highlighted by study days based on a particular composer that could last 12 hours. Jack's insights into Bruckner, Sibelius and Carl Nielsen were particularly memorable.[1]

The 'Prod' diet was highly academic, completely rigorous, and in every way exacting. Entry to his classroom required clean and shiny shoes, and entry to his world involved the textbooks of Annie O. Warburton, digested whole.

She taught music at Manchester High School for Girls, made the most of Manchester when the Hallé Orchestra had Sir Malcolm and Sir John; between 1921 and 1946, she wrote 16 books about music for use in schools. These range from treatises in harmony and melody-writing, through ear-training, to the four later volumes of *Analyses of Musical Classics* (Warburton, 1963; 1967; 1974; 1975), accessible but rigorous works of descriptive scholarship.[2]

Jack Longstaff and Annie Warburton believed in standards, clearly defined and applied meticulously. They opened doors to great things, but, to pass through, you had to work in the development of your craft, work hard. They would both have agreed with Roger Sessions.

In 1967, American composer Roger Sessions wrote to the editor of *Perspectives of New Music*, asking 'What Can Be Taught?' (Sessions, 1979). His answer, 'the central issue' in the teaching of composition, is craftsmanship; which he defines as 'the ability to cope, successfully and with assurance, with any problem with which a composer may be confronted' (1979: 205). Young composers need 'precision, fluency, and resourcefulness in the highest degree', and composition is 'a craft mastered through prolonged practice' (1979: 205).

All of this hints at a very different world of teaching to ours. For, on the other side of the Pennines from Blackburn and Manchester, the revolution was only just beginning.

Music in the secondary school curriculum

There was a decade, running from 1972 until 1981, when remarkable things happened in music education at the University of York. The creativity centred on John Paynter, composer and teacher, whose 1970 book *Sound and Silence* (co-written with Peter Aston) had caught both the imagination and the *zeitgeist* (Paynter & Aston, 1970). The book led to a nine-year project, run under the aegis of the Schools Council, which is described with great passion and insight by Paynter in *Music in the Secondary School Curriculum* (Paynter, 1982).

The project was quite a thing: contributors included Wilfrid Mellers, Harrison Birtwistle, John Paynter, Bernard Rands, George Self, and Trevor Wishart, and it reached directly some 200 secondary schools.[3]

Musical curriculums

After more than three decades, the most striking thing about the project is its idealism. Paynter quotes with approval the 1931 Hadow Report: 'The artist is strong in the child and it is to this side of the child's nature that the teacher should appeal' (1982: 10). Every child-artist is capable of musical expression, and to every child should be afforded the opportunity to make music creatively, to improvise, compose, and perform. This opportunity should not only be for the minority who take public or graded instrumental examinations, and the chance to perform should not be confined to the 'special occasion music' (Paynter, 1982: 23) of show, concert, or service.

Music's fundamental means is sound:

> Music is a way of listening to sounds, and musical experience is primarily a matter of working with sounds and of learning to control the medium.
>
> (Paynter, 1982: xiii)

We learn this working through the 'direct experience' of music, through experiments to 'try things out for ourselves' (Paynter, 1982: 24). There are very few who listen to music with analytical intent, noting the invertible counterpoint or the clever use of the Neapolitan; music, rather, is a sensation, as capable of evoking feeling as it is of understanding. And listening should be live, not the 'unreality' of recorded music (Paynter, 1982: 25). A recording loses the 'subtle inter-action of performers in the same room re-creating the music *together*' (italics original; Paynter, 1982: 25). Recordings have their use for those already familiar with a work, and an experienced listener might be able to recreate somewhat the communicative power of live performance; but that first intoxicating encounter with a work for a young listener should be live.

This is the antithesis of what Paynter describes (in slightly withering terms) as the teaching of 'Music Appreciation' (Paynter, 1982: 25). Paynter suggests moving away from the idea (echoing the language of Roger Sessions) of the teacher as 'Master Craftsman' (Paynter, 1982: 25), and suggests that these authorities offer a 'dated manner of expression' (Paynter, 1982: 33) as out-of-touch as the humour in nineteenth-century *Punch* cartoons, or the jokes in old television programmes. Artistry should come before the 'mastering of certain technical tricks':

> In his training a musician must acquire craftsmanship, but in the end he is an artist primarily
>
> (Paynter, 1982: 33)

A broad musical education consists in:

> music-*making* (performing, improvising, composing) and, in the forefront of all activities, the development of aural sensitivity and awareness. Keeping our ears open to sounds — all sounds, any sounds — is the most basic and therefore the most 'real' of musical skills.
>
> (italics original; Paynter, 1982: 28)

There is a lot which the pupils themselves bring to the project:

> The teacher's principal task is to draw upon the resources of ideas and imagination which the pupils themselves can bring to the work.
>
> (Paynter, 1982: 50).

Teachers should '*start where our pupils are*' (Paynter, 1982: 118), using composition and improvisation, intuition and the innate excitement of musical sounds to explore the coherent ways in which they might be put together.

One way of planning a pattern for the year or years is to constellate teaching around 'musical concepts', foundational elements of music. In reality, these flow one into another (harmony informs melody and *vice versa*), but separately allow clarity of focus in organisation. Here's a possible sequence, moving from simple to more complicated:

i. pulse and rhythm

ii. pitch and melody

iii. timbre and texture

iv. density, harmony, and counterpoint. (Paynter, 1982: 35–6)

At each stage, Paynter's prescriptions are wide and various. Here, for instance, are his suggestions for *timbre*:

> Leading on from the relationship between instruments and melodic characteristics (e.g. sharply disjunct and 'jagged' melodies on 'dry' instruments such as xylophones; flowing conjunct movement for wind or strings or the 'sustaining' sounds of the metallophone) concentrate next on *timbre*. Explore the different 'colour' effects of whatever instruments are available in the class. Try out various effects in the contrast and combination of timbres, and in the articulation of sounds (different ways of making sounds — e.g. different ways of striking

percussion, variety of beaters, etc.). Making improvisations and compositions for single timbral ensembles (e.g. a piece for a group of cymbals of different sizes or various kinds of drum; a piece for many *different* metal sounds or glass sounds or wood sounds as can be assembled). Explore different kinds of *vocal timbre* — relate this to style in songs (e.g. voice qualities most suitable for folk music, c.f. the techniques of folk 'revival' singers such as The Watersons; scat singing in jazz; 'toasting' in reggae); other uses of voice sounds (not necessarily singing voices, e.g. in the music of Luciano Berio. Bernard Rands, *et al.*)

(italics original; Paynter, 1982: 36).

These ideas can be spread over a number of school years, or might be the basis of just one – at the start of each school year perhaps beginning the sequence again, and working through it in ever more detail, complexity, and richness. The priority is working with sounds, and Paynter accordingly suggests that, if time is short, reducing the number of examples is preferable to reducing the time allocated to the children's explorations.

Paynter's model is inspiring in that it assumes that every pupil will be involved in classroom music through their school careers – at least until the equivalent of year 11 (Paynter, 1982: xii). Although not blind to the possibilities of music in developing contentment and character in our pupils, Paynter's central argument is for music as a thing-in-itself, intrinsically valuable, one of the great humanising forces. Perhaps this confidence is something we have lost?

Planning a curriculum using 'musical concepts' is but one way to achieve similar results. Another, enacted by Tom Gamble and reported by Paynter (1982: 39), takes its structure from a series of experiments with individual instruments. Gamble suggests that working with a single sound-source – voice, piano, or an invented instrument built by the children themselves – helps pupils both to concentrate, as well as to build their 'aural imagination'. The advantage of a newly-invented instrument (a 'piano-harp' was the frame and strings only of a dismantled piano) is that pupils approach it with no pre-conceptions about technique, no inhibitions about how the instrument should be played or what it should sound like. Each single-instrument experiment results in a group composition, which is then refined and preserved in a graphic notation. (It's striking how often invented notation appears in this approach, striking as Paynter is very happy to forego standard notation, saying that 'laboured exercises in notation can so easily kill interest and involvement' (Paynter, 1982: 38).) Then, and only then, does the teacher introduce the work of other composers ('long/short sounds' lead to Xenakis's *Akrata,* for instance).

The first year of this scheme asks pupils to experiment with sound as sound alone; ideas and images from outside music are then introduced in later years (the equivalent of years 8 and 9). Ideas from Western classical music are also used, forms such as rondo, and techniques such as twelve-note composition. But again, the children are taught first themselves to experiment, before listening to and exploring examples by established composers. For work on twelve-note techniques, for instance, the pupils first improvise using a row, each in turn, in effect, creating a set of variations; they then complete their own pieces; and finally, and only when the moment is right, are they introduced to the music of Schoenberg, Webern, and Berg. When the moment is right means that the listening must be apposite to the pupils' compositions. In turn, this means that the teacher's knowledge (or planning) must be very good indeed. A pupil writing about her own work as a member of a group of composers talks about the way the broken-chord figure she has developed reminds her of 'Stravinsky "Pagan"' and a moment of dialogue makes her think of *Scheehrazade* (Paynter, 1982: 130). The group's own composition first, the stylistic apportionment later.

In years 10 and 11, the choice becomes wider still, starting with the pupils' own compositions in their own chosen styles (from rock music, through the 'prepared' piano, to Balinese gamelan). A syllabus is thus constructed from the pupils' compositions which 'leads along many creative paths' (Paynter, 1982: 43).

From the last two paragraphs one can infer significant demands on the teacher – both in the planning of lessons, and in the mastery of their subject. You can see this in a sample lesson plan, week nine of a twelve-week term on the subject of texture and timbre:

> Listen to [the] use of the solo voice in selected sections of Schoenberg's *Pierrot Lunaire* (e.g. 'Die Nacht'), and the choral textures in Ligeti's *Requiem*, David Bedford's *Two Choruses* ... Berio's *Visage* or the same composer's *A-Ronne* ... Alternative examples could be found in the music of jazz singers (e.g. scat singing), in reggae (e.g. 'toasting') and *avant-garde* rock music. Draw attention to the variety of techniques possible between whispered sounds, spoken sounds, half-speaking/half-singing (i.e. 'sprechtstimme') and sung sounds. 'Commission' two voice pieces for next week. These could be made by individuals for the whole class to perform, or by very small groups (of two or three pupils) or by two of the usual working groups (five or six pupils). Suggest themes, e.g. 'Water Music', 'Fog', 'Star', '100 MPH'.
>
> (italics original; Paynter, 1982: 45)

The other demand made of the teacher is that they are creative musicians themselves. It's an inspiring idea, that we can teach young composers how to decide:

from the substance of a single musical idea how it shall go on in time. To develop that skill the material itself must be the starting point, because form is content not a pre-ordained pattern.

(Paynter, 1982: 51)

Inspiring, but also daunting, and requiring a total level of commitment to the project; without 'a clear picture of what his musical objectives were' and without 'conviction that the activities would really lead to musical understanding' then things might go wrong: as one participant reported, '[the children] are happier singing traditional rounds rather than "messing about" as they put it.' (Paynter, 1982: 51–2). If the project worked for you, the results could be transformative; other schools tried the materials, but found the ideas not suitable for them (Griffiths, 1977).

Finally, it's fascinating that the 'professional' music on which much of the book draws is that of the twentieth-century *avant garde*. Tom Gamble again:

Music of the twentieth century, and particularly the past twenty-five years, will have a special relevance to children's work in class — not only because of the emphasis on timbre and texture but also because the new solutions which young people adopt to old problems are so often refreshingly original and imaginative.

(Paynter, 1982: 39)

This is about as far from the 'canonical', *Musical Classics,* approach of Annie Warburton as it is possible to get. She would probably be much more content with *The Model Music Curriculum* (Department for Education (DfE), 2021).

The Model Music Curriculum

It's probably fair to say that John Paynter and the Paynterites would not have thought much of DfE's *Model Music Curriculum (MMC)* (DfE, 2021). The York school compared 'knowing about' unfavourably with 'experience of': the former a selection 'of techniques and points of musical history'; the latter the result of direct, first-hand contact between pupil and music:

It would be possible to 'feed' young people with information on virtually any musical topic or technique, and by frequent testing we could try to ensure that they 'knew about' these things. Musical experience need not be part of the process at all. But there is little virtue in knowing about pulse, rhythm, harmony, timbre, etc. unless we can make musical (i.e. artistic) use of these concepts, and unless the insight derived from the experience is such that it enables us to deal with other and varied use of rhythm, harmony, timbre, etc. as and when we meet them

(Paynter, 1982: 34).

In Key Stage 3, rather than exploring music as sensation, as sound, the *MMC* aims to build 'a universal foundation of musical understanding' (DfE, 2021: 37). It suggests that pupils should develop knowledge through performing, composing, and listening; and they should be able to read staff notation:

Staff Notation not only complements developing aural skills, improvisation, memorisation and composition, but provides the opportunity for pupils to be taught music independently both in class and after they have left school.

(DfE, 2021: 5)

Knowledge of notation might be the result of laboured exercises, and all teaching everywhere has the potential to 'kill interest and involvement' (Paynter, 1982: 38); but notation can 'grant access to a lifelong passion for music making if this skill is nurtured' (DfE, 2021: 37).

Class singing is an unbroken strand in the *MMC*, starting in primary schools, and continuing until the end of year 9. As pupils become more self-conscious, and boys' voices narrow in range and lower in pitch, it becomes harder, of course, but carefully-planned repertoire makes it possible (DfE, 2021: 39). The key is to provide 'regular opportunities', as, once lost, the confidence to sing will 'take significant time and encouragement to reinstate' (DfE, 2021: 39). Pupils should learn to sing in two or three parts, and regularly perform three- or four-part rounds. (Perhaps the dissenting voice quoted by Paynter had a lasting influence: '[the children] are happier singing traditional rounds rather than "messing about" as they put it.' (Paynter, 1982: 51–2).)

Over the course of the first three years of secondary school – and one notes with sadness that here there is no idealistic talk of classroom music continuing for all through until the age of 16 – pupils will have been exposed to 'some of the great output of human civilisation', have developed their knowledge of 'creative processes through improvisation and composition', and 'have built an understanding of how musical elements work and discussed how these interact with subjective and objective models of musical meaning' (DfE, 2021: 37).

In studying the 'great output of human civilisation' the *MMC*, first, aims to 'give pupils a core knowledge of music in many of its forms' (DfE, 2021: 39). The material suggested includes works from the classical canon, film music, popular music, and the music of diverse traditions from around the world. Listening to this 'great output' combines both technical and semantic elements. In common with Paynter, the MMC's starting point is the 'musical elements' (Paynter's 'musical concepts'):

i. tonality

ii. texture/instrumentation

iii. metre/rhythm/tempo

iv. pitch

v. harmony

vi. dynamics (DfE, 2021: 40)

But alongside the technical comes the semantic, the 'meaning of music' (DfE, 2021: 40). Pupils discuss geography and history ('Where does the music come from?'), the music's genesis and purpose, and 'How is this music expressive?' (DfE, 2021: 40).

This is difficult territory, difficult and important. The first thing to say is that to ask questions of meaning and expression (two categories which are not quite the same thing) is a good way of helping pupils to recall, practise, and articulate technical knowledge. Through questioning, it's possible to move a pupil's responses through a virtuous progression, of thinking, of remembering, and of refining:

> I don't like it.
> I don't like it because it makes me feel sad.
> It makes me feel sad because it's in a minor key.
> The minor key, and descending melody make me feel sad.
> The chromatic harmony and descending melody, sung in the low register of the mezzo-soprano's voice …

As well as this, hiding, as it were, in plain sight, is an idealistic commitment to a view of art articulated beautifully by Tolstoy; that, by definition, art is a means by which feeling is elicited in one human by another, an act of communication (Tolstoy, 1962). This matters because art is:

> a means of union among men, joining them together in the same feelings, and indispensable for the life and progress toward well-being of individuals and of humanity

> (Tolstoy, 1962: 123).

But Tolstoy died in 1910, and his idealism has been tempered somewhat, both by the shattering events of the early twentieth-century, by war-fuelled scientific and societal change, and by a new interest in the human psyche and brain.

Ofsted

Tolstoy might recognise the idealism in Ofsted's 2021 research review in music: 'Playing the piano ... singing in a choir ... writing lots of songs ... These are wonderful things in and of themselves and need no further justification' (Ofsted, 2021). But, in common with Wiliam (2013), the report leaves Tolstoy behind, and goes further even than Paynter and the DfE in relating musical teaching, and music curriculums to the mind:

> 'The central finding of this review is that, to become successful musicians, pupils must use both their conscious and unconscious minds, with the latter being developed by learning and experience'
>
> (Ofsted, 2021)

The unnamed authors suggest that academic progress in music builds on three 'pillars' (Ofsted, 2021): the 'technical' ability to play an instrument, to sing, or to use music technology; the 'constructive' pillar, important in listening, performing, and composing, which comprises the knowledge and understanding of how musical elements 'come together'; and, the 'expressive' pillar, which encompasses the 'more indefinable aspects of music' (Ofsted, 2021).

They then define three types of knowledge which combine to build each 'pillar' (Ofsted, 2021): first is 'tacit' knowledge, in the main acquired 'through enculturation, whereby members of a culture gain some tacit knowledge of the working of the main musical systems they hear' (Ofsted, 2021); the second is 'procedural' knowledge, built in tiny increments over time; it's largely knowledge of how something is to be done (the authors' example is playing the piano), learnt to the point of automaticity; the third type of knowledge is 'declarative' (Ofsted, 2021), the material which is taught explicitly and practised over time. In music 'examples of declarative knowledge might include that of notation, keys and chords or of the works and songs that illuminate musical culture' (Ofsted, 2021).

There are significant constraints on how this knowledge comes together in a curriculum, not least of which is that of contact time; which amounts merely to 'between 20 and 40 hours a year' in key stage 3 (Ofsted, 2021). Time is needed to embed all three types of knowledge, to teach, practise, test, and re-enforce learning, and its paucity means that not everything is possible; to echo Sir Richard

Musical curriculums

Livingstone, we need to be known by quantity of valuable music we decline to teach (Wiliam, 2013: 36).

And because the musical domain is so vast and so varied, it pays to remember that knowledge from one genre does not necessarily transfer successfully to another (Ofsted, 2021). This means that the teacher's clarity in explaining the curriculum to pupils is vital; clarity about when and how new material is related to old (to 'prior learning' (Ofsted, 2021)), and when it is not. It means that it's hard to make statements about musical principles and procedures which are generally true: a different generic context of a consecutive pair of perfect fifths, for example, might transform them from solecism to strength.

The authors take great pains to relate our teaching to 'current research on human cognition and the role of the phenomenon that cognitive psychologists refer to as working memory' (Ofsted, 2021). This is the heart of Ofsted's advice about developing a curriculum: that it should explicitly seek to build the long-term-memory knowledge-structures known as 'schemas' (Ofsted, 2021); and that, when delivering the components which are intended become the basis of or add to existing schemas, the significant limits of working-memory need to be mitigated (here associated with the concept of cognitive load). Within a curriculum, to this end, Ofsted recommends 'plentiful opportunities for pupils to return to and consolidate their short-term learning' (Ofsted, 2021) as well as 'repetition of key curricular content with the gradual introduction of new ideas, methods and concepts' (Ofsted, 2021).

The authors' suggestion for the development of the 'technical' pillar of the musical curriculum makes an interesting comparison with Paynter's recommended approach. Both are distinct products of their times. Whereas Paynter deals with the child as an artist, exploring the musical world; Ofsted draws on research in music psychology, expertise, and neuroscience to suggest that technique – taught directly and explicitly – is essential in every part of musical understanding:

> The ability to manipulate sound is central to both performing and composing. It also impacts on how we listen. Performance is unlikely to be an entirely satisfying experience for performers or listeners if it is undermined by technical inaccuracies. Composition flows from explorative improvisations and technical expertise expands the range of compositional possibility
>
> (Ofsted, 2021).

Again, the authors recommend that the musical curriculum is designed over time 'to gradually develop [pupils'] control over the sound they are producing'. And again, they caution that skills pertain only in a very limited set of circumstances – and that 'shallow encounters with lots of instruments will limit pupils' musical outcomes to the most mechanical and least expressive level' (Ofsted, 2021).

Early encounters with music should be as aural artefacts, but the authors also suggest that staff notation should be a significant part of our curriculums (Ofsted, 2021). An analogy is drawn between reading staff notation and early reading – both are symbolic systems made possible by explicit teaching. Early reading starts from the smallest perceptible units of sound in language, phonemes; the relating of symbol with sound is practised the to the point of automaticity; those sounds are associated with larger components; and finally, as fluency grows, higher-level structures can be considered. In sound the progression would be from sound, to motif and melody, through scales and chords to larger structures.

Reading music has a role in perception:

> notational systems ... change our internal conception of musical features rather than merely representing them
>
> (Ofsted, 2021).

As in mathematics, such 'symbolic systems are helpful in developing abstract concepts' (Ofsted, 2021), and higher-level understanding.

Having diverged so much, there's a moment of agreement between Paynter and Ofsted:

> high-quality music education may have ... space for exploration, inconsistency and independence
>
> (Ofsted, 2021).

This is a good lesson for us all.

Our curriculums?

This musical world is so multifarious, so varied, that it's near-impossible to come to a common agreement about what it is like. The autonomy many of us enjoy as individual teachers is the most-important lesson of this chapter, and it's easily forgotten. We are ourselves neither 'Prod' nor Paynter, but if we are offered the gift of significant freedom, we should choose to accept it. Used well, that freedom is stimulating for us as teachers, thinkers, and musicians, and has the possibility of igniting in our pupils the enthusiasm and passion which is the basis of all learning.

How to make the curriculum real in the classroom is the subject of the next chapter.

Notes

1. https://www.thetimes.co.uk/article/jack-longstaff-98-inspiring-blackburn-music-head-0d9btdljd [Accessed: 24 January 2022].
2. https://www.manchesterhigh.co.uk/hiddenarea/manhighmusings/taking-inspiration-from-annie-o-warburton [Accessed: 9 March 2022].
3. There is more posted about the project at: https://borthcat.york.ac.uk/index.php/university-of-york-music-in-the-secondary-school-curriculum-project [Accessed: 8 February 2022].

References

Arendt, H., 2006. *Between Past and Future*. London, Penguin.

Arnold, M., 2009. *Culture and Anarchy*. Oxford, Oxford University Press.

Department for Education (DfE), 2021. Model Music Curriculum: Key Stages 1 to 3. Available at: https://assets.publishing.service.gov.uk/government/uploads/system/uploads/attachment_data/file/974366/Model_Music_Curriculum_Full.pdf [Accessed: 14 December, 2021].

Education Act, 2002. Available at: https://www.legislation.gov.uk/ukpga/2002/32/contents [Accessed: 31 October 2022].

Griffiths, P., 1977. The York Project. *Music in Education*, 41, May/June.

Ofsted, 2021. Research Review Series: Music. Available at: https://www.gov.uk/government/publications/research-review-series-music/research-review-series-music [Accessed: 14 August 2021].

Paynter, J., 1982. *Music in the Secondary School Curriculum*. Cambridge, Cambridge University Press.

Paynter, J. & Aston, P., 1970. *Sound and Silence: Classroom Projects in Creative Music*. Cambridge, Cambridge University Press.

Sessions, R., 1979. What Can Be Taught, in Cone, Edward (ed.). *Roger Sessions on Music: Collected Essays*. Princeton, Princeton University Press.

Tolstoy, L., 1962. *What is Art and Essays on Art*. Translated by Maude, Aylmer. London, Oxford University Press.

Warburton, A.O., 1963. *Analyses of Music Classics*. London, Longman.

Warburton, A.O., 1967. *Analyses of Music Classics; Book 2*. London, Longman.

Warburton, A.O., 1974. *Analyses of Music Classics; Book 3*. London, Longman.

Warburton, A.O., 1975. *Analyses of Music Classic; Book 4*. London, Longman.

Wiliam, D., 2013. *Principled curriculum design*. SSAT The Schools Network. Available at: https://webcontent.ssatuk.co.uk/wp-content/uploads/2013/09/Dylan-Wiliam-Principled-curriculum-design-chapter-1.pdf [Accessed: 11 October 2019].

Chapter 4

Mastery in music

This chapter is about making the curriculum work in the classroom. It will define learning as a change in long-term memory (Kirschner *et al.*, 2006), and seek to explore the ways to plan lessons and sequences of lessons, how to exploit the findings of cognitive science (Willingham, 2009; 2015).

i. The long-term

It was Mr. Taylor and Mr. Young for me. Mr. Taylor was the embodiment of cultural sophistication, swirled around my traditional grammar school in gown and a miasma of learning. He shared with his form his subscription to *Private Eye* and *The Spectator*, and plied us with Evelyn Waugh and Sartre. Mr. Young was a model of precision and generosity. In his spare time he both travelled the country photographing things geographical, and made meticulous maps of fictitious places with the finest of pens and the steadiest of hands.

There is a mystique about great teachers and about great teaching which gathers power and significance over time. And our memories of teachers reinforce that mystery, as we ourselves seek to become teachers. But teaching is both an art and a craft. It's an art because it involves communication, and because, when practised at its highest levels, it seems just a little like magic. But, like all great art, it's a craft, too, and can be improved by study, attention, and most of all, by practice.

Musicians understand this very well, certainly those who are or who have aspired to be accomplished instrumentalists or singers. We know that mastery requires repetition and drill, daily work with absolute concentration, working towards and testing ourselves against goals. If we aspire to become master teachers, artists in the classroom, then we need to work on our craft.

Planning is such a desiccated and manilla-folder word, and it's a shame that we can't call it something else. But planning is where we can seek most immediately to improve our work.

DOI: 10.4324/9781003112402-4

We start from the highest of expectations, and from an aspiration to share our passion for and understanding of music with every child in our schools.

Planning should use language with the greatest of care – the language we use first betrays and then becomes our thoughts. It's all-too-easy to prize more- and demean less-able pupils, to celebrate the top end, bemoan the long tail, and most damagingly of all, to speak figuratively of talents and endow children with gifts. These last two are ideas which originated in Christian doctrine, which were subsequently appropriated by the romantic movement in the arts. It's our great gift that we can now begin to move away from them, begin to hold more utopian tenets – that with searing hard work, with years of persistence, and with an enormous dollop of luck, most things are possible for most people. Throughout this book, you will find the expressions 'more-experienced' and 'less-experienced'. They are not in any way ideal, but they do radiate a sense of possibility, of not-quite-yet, of experience earned through time.

ii. Planning for assessment

That is a deadly sub-title if ever there were one, but planning and assessment are integral parts of an educational whole. Teachers select and arrange knowledge, and make out of it an upward ascending staircase which pupils tread to move from beginner to expert. Each step relies on the last, and it's good to make sure that the footing is secure before reaching for the next. It's assessment which tests the safety of the present, makes possible the future.

It's assessment which moment-by-moment in the classroom determines where the lesson will travel, and how fast it can move; and it's assessment which confirms, validates, and celebrates the major rites of each pupil's passage. Both need to be incorporated in a teacher's plans.

Both types of assessment need to be simultaneously reliable and valid, terms borrowed from statistics. A reliable finding simply means one which can be repeated; a valid finding measures that which it claims to measure.

In moment-to-moment assessment, the reliability of a pupil's answer depends on the quality of the question. Asking, 'Is the pentatonic scale used in Chinese music?' will not elicit a reliable answer – the pupil has a 50% chance of guessing the correct answer. The likelihood of guesswork can be removed, and the possibly of reliability made more certain if you ask the same question in a number of different ways. Better still ask questions which give pupils the chance to demonstrate their thinking: 'From what culture does this piece come?', or 'what does the scale used in this piece suggest about its origins?'

There is a real danger here that a teacher hears what they want to hear, moves onto the next step without being truly certain that a pupil really knows what they have been taught.

Reliability is also a concern in more-formal assessment. But it's validity which is a bigger concern. Testing – whether the informal low-stakes testing, which provides such useful practice for pupils, or whether the more-formal end-of-module assessment – the results need to tell a truth about learning. Unless they are designed with great care, multiple-choice questions can be a problem – especially if used as the only or the principal means of assessment. The problem is that a multiple-choice question presents pupils with the correct answer, removing some of the intellectual struggle which is required in the building of permanent knowledge. Multiple-choice tests are only truly successful if the correct answer is mixed with both highly-plausible alternatives and common misconceptions, meaning that the pupils have to think quite hard about which is actually correct (Little *et al.,* 2012).

It's easier to plan for validity using questions which are much more open, which expect pupils to tell you why, to tell you how, and to make conceptual links between different pieces of knowledge.

You can plan to make assessment more efficient, too. If pupils are to produce a piece of analytic writing, then make sure that the piece of information you need to check is in the same place on the page, easily available at a glance as the teacher moves around the room; make sure that it's easy to track a class's progress through a work-sheet, in case the lesson needs to be adjusted for the particular group taking it, or if some aspect needs to be taught again.

iii. Mastery

There is something simultaneously inspiring and daunting about so-called mastery learning, but it's something which should have a place in the music classroom. The first problem is with its name. Psychologists who are concerned with motivation make a distinction between ends which are driven by performance and those aiming for mastery (Didau & Rose, 2016). Performance seeks affirmation from others, praise, acclaim, or good marks in a test; mastery is the pleasure of getting better at something, of cracking a code for oneself, of finding out things.

The mastery approach is usually associated with Benjamin Bloom (1968). He challenges us to believe that the most important variable within the classroom is the teacher, that deep knowledge of our subject combined with significant craft will make it possible for the overwhelming majority of our pupils to learn everything which we teach. This undermines some of the assumptions on which the conventional curriculum is based: we will spend three weeks' lessons learning about the blues; then three on twentieth-century art music; then nineteenth-century programme music. Apportionments of knowledge (the blues) are to be learnt in a set period of time (one 50-minute lesson each week for three weeks, for instance). Bloom's mastery approach says that we will spend as much time as it takes for almost all the pupils, 80% or more, to be able to succeed in the assessment we have set. This has been an influential finding: Rosenshine's 'obtain a high success rate' (2012: 12) but one recent and much-debated offspring.

Bloom suggests that very pupil will need to take a slightly different path through each chunk of knowledge, and that the ideal for every child is one-to-one tuition (1968). His fascination with this '2 sigma problem' ('2 sigma' meaning that something is true 95% of the time) leads to his suggestions about making each pupil's experience more individual, even within a busy class of 30.

This inspires for two reasons: first, it places high expectations at the heart of our work – and not just wooly statements, but pupils' scores in an assessment which are to exceed a certain number. Secondly, there is an inspiring body of evidence suggesting that this approach is probably most effective for less-experienced pupils, perhaps the ones who are too-easily excluded from the highest of expectations (EEF, 2018).

This daunts because of its practical challenges – what if it takes four weeks rather than three to teach a topic? – and because of the demands it places on the teacher.

How might this work in music? Mark McCourt (2019) suggests a six-stage process:

Preparing to teach

The first stage is to make sure that the pupils are ready to learn. When we start a new topic, we often assume that the foundational knowledge is in place – if it's not, then the walls quickly come tumbling down. Pupils test each atom of new material against what they already know, assimilating it with other covalent molecule structures, and grow each in turn, building wide and grand structures of knowledge (Ausubel, 1968; Willingham, 2015). Testing our assumptions about the pupils' prior knowledge, a 'diagnostic assessment', is the first step (McCourt, 2019: 22).

An early assessment is a good thing for two other reasons. First, testing provides pupils with another opportunity to practise their knowledge – effortful remembering and attentive calculation are what learning looks like (Roediger & Butler, 2011; Rosenshine, 2012). Secondly, it's an opportunity to set out the stall of knowledge, to help pupils to understand the nature of what's coming next, and even to show them its overview. The testing might be associated with an overview of the new topic, a story, a set of topic headings, or some sort of map showing its contours (Ausubel, 1968).

Direct instruction

At first glance this is very simple – at this second stage, the pupils are taught something new. But Bloom's emphasis on the teacher's responsiveness, on the combination of knowledge and craft, makes this rather fascinating. The teacher is expected to work in a way which is appropriate to the pupils, responsive in a way which goes beyond the normal definition of good teaching (Hattie & Timperley, 2007; Coe *et al.*, 2014). It means that the teacher's subject knowledge is sufficient that they are able to offer not only one single well-practised explanation of a new idea, but many; not just a single analogy or explaining metaphor, but a variety; not one example of a way around a problem, but several, each of which is intricately-nuanced, and responds directly to the immediate needs of the pupils.

And, of course, this instruction will contain numerous opportunities for and feedback on deliberate practice.

First assessment

The teacher then tests what has been learnt. The nature of this first assessment is important: it's closer to an informal quiz or low-stakes testing than it is to a formal summative examination. It's the opportunity for the pupils once more to practise and rehearse their knowledge, and for the teacher to 'notice and act' (McCourt, 2019: 22) – notice those who have not yet understood, those who have fallen into misconceptions, and those who are flying; act to give 'feedback in the moment' (McCourt, 2019: 22–3).

More teaching (and a digression about adaptive teaching)

This is a moment of humility and excitement for the teacher. Informed by the assessment, the same material is taught again, but this time using different means. Some talk of re-teaching, but that is not at all the point: re-teaching could simply consist in teaching the same material again in the same old way. The flexibility required here is to teach the same material again, but to deliver it in a *different* way, a new approach which takes into account both what the pupils have thus-far learnt, as well as the means by which it was taught first time. There is a sense in which this corrects the teaching which has gone before, a humbling and educational experience for every teacher. It forces the teacher to take pride in what has been learnt, and responsibility for what has not been understood. It's also a moment of excitement: there is nothing humdrum or dull about being forced to delve deep into your own knowledge and to draw on every resource of your craft as a teacher – this is the fun bit.

There are often caveats raised at this point: what happens to the pupils who have genuinely mastered the topic? The distance between the most- and the least-experienced musician in the music classroom is probably wider than in any other space in the school. Mastery's advocates would specify that all knowledge is partial, that we can teach our more-experienced pupils both humility and awe about the sheer heft of what there is to know, even in the seeming-simplest of topics.

But this is a really interesting and important question for all music teachers. There is much loose talk about adaptive teaching (sometimes called differentiation) in our classrooms, all well-intentioned, some downright dangerous. It might first be easiest to say what adaptive teaching is not. In the music classroom, adaptive teaching is not giving different work to pupils in possession of different levels of musical experience, nor is it a series of colour-coded worksheets – daunting to some, a race for others, substantive learning for only a few. Neither is it setting different goals for different pupils. The observation-friendly 'all', 'most', 'some' is a pedagogical manifestation of low expectations, just plain wrong.

At best, adaptive teaching in music is about making it possible for all pupils to reach the same goal, about setting a goal which is both realistic and challenging for every pupil; a goal of sufficient merit and depth that it will be valuable for all. If we are any kind of musician, we know that the simplest thing can be refined infinitely, and that there is great joy in the work of that refinement (again mastery is not, in the pedagogic sense performance) – we also know that musical greatness does the most astonishing things using apparently rudimentary means. This has a place in our classrooms.

Once the goal is set, then adaptive teaching comes in, recognising that every pupil is an individual, an autonomous thinker, recognising that each will find a different way of achieving that aim. Each pupil will need different *levels* of support from the teacher, and all will need different *types* of support from the teacher.

This approach naturally escapes the confines of a single lesson, is possibly greater even than a sequence of lessons. And its planning requires some deep thinking, both about defining a goal of nuance and substance, and a consideration of the multiple means by which pupils will reach it. It needs a two-fold planning of lessons, too. This approach to planning is not merely concerned with the teacher's actions, but simultaneously with what the pupils will be doing in response (Lemov, 2015: 143–5). It should consider the activities mandated by the teacher – whether they should be answering questions or writing notes, trying an exercise, or listening attentively to a piece of music – but at the same time be aware of their 'hidden lives'. It's invisible to even the most-experienced teacher, but whilst doing the teacher's bidding, in lessons pupils will be thinking for themselves, may well be talking (or singing) to themselves, as well as interacting with their peers (at best asking questions, seeking clarification or confirmation, helping and encouraging) (Nuthall, 2007).

At the end of this section is a short practical experiment in adaptive teaching.

More assessment

After more teaching, there comes a second group of assessments. The everyday nature of these assessments is important – unlike a traditional end-of-module test, they make testing just one more of the habits of the classroom, associated more with learning than with judgement. They are a new opportunity for pupils to demonstrate their mastery of the material, and for the teacher to check that the teaching has been successful. If the latter has not been successful, if a compelling majority of the class has not yet obtained good results, then the cycle is repeated. McCourt uses the diving test as an analogy (McCourt, 2019: 25). Once we've passed the driving test, we all have equal rights on the road – but it takes many of us several attempts to pass, and between each attempt come more individualised lesson with a teacher, helping us to practise and master the clutch, the indicator, and the mirrors. But being let-loose on the road is not the end of the story. Once licensed, we are permitted to drive, but we are not yet Lewis Hamilton – the test is merely one more stage in our development.

Beyond mastery

For the pupils who have been successful, either on the first or second assessment, there are other things to do. This should not be new material; rather it should be the same ideas treated with greater depth and in new ways. The idea of practice is to build stronger knowledge schemas, and to build stronger links between schemas. This is one of the easier things in music. We are a repeating and refining art, and there are always ways in which we can seek to improve; our pupils need to experience and begin to learn that discipline.

Mastery in music

A short and practical experiment in adaptive teaching.

The following is an experiment in adaptive teaching and mastery. It is an exercise in composition, focusing on melody writing, and on the use of systematic repetition of musical materials. Depending on the experience of the pupils, this might be used from year 7 upwards.

Plans are often best built backwards from their intended goal. The long-term aim of this particular experiment is to teach pupils to become composers. The particular way-marker here on the road to that distant goal is to understand the properties of and to be able to compose an eight-bar question-and-answer melody. A good final response would be this:

Pupils might be shown this melody as a model, and helped to understand what makes it good:

A phrase is a component part of a melody which belongs together. A great deal of music deals in four-bar phrases, and this is a pair of them. The second four-bar phrase balances the first, a question followed by an answer. This means that in the balancing second phrase there is more repetition of material heard in the first phrase than there is new and contrasting music.

Melodies are built on scales, and some notes in each scale are more stable than others (this explanation is clearest when seated at the piano). You can test for stability by putting it at the end of a phrase: if the phrase sounds complete then the note is stable, if incomplete it's unstable.

Stability and instability are predicated on harmony, which is the use of chords. The context of a chord explains why some notes can be both stable and unstable. In this melody, the first phrase ends on a note drawn from chord V (the dominant), and the second on chord I (the tonic).

In speech, questions end with an upwards inflection; when you write a musical question you end with the notes of chord V (the dominant); an answer needs to be more definite, and the notes of the tonic chord (I) come at its end. Answers often conclude with a musical full stop (a perfect cadence).

This explanation should be accompanied with a detailed annotation of the melody. The finished board might look like this:

There are conventional patterns of melodic repetition which pupils should understand and can use:

In an eight-bar phrase there is space to include both basic principles of composition – repetition and contrast. There can be direct repetition: the first-bar motif is repeated in the fifth. There can be repetition by motivic development: the first-bar motif (x) has a dotted rhythm and mainly-conjunct movement. In bars 3 and 7, the rhythm is the same but the pitches are developed, becoming a descending scale (x'). There is contrast, too: motif y has a simple rhythm consisting in two crotchets and disjunct movement. It, too, is repeated, in bar 6.

All of the foregoing is quite a detailed explanation, and its use depends of the experience of the class. A simpler version of this can work almost as well:

Melodies are built on scales. Here's a five-note scale starting on 'middle' C. If your melody ends on C, the first note of the scale, it will sound complete; if you reach G at the middle of the phrase, it will sound incomplete.

Your first bar should be the same as the fifth; the second as the sixth; the fourth as the seventh.

But this comes with significant caveats: with a little thought, skill, and luck, it's quite easy to help pupils to write music which is convincing and often attractive. A basic stage-by-stage approach like this is really helpful in building pupils' confidence, and that's a really big part of composition. It shows them that the teacher's highest of expectations of them are not misplaced. But pupils need to understand the craft of music, too, how they've made an attractive piece, and how they might use and build on those processes and conventions to do still better next time.

Mastery in music

Once pupils have seen and analysed a good outcome, they can start themselves. And every pupil will likely start in a slightly different place. What follows is a set of possible starting-points for the exercise. It is designed to be used sequentially, starting from those which offer only rather abstract suggestions, and moving through a progression to those which are much more prescriptive.

The task might be introduced with an outline: time- and key-signatures followed by eight empty bars divided four plus four; a plausible harmonic structure is suggested. This might be all the instruction needed by the most-experienced composers:

Slightly-less experienced composers might be helped and encouraged by a pattern of melodic repetition which looks like this:

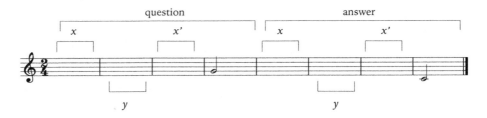

This specifies that the first phrase finishes in bar four on the dominant, and the second on the tonic in bar eight – represented on the example by the fifth degree of the scale and the first, respectively. Because repetition is an essential component of all composition, it shows that the only two different bars need to be invented (x and y), and that the rest is simply duplication. It shows that the first bar and the fifth bar should be the same, the second and the sixth, and the third and the seventh too. But because contrast is the second essential component of all composition, it shows that the repetitions should ideally be varied slightly (x').

It's also possible to give a little more help by specifying the motif which is to be used in four of the eight bars:

Aside from completing the missing bars, pupils can be helped to build contrast into the third and the seventh bars. A possible solution, altering the third, and improving the contour from the last beat of bar seven into bar eight, is shown below:

In composing the missing bars, pupils can be given notes from which to choose, and even have a rhythm specified.

Remember that the final goal of this exercise is for the pupils to become better composers, and the specific aspect practised here is the composition of eight-bar question-and-answer phrases. The foregoing has concentrated on different ways of explaining composition to less-experienced musicians; some of the more-experienced will have galloped through the exercise already – what of them?

Well, there are two things which mastery requires of the teachers. The first is to make sure that the melodies written by the more-experienced musicians, the simple tasks which have been completed so quickly, are both correct and as good as they can be. Experienced musicians feel such confidence in our lessons, and that is a wonderful thing; but it does lead to mistakes, often mistakes which are based on misconceptions about rather simple things. Once those are corrected, then the melodies should be improved and revised. Revision, re-writing, and re-composition are the true secrets of every artistic pursuit – scribbling-out and making it better, scraping-off the paint, withdrawing the five-act version because it's not quite right – and the sooner young composers learn to evaluate and endlessly improve their work, the better. Ron Berger's (2004) example of Austin's butterfly may be a staple of after-school training, but it's truly inspiring, and easy to see the improvement in one boy's work with the help of superb feedback and constant revision.

The second part of the mastery approach is to make the exercise endlessly deeper. For these more-experienced musicians it might be to add dynamics,

Mastery in music

articulation, and phrasing – simply, elegantly, and with proper consideration for the musical substance – or to use the chords to make an accompaniment, bass-line, or contrapuntal second part. Pupils might then take their eight-bar unit, internally balanced, and build it into a 16-bar phrase – a balanced pair of eight-bar phrases. Something really simple can quickly become something far-more ambitious – and when it happens, it's invariably an inspiring moment.

Mastery in the curriculum

This all might take a great deal more time than conventional approaches, perhaps as much as 20% (McCourt, 2019). The proponents of mastery suggest that the extra time spent now will save time later; that subsequent units of work might be shorter as a result of pupils' increased confidence in what comes before. They also argue that the stronger the foundations, the more-imposing and high-reaching the eventual structure will be.

Which takes us back to the psychologists, to the difference between mastery and performance. This mastery approach has to be used with great care within the curriculum. The teacher has to be near-certain that the 80% who have passed the test have actually learnt something – effected a permanent change in long-term memory; near-certain that they have not merely been taught to perform well in a test.

The trick here is to combine the mastery approach with other means of teaching, perhaps to reserve it for knowledge which is truly foundational to the music curriculum – the use of staff notation. And it can only work if the curriculum is built in such a way that the pupils return again and again to deeper iterations of the topic; making deliberate practice of the knowledge, well-spaced, an intrinsic part of their work over the course of several years (Dunlosky *et al.,* 2013). This resonates strongly with Bruner's (1960) idea of the spiral curriculum.

Mastery learning is thought-provoking, and potentially a useful component of the music teacher's toolkit.

iv. The medium term

It matters very much how pupils write and speak, and we do young people a tremendous disservice if we do not expect from them the highest of standards. Language matters for two interlinked reasons: because a person's skilled use of language is the only real way we can test their thinking; and because the use of good conventional language will help our pupils to succeed in life.

The great essayist, poet, and farmer Wendell Berry reminds us that the etymology of 'sentence' has *sentire*, Latin 'to think' as well as the Middle English, 'way of thinking'. He puts it perfectly:

A sentence is both the opportunity and the limit of thought

(Berry, 2011: 53)

We should expect from our pupils written and spoken answers in full sentences, using correct and formal language, because only from this we can see the clarity of their thinking, teach them how to improve.

Language denotes and earns respect, too. The answer 'fast' might well be correct when discussing a sonata by Mozart, but far better would be:

'In this song, the tempo Allegro means that it is to be played quick.'

'Fast' is a little derisory as a stand-alone answer. The fuller answer is far more revealing, and in its way impressive. The heart is very good ('tempo Allegro'), but the beginning ('song' instead of 'piece' or 'movement') and the end (the mangled adjective) are not. The latter is possibly careless – and carelessness with language might mean carelessness of thought; the former might help someone looking to make a judgement come to an incorrect opinion of the pupil. We want our pupils to show their best selves under pressure; correcting them now, in our classrooms, and in their homework, is the best way to do it.

It's a question of character, too. Humans are remarkably perceptive in their relations one with another, can adapt chameleon-like to circumstance, and perform accordingly. As teachers, we speak in different ways to each other, to our pupils, to the headmistress, and to the governors. This we do almost without thought, because of the experience we have, and because we've made a few mistakes in our time. In insisting on formality from our pupils – full sentences, correct grammar and syntax, careful and very-sparing use of slang – we give them the opportunity to practise relating to others formally, which practice will help them to thrive at interviews for jobs and universities, and beyond in their professional lives.

Experts speak to each other in code, using short-cuts, and assuming shared knowledge. It saves time, words, and thought (yet another example of knowledge mattering). The name for this, jargon, has an older meaning, too, implying barbarity and debasement, and the negative connotation is apt to stick. Rather than excluding, however, in reality this invites: if our pupils have sufficient knowledge, even if that knowledge is passing, then they are part of the closed circle; invited to belong to a group which can discuss either Bach's counterpoint or the latest

Mastery in music

NME review of Pom Poko's Norwegian strangeness. Planning for the medium-term helps to include in this as many pupils as possible.

Little details should be part of this planning, too. Having worked in and recruited for two schools whose names contain the apostrophe, I know how easy it is for the busy recruiter to reject an application which does not spell or punctuate the schools' names correctly. Build habits of literacy from the very beginning, and your pupils will have one fewer disadvantage in life.

Teaching difficult things

Alongside the opportunity of language, there are other considerations in the medium term. Music is a vast and rich landscape, simultaneously part of people's lives and subject to scholarly attentions of the highest order. A fascinating question in planning asks how to find the right level of material.

There are two pernicious traps which we should seek to avoid: either denigrating a topic because we ourselves lack confidence in its teaching; and telling our pupils that something is too hard.

Because of the breadth of the landscape we inhabit, it's impossible for any one music teacher to be truly expert in all of its particulars. It's important and good that we are compelled by examination syllabuses to teach a variety of music with which we are less familiar – it allows us to be reminded just how hard it is to be a novice in any subject, and builds in us greater empathy for our pupils. But it also opens a world of music for our pupils; the possibility of sparking in them that lifelong passion which is the ideal aftermath of teaching.

We can teach music we do not know well with curiosity and wonder, with respect for its cultural background, and with proper humility about the depths of our own ignorance; or we can denigrate and teach because the syllabus tells us to. Either way, the choice is made by the teacher.

Music is a technical subject which deals with the biggest ideas and the headiest passions. It's constructed using formulas and conventions, using a language with its own grammar, syntax, and morphology, and it whispers secrets of what it means to be human. These are big, nearly overwhelming ideas, and that's the wonder of it.

But, I'll warrant that in every one of our schools there is a pupil or a handful of pupils who are already masters of their own distinct musical territory – who know as much as anyone about it. There is only so much to know about *The 1975*, and perhaps only so many people who would care to know, but meet Oliver in my class and he can tell you most of it.

Why should pupils not try things which are 'too difficult' for them? Barnaby Lenon (2017) tells of challenging his year 9 classes to learn the name of every country in the world, some 200 or so; Doug Lemov (2015) is proud that students from Newark New Jersey in the first school he founded could order lunch in Mandarin; I taught A-level harmony to year 7 pupils (Leigh, 2020).

We should present 'difficult' material without apology or simplification (although, it should be said that, in some boys' schools, forbidding boys from reading something is an effective incentive), and certainly without telling pupils that anything is beyond them. The level of enthusiasm is palpable for material which goes beyond expectations, or which allows children to peer into the world of university and beyond; when a teacher 'trusts' a class with something which is challenging, the education is also something about confidence, belief, and ambition.

Making a plan realistic

Music teachers might have the best job in the world, but they also tend to be the busiest person on the staff. (Please accept a little hyperbole, but that often seems to be near enough to the truth properly to be stated here.) A lunchtime spent rehearsing the wind band, a few seconds of caffeine, then the double with year 8, some time on administration, and an evening's concert – this is the nature of our days. And it's all-too-easy to rush into the double lesson, with only a hazy idea of what the lesson is about, certainly without a plan, relying on enthusiasm and experience to carry the day.

Whisper it quietly, but sometimes that's fine, when self-preservation is the order of the day and more-important than meticulous planning. But there are many other times when a little planning can simultaneously come to the rescue and result in a really strong sequence of lessons for our charges. There are two ideas here.

The first, is that no lesson is an island, isolated and lonely. The means by which islands become archipelagos is through clarity of purpose, through having clearly in mind the eventual aim of the sequence of lessons. This is very hard to do in a subject where the outcome is quite so tangible: the aim of these four lessons is for all pupils to have composed an eight-bar question-and-answer phrase using an Alberti bass; the aim of these six lessons is to prepare pupils to answer questions about the GCSE set work (a Vivaldi string concerto) – both of these might result in good lessons, but neither represents clear-eyed thinking about what the pupils will have learnt, and both rather conflate what the pupil is doing in a lesson with what the pupil will have learnt by the end of the series of lessons.

Are the lessons about question-and-answer primarily concerned with the economy of materials in composition – in teaching our pupils that repetition is both at the heart of great composition, and that it itself makes the act of composition easier? Or is it teaching about balance and proportion in music? Or is it a composition exercise exploring, practising, and deepening knowledge of the classical period?

The GCSE syllabus might well require that pupils can identify the *ritornello* and episode, the *ripieno* and *concertino*, continuos and cadenzas, but what more do we want them to understand, feel, and do? When they come across the work in years to come, what do we want them to remember, recognise, and comprehend – what in our teaching will make them passionate and informed future listeners?

Further, what is the place of assessment in these lessons: assessment not just of the final outcome (the composition or the GCSE past paper) but an ongoing process of practice for the pupils, and feedback for the teacher.

The simple act of thinking hard about an aim for a sequence of lessons, and repeating it to ourselves when taking-on caffeine before year 8, has the potential to make all the difference.

The second idea is that there is very good work to do as part of our daily commute. Musical stories about this abound: whether the value of practice snatched whilst waiting for the carriage to arrive, or learning a piano concerto in a train-compartment on a long journey, without an instrument. These are simultaneously apocryphal and true.[1] But the time in the car practising, simplifying, and making automatic our explanations of the Alberti bass, of the use of the continuo section, of repetitions are hugely valuable. A well-practised analogy helps the lesson in both flow and substance, frees time in the classroom, which might be used more effectively.

Making a plan practical (or how not to do what I do)

In a storm of idealism, it's very easy to become somewhat carried away; this is one subject upon which I speak with real authority. But plans have to be practical as well as realistic. The idea of teaching even a working knowledge of 1960s pop, or Klezmer, or the eighteenth-century symphony in one cycle of lessons may well be commendable only for its ambition.

The aims in each sequence of lessons need to be practical, and to fit within the allotted time. There are here two realistic constraints, and two great opportunities.

The first is the constraint of a single lesson. There is only so much which can be accomplished in a 40- or 50-, or 55-minute period, and within it time is precious. If possible, lessons should begin and end by reviewing knowledge: at the beginning to make sure that the pupils have the knowledge and understanding which are the underpinnings of what comes next; at the end to check again what has been taught. At the heart of the lesson comes the three-part delivery of the new material: an explanation of new material by the teacher; guided practice shared between teacher and pupils; and the pupils' own practice. Even to aspire to this ideal poses considerable limitations on the amount of new material which can be taught.

The second constraint is the sequence of lessons, by how much material can be contained within even several lessons strung together. There's clearly more time in four lessons than in one, but it's not quite that simple; the time is certainly not four times as much. For within that sequence of lessons the balance of reviewing the old and teaching the new shifts subtly towards the former; and within that sequence there needs to be some sort of testing, which itself takes time. The teacher needs formally and informally to measure progress towards a goal, needs to mark and celebrate success, needs to identify those elements which require more practice and work. That testing can be a simple answer-this-question-before-you-leave activity, or it can be a more formal submission of written- or composition-work. All of this takes time, and reduces the amount of material it's possible to teach.

The first great opportunity is this: that once interest is sparked, the resources available to pupils today are unimaginably rich. There is much talk of flipped classrooms, of pupils learning new material beyond the classroom: if the technology and the culture of a school allow it, this has rich possibilities in the music classroom. It can allow pupils to have at least encountered new material before each lesson, and means that the teacher's time is spent guiding pupils' practice rather than explaining material. If the teacher makes a video explaining the next stage of a composition, and the pupils watch and take notes from the video for homework, then the lesson can begin immediately with composition, and more of the teacher's time can be spent giving individual feedback.

The constraints, then, are considerable, but nothing is impossible, and it's instructive to see just what can be done. Just how much about the eighteenth-century symphony might it be possible to teach in four short lessons? Very little is the answer, but the lessons might nonetheless be rich and valuable ones. The sum total in year 7 is probably this:

> *The eighteenth-century symphony, as composed by Joseph Haydn and Wolfgang Amadeus Mozart, is a work for a small orchestra in four movements: the first movement is fast and in sonata form, the second slow and song-like, the third a minuet and trio, and the fourth a rondo.*

It's very little, but it's not nothing. It constitutes one foundation of the Western cultural inheritance, and, if taught and learnt well, gives pupils knowledge which, later in life could be the basis of a passionate enthusiasm, could help them make informed small-talk with a potential employer or partner, or could make them a champion in a pub quiz.

Neither is it quite as little as it first appears: pupils need to understand as part of it a little about the history and instruments of the orchestra; need to be able to listen for tempo and metre; to know some of the basics of form. It's important to note here that the plan starts with knowledge, and that the activities are used to practise the knowledge are secondary: the decision to teach rondo form comes before the means by which we do it. And all the time, we are teaching, almost incidentally, the skills and knowledge required of a musical being: Italian words for tempo and dynamics; notation; melody, harmony, and all the rest.

The second great opportunity is this: that the year 8 curriculum might be this:

> *The eighteenth-century symphony, as composed by Joseph Haydn and Wolfgang Amadeus Mozart, is a work for a small orchestra in four movements: the first movement may start with a slow introduction which is then followed by quicker music in sonata form, the second movement is slow and song-like, the third a minuet and trio, and the fourth a rondo. The first, third, and fourth movements will be in the tonic, but the second is likely to be on a contrasting but related key.*

The essential similarity is powerful: it re-visits the material a year later, gives pupils the chance to practise once more the knowledge and skills learnt in year 7, provides an opportunity to refine and make them permanent. But there is a difference, too: not just the nuance of a slow introduction, but also the essential knowledge that key and form are inextricably linked.

The year 9 curriculum is familiar, but once-more growing in its ambitions:

> *The eighteenth-century symphony, as composed by Joseph Haydn and Wolfgang Amadeus Mozart, is a work for a small orchestra in four movements: the first movement may start with a slow introduction which is then followed by quicker music in sonata form, the second movement is slow and song-like, the third a minuet and trio, and the fourth a rondo. The first, third, and fourth movements will be in the tonic, but the second is likely to be on a contrasting but related key. The symphonic genre is a significant part of the rise of instrumental music in the late eighteenth-century, and paved the way for the nine revolutionary symphonies of Ludwig van Beethoven.*

The chance to return to material three times before pupils choose their GCSE options is the greatest of opportunities.

v. The short term

The next stage is the moment-to-moment enactment of a plan, whether it survives 'first contact with the enemy'. Which, of course, it does not. Every class and every child is different – the 'crooked timber' of humanity an intrinsic part of its glory – and no one lesson will ever be the same twice. Being a music teacher is the best job in the world, and this is part of the reason why.

Using a plan is about 'sensitivity and adaptation' (Nuthall, 2007); it's about the awareness of what is happening in your lesson, and what you might do to help your charges as they take their next steps. Such awareness may come with experience and introspection, can be the result of 'blind trial and error'; but there are principles and ideas which can help to make the errors fewer, the trials more successful, and provide moment-by-moment feedback which responds to your teaching, and which can help to shape the lesson. Some of these are examined in chapter 5.

When I was a boy, my friend and I treasured books of adventure, ones in which you, as reader, helped to determine the plot. At the end of each corridor, seeing passages to left and to right, the reader chose which to take, and turned to a certain page to reveal the consequences of their choice. Whether fearsome monster or golden treasure, it seemed that the reader enjoyed some sort agency.

The teacher's role in the plan is to make the choices for the class, and, maybe, to avoid the foulest of monsters. An activity at the beginning of a lesson can determine where that lesson needs to go. Let's assume that the activity is paper-based and that the teacher is able to circulate and take note of the pupils' work. It's good to take note physically, rather than mentally, of those things which the class find most difficult. The tally can determine whether the lesson moves to the next thing, or whether it's necessary to return and teach something again. It does not matter why the pupil has misunderstood – although a good teacher will take note of those things which their classes often fail to grasp, and think about better ways to teach them in the first place – it matters that those deficiencies are addressed, and quickly.

It's a good idea to start a lesson this way, with some sort of informal, low-stakes assessment, an activity to test understanding. The word 'test' is best avoided, as this work has much more to do with practising understanding and building memory, than it does with collecting marks. It's also good to test for, and have a plan to address the mistakes which pupils most commonly make. These might be simple failures of logic or memory – conjunct versus 'disconjunct' melodic movement – or places where the English-language conventions of music are quite strange – root, then first, then second inversions of a triad – or when the same word can mean many different things (polysemy): the meanings of inversion is a troublesome example, although dominant, and perfect also cause problems. Whatever their type, a rehearsed explanation or quick exercise, held in reserve, can save a great deal of time, and can make a huge difference to the pupils' experience in a lesson. Perhaps there are as many ways through the lesson as there are teachers who teach them.

It is also a good idea temporarily to stop a particularly tricky activity regularly, to make sure that the pupils' path through it is straight and direct. For those doing well with it, encouragement and affirmation are always welcome; for those about to plunge into a thicket of misunderstanding, this can be a moment of rescue. When pupils are composing using a model, for instance, there are moments when predictable mistakes, ones which have the potential to waste a great deal of time, can be avoided. If the pupils' composition is modelled on an extant piece of music, there will be moments when composers' mistakes or their deliberate (and unhelpful) rule-breaking need quietly to be glossed over.

Planning

Planning aims to effect changes in our pupils' long-term memories, and it's a complicated business, and hard to do well. But what happens to the plan when it encounters the classroom, how it is made real, depends on what the teacher does every day.

If our aim is to become the best version of our teaching selves, then we have to ask ourselves a question: what does a great music teacher do?

Note

1. I've heard these stories told about Ignacy Paderewski, prime minister and pianist, about Hans von Bülow who conducted Brahms and married Wagner's daughter, and about Rakhmaninov.

References

Ausubel, D.P., 1968. *Educational Psychology: A Cognitive View*. New York, Holt, Rinehart and Winston.

Berger, R. 2004. *Austin's Butterfly*. Available at: https://modelsofexcellence.eleducation. org/resources/austins-butterfly [Accessed: 19 March 2019].

Berry, W., 2011. *Standing by Words: Essays*. Berkeley, Counterpoint.

Bloom, B.S., 1968. Learning for Mastery. *Regional Education Laboratory for the Carolinas and Virginia, Topical Papers and Reprints*, Number 1.

Bruner, J., 1960. *The Process of Education*. Cambridge, Mass, Harvard University Press.

Coe, R., Aloisi, C., Higgins, S., & Major, L.E., 2014. *What Makes Great Teaching? Review of the Underpinning Research*. London, Sutton Trust. Available at: https://www.sutton-trust.com/our-research/great-teaching [Accessed: 15 May 2020].

Didau, D. & Rose, N., 2016. *What Every Teacher Needs to Know About Psychology*. Woodbridge, John Catt.

Dunlosky, J., Rawson, K.A., Marsh, E.J., Nathan, M.J., & Willingham, D.T., 2013. Improving Students' Learning with Effective Learning Techniques: Promising Directions from Cognitive and Educational Psychology. *Psychological Science in the Public Interest*, 14(1), 4–58.

Education Endowment Foundation (EEF): Mastery Learning, 2018. Available at: [https://educationendowmentfoundation.org.uk/pdf/generate/?u=https://educationendow-mentfoundation.org.uk/pdf/toolkit/?id=156&t=Teaching%20and%20Learning%20Toolkit&e=156&s=] [Accessed: 26 January 2021]

Hattie, J. & Timperley, H., 2007. The Power of Feedback. *Review of Educational Research*, 77(1), 81–112.

Kirschner, P.A., Sweller, J., & Clark, R.E., 2006. Why Minimal Guidance during Instruction Does Not Work: An Analysis of the Failure of Constructivist, Discovery, Problem-Based, Experiential, and Inquiry-Based Teaching. *Educational Psychologist*, 41(2), 75–86.

Leigh, M.D., 2020. How to fail perfectly, a research review. *TES*, 20 November 2020.

Lemov, D., 2015. *Teach Like a Champion 2.0: 62 Techniques That Put Students on the Path to College*. San Francisco, Jossey-Bass.

Lenon, B., 2017. *Much Promise: Successful Schools in England*. Woodbridge, John Catt.

Little, J.L., Bjork, E., Bjork, L., & Angello, R.A., 2012. Multiple-Choice Tests Exonerated, at Least of Some Charges: Fostering Test-Induced Learning and Avoiding Test-Induced Forgetting. *Psychological Science*, 23(11), 1337–44.

McCourt, M., 2019. *Teaching for Mastery*. Woodbridge, John Catt.

Nuthall, G., 2007. *The Hidden Lives of Learners*. Wellington, Nzcer Press.

Roediger, H.L. & Butler, A.C., 2011. The Critical Role of Retrieval Practice in Long-Term Retention. *Trends in Cognitive Sciences*, 15(1), 20–27.

Rosenshine, B., 2012. Principles of Instruction: Research-Based Strategies That All Teachers Should Know. *American Educator*, 36(1).

Willingham, D.T., 2009. *Why don't Students Like School?: A Cognitive Scientist Answers Questions about How the Mind Works and What It Means for the Classroom*. San Francisco, Wiley.

Willingham, D.T., 2015. Ask the cognitive scientist: Do students remember what they learn in school? *American Educator*, 39(3) 33–38.

Chapter 5

What does a great music teacher do?

A great music teacher makes an impact beyond their classroom and we're all different. But we all seek to build relationships with pupils and colleagues, and we all manage spaces – be they classrooms or rehearsal spaces; there are key things which we all have in common.

Managing the classroom

'Wingèd chariot'

Time is the most precious asset in any classroom. Waste time and the children in your class will never get it back. There are about 22 hours to learn music with me in year 7. If I fail to make the most of even a few minutes of every lesson, say a total of six or seven minutes in each, then the cumulative result is that my 22 hours quickly becomes 18 and my pupils' education is measurably worse.

It's good, then, that the small changes can make a very big difference.

At the beginning of lessons we need folders, keyboards, and headphones, all three taken from their storage-places and given out to every pupil. Our lessons are only 40 minutes long, and time spent taking-out and packing-away needs to be kept to a minimum. The boys are trained at the beginning of the year, given roles in the operation, and expected to perform their duties quickly and quietly. Lest it become too much of a chore, and to help them remember, a stop-watch is used, and records are kept (and often broken).

You can save time, too, by establishing other types of routine. If you need to give instructions, it's a good idea to stand still, at the front of the class, show in your physical behaviour that what you are saying is worth listening to. If you ask for headphones to be removed before you speak, then make sure that it's always done the same way, and that you can check with a glance for compliance. If you need the swivel chairs of a music IT room to face you when you speak, then make sure that every pupil does the same. The cognitive resources of the teacher are

DOI: 10.4324/9781003112402-5

just as limited as those of their pupils, and the more that can be done to use them efficiently – to think about the next explanation rather than managing the classroom – the better.

The way pupils learn and study should also be subject to time-saving routines. There are simple things about written presentation – dates and underlined titles, writing in ink and not biro – which serve to remind pupils that they are to take pride in their work. It also means that their exercise book becomes a usable resource for later revision and, at the same time, a record of progress through time. There are further practical questions here too: do the pupils have folders or do they stick hand-outs into their exercise books? Do you dictate (literally or metaphorically) what goes into their books, or do they take notes? Have you taught them how to make notes?

The way you ask questions of a class can also save considerable time. Asking pupils to put-up their hands potentially consumes more time. Often it's better to ask pupils directly to respond, ask using their names, and make especially sure that every pupil speaks in a lesson (this is Lemov's 'Cold Calling' (2015: 249–62)).

Running a lesson

A music lesson starts even before your pupils enter the room. What happens at the beginning of a lesson depends a great deal on the culture of the school. Ideally your class will arrive as one, and you can greet them *en masse*. Work out the geography of your room, and find a place in the doorway where you can see both corridor and classroom, and greet the pupils as they enter. You can congratulate a pupil on their performance in last night's concert, pass on a message from a visiting teacher ('Did you practise your scales last night, Christopher?'), correct uniforms, and set the mixture of welcome and control you want to exert throughout the lesson. Irrespective of what happened in the language laboratory in the previous lesson, you remind your pupils what we do in music. Pupils are apt to forget, and the culture of every lesson is created anew at its start.

Meeting your pupils at the door is also about building relationships with them, reminding them that you are firm but warm, that the task of learning is shared between you and them. Once in the room, the pupils move quickly to their assigned places. Seating plans are essential in music. We work with a greater range of prior experience than any other department in a school, and in every one of our classrooms are both children who spend lives immersed in music, and others where there is none. For some tasks, carefully seating more- and less-experienced musicians next to each other helps both – one by having help on hand should it be needed, and the other by practising their knowledge through teaching.

What does a great music teacher do?

If you're suitably attuned, there's a palpable sense of possibility hovering at the beginning of each lesson; it's one of the most exciting things about teaching. Maybe this one lesson is the one in which Solomon will understand the bass clef, or Simone will discover Handel, or Tade will understand why spelling matters. Keeping the energy and excitement easily found at the beginning of a lesson for its entirety is a difficult trick to perform, especially when practical matters intervene. The start of a lesson is the perfect moment for pupils to practise their knowledge (see chapter 7). Display a slide on the board which contains some music as well as some simple questions. Make it routine that, without asking, the pupils write the answers to those questions. The activity can be as simple as practising the treble clef and rhythmic values, or as complex as asking by whom a piece is written, and giving three reasons why. Putting children to work immediately sets the tone, and helps to sustain the possibility – but the teacher needs to be highly disciplined in keeping the duration of the task within its set bounds. The more demanding the question, the greater the danger of digression. And I speak with real authority on this subject.

During the lesson

The seating-plan has another advantage: it means that you can easily and constantly use the pupils' names. Music teachers often teach whole year-groups, and learning 150 names, especially when you see the pupils only once each week, takes significant effort and commitment. A photo-book and a seating plan can sit unobtrusively on the piano, or near your desk; both help to sustain the illusion that you know their names, especially if it's early in the year (or late in the week), and you are struggling. Getting the names right is the biggest thing you can do to show that you value every pupil. Take care with shortening names and don't be afraid of the difficult ones. Too-often teachers are worried about using names they find hard, and as a result, don't call on those children. Pupils appreciate you taking the time to get it right.

Control in the classroom does not mean that you are fearsome – I will tell more of Mr. Edmonson's reign of terror in chapter 7. It means pupils knowing what they should be doing, and you holding them to account if they are not. We expect our pupils to look smart and be prepared, to sit up and look interested, to make eye contact, to listen attentively. From this follows two things. The first is that they may not know how to do these things or why they are important. If we don't break down the larger task of attending into smaller actions, things which they can immediately do, telling them to pay attention to our teaching is not enough; neither will they learn that appearing interested is both a useful social and professional skill, and that it's a way to get on in the world.

The second thing is that we should, as teachers, hold ourselves to higher standards than we do our pupils. If we want our pupils to read silently or dress smartly, to refrain from using mobile devices, or – and this is the hardest – not to speak when others are speaking, then we should do these things ourselves. How often, as teachers, do we speak rather than listen, do we interrupt our pupils' answers, do we fail to help them to develop their ideas by precipitously supplying the correct answer?

This holding ourselves to higher standards also means that our lessons are purposeful and demanding. It's really no wonder that pupils drift away if our lessons are thin gruel. If there is insufficient challenge for the more experienced, or inadequate support for those new to music, then children will find other ways to fill their time. There are particular difficulties in music, and not only because of the disparity of experience inevitable in every classroom. It's hard to find accessible and practical exercises, hard to communicate to impatient young minds the delights of perfecting, of really mastering, even a very simple piece of composition. It's hard, too, to teach good lessons in the midst of the whirlwind which is every good music department. The subject suffers the moment the children know that you've 'parked' them in front of a computer, parked with insufficient idea of what they are to do, and why they are to do it.

These high expectations often seem quite bewildering to the beginning musician, especially when there are clearly exceptional young players and composers in the same class. With them, the teacher has to work particularly hard, demonstrating to them their progress, praising commitment and effort, and helping them with the patient work of becoming better. The record of progress constituted by their exercise book is quite powerful – at least if the curriculum is planned carefully enough: 'Look at this, just six weeks ago, look how hard you've worked and how far you've come'.

In the classroom

The pupils have arrived, prior knowledge is practised, and the lesson continues. The music classroom should be a place which combines collective engagement, intellectual rigour, and a little fun. There's nothing natural about this, a group of 30 children working diligently, listening hard, acting collectively towards a positive end – it's an entirely manufactured environment, built through the year and built anew with every lesson. And it's an environment of agreed purpose, not one of tyrannical power. A disruption might not be what it seems. Pupils who talk to each other may well be discussing the latest signing for the local team, but might equally be helping each other with the task in hand. And it's possible that the help of a fellow pupil is more valuable than that of the teacher (Nuthall, 2007). Such talk might, in carefully-monitored circumstances, be understood, tolerated, and even encouraged.

You know that pupils are attending by looking, and by being seen to look; and there is a technique to it. Watching the room, and being seen to watch the room are both intentional habits, which can be learnt and practised. This is harder for music teachers, especially when you are seated at the piano, and the pupils have classroom instruments to hand. Eye contact is very powerful (as is the skill of playing the piano whilst looking at your pupils). And the 'look which applies just the right amount of pressure' should be a developing part of every teacher's arsenal (Ashman, 2018: 108).

Music teachers can also conduct the room. A gesture of encouragement or suppression can be very powerful. The gesture which accompanies the instruction to remove headphones re-enforces that instruction, and also has practical value if the pupils can't hear you. A gentle knock on the desk can bring the day-dreamer back to full attention (or wake them from their slumbers). You can change the weather with a smile, cause clouds to form with a frown – and you should use this power deliberately and to the advantage of your pupils' education.

And music teachers' language should be very precisely controlled: it's 'our' choir, not 'yours', your pupils are all 'musicians' of varying degrees of experience. The trust embodied in this statement should be one of a wider set of actions in which pupils show themselves to be trustworthy by being first trusted by the teacher.

Teachers should be kind; polite, but firm. With at first a little courage, and some of the skills of an actor, every teacher can cultivate these habits. The perception of strength in a classroom comes from a few little steps: from speaking without undue volume, sometimes quite slowly; from using words sparingly and precisely (particularly in your instructions) and avoiding undue informality ('okay guys' and 'kids' is less effective than 'boys and girls' or 'pupils'); from standing still as you speak; from waiting until everyone pays attention before you speak (Lemov, 2015). The politeness at the heart of this is merely treating your pupils as you would wish yourself to be treated. Say thank you with warmth and sincerity. Education is about preparing the citizen, too, and teachers should help to build the society which they themselves wish to inhabit and pass to their own children.

Leading a department

Music teachers like to think ourselves different, and, to a point, we are. With advancement, the outstanding music teacher moves on from 'teacher of' towards 'head of' or even 'director of'. With the new title comes the responsibility of leading a department. And it's often the leadership of quite a large and notably disparate group, consisting of classroom teachers, instrumental teachers, and, if you are really lucky, technicians and administrators. This group will be a mixture of part- and full-time colleagues, and some might even be volunteers and helpful parents.

It's worth spending a moment before you take the new job to think about what you are going to do; the culture you want to create, and what you might achieve in the first year, the first three years, and the first five and longer.

At the beginning, the temptation is to announce revolution, make sweeping and eye-catching changes; this type of leadership briefly glitters and draws attention to the leader, but tends not to build a department which, in the long-term, helps children to succeed. In any new position, there will certainly be things which need to be improved, things to change, and things whose purpose has been forgotten in the mists of the past, and which consume precious effort and time. We know as musicians that real progress is earned by sustained and incremental work, and altering a department's culture and the habits of others are no exception to this. Colleagues in your team come to trust you when they see at first small changes brought successfully to a conclusion (and there is an art to communicating these, too). In the ideal situation, it should be possible to measure the changes (attendance at choir, results in aural tests in ABRSM examinations), they should be credible (caused directly by a small intervention), and they should be true to the leader's ideals (that children are learning more) (Collins, 2001).

The people with whom we work are key to this, and musicians are lucky in this. We are invested deeply in our subject, are enthusiasts for it, and, as teachers, we want our pupils to succeed. There are exceptions to this, of course, but look around at your musician colleagues, set aside the petty irritations about the stolen coffee cup, the double-booked room, and that awful woollen jumper, and you will see good things. These are people who want to be part of something, believe in something, and it's the job of the leader to help them to remember this and to help them become the best versions of themselves.

People are the key to this, and the new leader has very quickly to understand the musicians around them. A single new instrumental teacher can make the most tremendous difference to a department, and the job of a leader is to recruit the very best when the opportunity arises. But that's arguably easier than finding the best in those already around you. It's your job to give everyone the opportunity to thrive: whether that's finding the right type of pupil for the instrumental teacher (some are brilliant with the less-experienced player, others only with older pupils); an enthusiasm for ensemble work (a recorder group, the ukulele, the harmonica); or encouraging a genre which the school does not yet offer which one of your team members spends her weekends playing (hard bop, anyone?). These steps are simple, and are consistent both in themselves and with your aim of improving the pupils' experience. They should taken diligently.

But musicians are a little different, and little things are important to us. There are never enough rooms even in the biggest and most lavish music centre, and musicians are creatures of habit. We like our own spaces, and it's a simple part of our contentment; a clear understanding of custom is a good idea before the altering the room-booking system. Coffee and tea, with fresh milk help, too – most noticeable, when it's missing. Access to a photocopier, if budgets and copyright allow, is near essential.

You need to work hard to make visiting teachers feel part of the school, valued for their work. They are such an important part of a school's ensemble work, of academic success, and of the pupils' wellbeing. It's worth taking a moment to say this to them. A culture in which you thank people for working hard is a good one: it shows that you know what's happening, and that you understand the skill, time, and effort it takes to help children thrive. Handwritten notes, if possible posted to their recipient, are striking in how much they mean to people; and remembering your team's birthdays is a good gesture.

There are practical things you can do, too. School e-mail messages are hard to ignore, especially if the account is linked to a personal device. It's a good idea think about how little you can use it. Most conversations are quicker, more pleasant, and more long-lasting in their effect if they happen face-to-face. If you do use electronic means, make sure that you keep civilised hours – many providers allow you to schedule messages to be sent later – keep the distribution small, so that people learn that a message from you is important. And don't ever clear your in-box on Friday evening: it eases your mind, maybe, but it has the potential to create weekend work for the recipients.

Organising yourself

It's a busy life, being a music teacher, or leading a music department, and it's good to have in place some systems and processes which will help – a little old-fashioned bureaucracy. The e-mail in-box is going to be the place where much of your work is concentrated, and it can feel at times like a steaming pressure-cooker poised for its moment of disaster. There are some who advocate making sure that the in-box is empty before the end of each working day; but there are also people who have tidy desks, and few of them are music teachers. Or normal. There are, however, useful ideas in this *Getting Things Done* method, and some of them are freely adapted below (Allen, 2015).

Allen's idea is that the capacity of the mind can be expanded using a mechanism of external memory. This sounds rather like science-fiction, but it actually involves a pen and a note-book – and everyone uses external devices to help us to remember all the time: diaries, and lists of telephone numbers, and the sticky-yellow note on the back of the front door.

The trick is to be a little more systematic about how to deal with any new item as soon as it arrives. The item might be an e-mail, or a telephone message, or a spoken request from a parent or a colleague.

The first thing to consider is if the item requires you to do something. If not, then it can either be ignored or recycled, retained for future reference, or put on a list of things which might be done at some unspecified and unlikely time in the future.

If the message does require you to do something, and it can be done very quickly (a task taking fewer than two minutes or so), and you have those minutes, then it's best to do it immediately. One fewer thing to do, and a little buzz of satisfaction about a job done. Tonight's rehearsal is definitely going ahead, and yes, some help moving chairs would be very much appreciated.

The next stage is to delegate. Ask the relevant person as efficiently as you are able, and make a note to check that, after an appropriate time has elapsed, the task has been completed. The new pupil for your guitar teacher is quickly allocated and, in the corridor, it's the work of an instant to check that lessons have started.

If the task is still yours, and there is a time when it needs to be done, then add it to a calendar or write in a diary, and forget it until the moment arrives. To make sure that a room is free for the harp to be delivered can wait until Monday.

The task is now yours, and if it's a more complicated one, then it needs to be broken down into steps which can be done one-at-a-time, ideally written on a list of projects, your mechanism of external memory. The cathedral is booked for the carol service; next the date is confirmed in the school's calendar; then the buses can be booked; then the organist – tasks are rarely completely sequentially, but one-thing-at-a-time makes big things seem possible.

Some music teachers have notebooks, some electronic reminders on smartphones or tablets, some clip-boards, and some have a jaundiced outbreak of sticky notes – all have some external way of calling to memory things which need to be done.

If you are lucky, you will have an administrator, the best of whom are worth their weight in platinum. If there is the smallest chance that your school can be persuaded to employ one, the pupils are the ones who will benefit most.

Photographs and videos

A good camera, or, better still, a good teacher-colleague who is an enthusiastic photographer, is a great addition to any music department. In some schools there is a demand for materials which can be used for publicity, to feed the beast of social media and recruitment. But this is not the most important reason for photography.

Photographs of the pupils taking part in and enjoying making music together are a powerful way to involve them in a department – if their images appear on its walls, it will become their space. A display board, or a framed photograph of an ensemble, or an electronic display screen will always attract a crowd, as pupils find themselves and their friends on it. The sooner you can do this in the pupils' careers, the better: if you ensnare the year 7 pupils early, they are less likely to escape later.

Photographs are perfect mementos of concerts – far better than audio or video recordings. Sound recording mercilessly seeks out imperfections; photographs, well chosen, can give a more-truthful representation of the joy and achievement of the moment.

Video recording has recently become a much more significant part of music teachers' lives. It's a mixed blessing. Concerts need audiences, and pupils need to play in public. They need to practise being nervous, and succeeding in public. A large audience teaches an ensemble its worth, that it is an important part of the school's community, valued in its locality. That magical communication between player and audience is broken savagely by the video camera's lens.

But video has the potential to reach a wider audience, and can sometimes engage with children in a different or a more effective way. But it also has its problems. If pupils are recording at home, take great care with their appearance, what appears in the background of their performances, and the video format.

The Apple ecosystem manages video very well, through smartphone, tablet, and desktop. PCs are cheaper, but much harder to use.

Be certain in all of this that you know intimately the school's policies about photography and videography, about using personal devices to record, especially whom you are not allowed to photograph.

IT

To generations gone by, IT in the music classroom today is little short of miraculous – both in its capacity, and in the possibilities it opens up for our pupils. This section considers how to make the most of its opportunities, both within the classroom and beyond.

The first lesson is that simpler is often better. Take the interactive white-board. This educational panacea was announced in English schools in 2004, and in that year £50 million was spent on them (Christodoulou, 2020). The idea was exciting and shiny, and almost completely unsuited to the teaching of music. Even with the latest iterations of the technology it's still near-impossible to write notation on an interactive-whiteboard stave.

The second is that a music classroom set-up need no longer be as complex as once it was. Jack 'Prod' Longstaff, my late, great music teacher, had a record player of great distinction, a carefully-chosen amplifier, huge and exquisite speakers. The music teacher's hi-fi – for it was that era – was precious, kept under lock-and-key, used only by an expert who could release the records from their sleeves in the prescribed manner, clean, and drop, oh-so-gently, the needle. The sound was wonderful, the ritual mesmerising to a class, and perhaps it's a representation of something we have lost today.

The technology needed in today's music classroom is a projector, beaming its images onto a white-board; a computer; and some sort of sound-system. Some portable speakers are so good that an audio system is almost redundant.

The heart of this is the old-fashioned white-board. Although it's possible permanently to apply staves, it's better to have a standard stave-slide in your presentation pack. A plain board is more versatile – used for the projection of video, for the annotation of scores, for musical presentations of all types – and it concentrates pupils' attention on one place. This last has important implications for the quality of learning – we learn that to which we attend, and looking at two boards simultaneously is not advantageous to this.

There are also significant possibilities in projecting lessons onto the board using a tablet and stylus; there is more about this in the next section.

It's a similar tale when it comes to capturing and editing sound. The high point of Prod's year was taking his meticulously-trained choir to the local cathedral, inviting players and soloists from Manchester, and giving performances of the great choral repertoire. The author was the treble soloist in *Elijah* – 'Behold, a little cloud ariseth now from the waters: it is like a man's hand!' – and it's been downhill for him ever since. These great events were faithfully documented using a stereo-pair and a reel-to-reel tape recorder. The in-school playback was an awesome moment.

But we now have the capacity in our pockets to record audio and video almost at will, both in truly astonishing fidelity. The problems we face are in their use, not least of which is the safeguarding of our pupils. Although a smartphone is good, it's probably best, if possible, to use a dedicated recording device – something small and with a built-in pair of microphones. This is for our security and for the protection of ourselves and our charges – our personal devices should be kept well away from our school lives. Some schools use a departmental tablet for recording, from which good results can be obtained.

What does a great music teacher do?

Quite what Jack Longstaff would have made of modern notation programs in the classroom, I don't know. Their widespread availability means that more pupils than ever can experiment as composers, can try something on paper, hear it played instantly, and thereby receive immediate feedback. The possibilities of play, of finding out for themselves, of writing for unimaginably-ambitious forces are truly glorious.

There are dangers, too. The first sounds better in German: 'Sibeliusmusik', computer-composed music which, owing to its difficulty and complexity, can and will only ever be played on computer. There's nothing inherently wrong with an artistic creation, which is unthinkable without technology – ask Conlon Nancarrow, the boffins at IRCAM, or any K-pop sensation – but we want our pupils to experience, understand, and be able to draw on a wider range of possibility than this.

Because notation programs can do most everything, it's more important than ever that we help our pupils to understand what makes a composition good. This is done partly by encouraging wide listening, but also by helping to build pupils' toolkits of compositional techniques and devices. Aesthetic judgement matters in the classroom – 'I like the sound of that' is a perfectly valid first response – but it's better still if pupils are able to explain why. When young composers can talk about repetition, contrast, development, balance, and form, talk from a position of knowledge and experience, then they are beginning to develop this critical discernment.

There should be a moment, too, in a young composer's development that they should create using an instrument, away from a computer. Some of the most-inventive thinking by the most-inventive composers was done at the keyboard. Debussy's sound-world surely comes from hours of experiment at the piano, from experienced fingers finding just the right sound in highly-unconventional ways; Stravinsky's octatonic wonders are the same, originating in doodling and messing, from uninhibited play and from hard listening. That young composers at the computer start with notation is a wonder, but there's something missing.

This thought leads to the next, which is a personal hypothesis: that notation programs are less good in the development of the musical ear, of the musical imagination, than direct contact with an instrument; that exploring a work, or composing using a piano, or a guitar, or a 'cello, offers a richer set of experiences – sense-data, the physical sensation of playing, where the playing takes place, and how the composer is feeling at the moment the string is plucked – than can be experienced underneath headphones sitting at a computer.

Notation programs and the computers on which they run have a great deal to offer our pupils, especially when they are becoming more accessible than ever:

at the time of writing, MuseScore (www.musescore.org) is a free and compelling alternative to industry-standards. Their use in the classroom is a particular skill required of music teachers.

Planning a music IT room

Managing an IT classroom starts with its layout. It's a significant opportunity for all music teachers when facilities are built or renewed. The best music IT suites are planned for teaching and learning. If it's a room specifically for music IT, then the management of the room is paramount: plan so that the teacher can see as many of the screens as possible at all times. It matters less that the pupils have to turn to see the board than this simple fact. The IT specialists will insist that there is software available which affords teachers the opportunity to see every screen in the class, merely at the touch of a button. This is useful, especially the facility to take over a pupil's machine, to share its screen with the class, and to lock every device in the class; but it's not the same as the teacher's intentional glance, understanding in a moment what feedback is required, or where work is being done less earnestly than it should.

The IT specialist will also insist that IT servers needs to be cooled with air conditioning, and that the box of mysterious flashing lights, with its seditious little fans, will need to be close by. The music teacher should resist: the music classroom should be a place of listening, and listening comes from silence. (Is it a coincidence that 'listen' is an anagram of 'silent'? Probably not.)

There is also the thorny problem of which ecosystem to choose, PC or Apple. The author can only write from personal experience of both, and certainly the one-time gulf between the two has substantially been narrowed. But audio is central to the Apple world, and there is an ease and a simplicity to teaching in it which helps children to learn more quickly and learn more. Apple computers are less prone to software problems, more reliable, and longer-lasting. They also add a kudos to a music department, which pupils and prospective parents like. The PC ecosystem is certainly cheaper, but the investment in a better machine is worth it. The IT specialist will also tell you is that Apples are harder to integrate with a school's PC-based network. This is not true, and reflects more on the capabilities of the IT specialist than it does on reality.

Everything matters when planning a room. It's a pet theory of the author that there is an inverse relationship between sitting on a swivelling desk chair and mental age. There is already temptation aplenty for pupils in the music IT room – buttons to click and on-line videos to distract – that not to slump and swivel is too much to ask. If practical, then stools (without wheels), the like of which are found in the classrooms of our science colleagues might well be the answer.

Teaching in the music IT room

The teacher manages two separate dimensions in the music IT classroom – teaching technology and teaching music. The technology is powerful and complicated, and its use certainly requires instruction; but the purpose of its use is to teach music, and the one must not obstruct the other.

In part these are questions of efficiency, of building in pupils good habits. When music teachers gather around the camp-fire to tell tales, one of the favourites is the loss of electronically-stored examination coursework. Every system is different, but finding ways to make sure that work is near-permanent should be the highest of priorities. For some this means saving to a shared network drive (backed-up by the school); for others it means coloured and named memory-sticks locked in the music office at night; for others still, requiring pupils to save work in the cloud, on Google Drives, or in the school's VLE.

Once the work is safe, what are the other good habits we should develop in our pupils? Modern notation programs come loaded with possibility and power; finding a quick and efficient way through to the essence of what we want to do with them is the next habit. Every department needs a single, simple work-flow for their use. This means agreeing and teaching ways of naming and saving work, of starting new compositions, of using short-cuts and work-arounds.

A typical work-flow when starting a new composition in a notation program might be this:

Let's start a new file.

Type 'notation program' in the search box and open it.

Click 'blank template' only once.

Go to 'change instruments', select piano and click 'add to score' then 'OK'.

Select a time signature. You may write in 4/4 or 2/4

Select any major key up to three sharps or three flats.

You do not need an anacrusis.

Your tempo is either Allegro, Moderato, or Andante.

The title is 'Theme and Variations' and you should add your forename and surname as the name of the composer.

Click create.

Type 'command-S', give your piece the title 'Theme and Variations', select your GCSE course-work folder on the school network, and press return.

Move the notation program to one side, open your GCSE course-work folder from the network, and wait for me to check.

This seeming-complex routine is actually quite quick, avoids some of the many pitfalls, and has the capacity to save time later – and keeps the pupils' safe. It's an idea to have a written version of this routine, to which pupils can refer as needed.

Once the file exists and is safe, there are many different ways to add notes. For some, a midi-keyboard works well, although recording live takes a certain precision. It's better to assume that the mouse will be the primary input-device, and teach accordingly.

Keyboard short-cuts are near-essential in developing an efficient work-flow. Choosing and teaching which short-cut to use requires a little thought, as does their teaching. Coining little catch-phrases works well:

Command-E for expression, then right-click

S for slur

T for time signature

K for key

Command-S for save

P for play

The latter is the most important. Fumbling with a mouse, selecting a place on a transport, and clicking a play-icon wastes too much time.

There are also tricks of processing and repeating music:

To select a unit of music, click the first note, hold shift, click the last note

Command-C to copy

Command-V to paste

Use the arrow keys to move notes up or down

Command-S for save

Many of these short-cuts are familiar to us and to some of our pupils from word-processing programs. But to assume that every pupil knows them is a mistake.

All of this is prosaic, dull even, but powerful. If pupils are taught consistently to do the same things in the same way, those seconds saved, added together over a pupil's school career, can make an appreciable difference to how well they succeed. They also mean that some of the actions with which pupils most often need help become automated; if automated, then the teacher's time is also freed to give musical feedback, rather than technical support.

Make them listen to good recordings

I feel quite old when writing this, remember when a long-playing record and the weekly trip to the music library were great highlights. Recorded music, and the rituals surrounding it, was special and to be treasured. That's about the only thing which has been lost to our pupils today.

For the wonder of recorded music, of video on-demand, of legal on-line scores is still thrilling and bewildering, the greatest of opportunities for the curious child.

But we need to guide them quite carefully. There are two particular pitfalls we need to help our charges to avoid; first, that not all performances are the same; secondly, that not every score they can so easily find, is a true and accurate reflection of the intentions of the composer.

In a world where manufactured music is everywhere – perfect every time, identical on each hearing – the variability of live performance is a vital lesson to teach our pupils. If they try something, and it seems a little dull, then there is every chance that they have happened on a dull performance. The more complicated the music, the harder it is to perform in a way which will bowl-over a new listener. Opera is the hardest art-form of all – singers, orchestra, sets, costumes, animals! – and the number of truly exceptional performances which balance each dimension are vanishingly small. Ingmar Bergman's film of *The Magic Flute* is perhaps one.

That we apply this quality filter is vital for our pupils. I can trace my musical enthusiasms to certain works and certain performances – to Carlos Kleiber in Beethoven, to Wilhelm Furtwängler in Brahms, to Julius Katchen, to George Szell, to Emil Gilels. These musical giants both taught me, and lit fires of enthusiasm which burn still.

I cannot recommend strongly enough the Petrucci on-line music library, *imslp. org*. At last count there were half-a-million scores legally and freely available there. There are the old, out-of-copyright critical editions of Bach and Mozart, usable Beethoven and Brahms, excellent Tchaikovsky; and one of the other riches is the presence of early editions and the composers' holograph manuscripts. A treasure-trove. But with this cornucopia comes the second pitfall. There is also an amount of less-good and misleading material. A weather eye needs to be kept on the inexperienced explorer.

What does a great music teacher do?

From all this it should be clear that we music teachers are a little different, not least in the sheer variety of things we do every day. But at the heart of everything is teaching, imparting to others knowledge and skills.

This is the subject of the next chapter.

References

Allen, D., 2015. *Getting Things Done: The Art of Stress-Free Productivity*. London, Penguin.

Ashman, G., 2018. *The Truth about Teaching*. London, Sage.

Christodoulou, D., 2020. *Teachers vs Tech? The Case for an Ed Tech Revolution*. Oxford, Oxford University Press.

Collins, J.C., 2001. *Good to Great: Why Some Companies Make the Leap ... and Others Don't*. London, Random House.

Lemov, D., 2015. *Teach Like a Champion 2.0: 62 Techniques That Put Students on the Path to College*. San Francisco, Jossey-Bass.

Nuthall, G., 2007. *The Hidden Lives of Learners*. Wellington, Nzcer Press.

Chapter 6

Teaching music

Belief

Whether in the classroom, in the rehearsal-room, or on the concert stage, a great music teacher believes that everyone can do well.

How does that manifest itself?

A teacher who has high expectations for their pupils knows that little is impossible, at least when the teacher gets it right; but there's an expectation on the pupils, too. This is obvious in an ensemble, when pupils practise their part between rehearsals, bring music and pencil, take responsibility for their own individual contributions. It's true in the classroom, too, and every pupil has a part to play. It's easy for pupils to choose not to be part of the lessons, neither to answer questions, nor to try; Doug Lemov (2015: 90–3) calls this opting out. It's easy to empathise, as we often opt out ourselves: remember the moment in the staff meeting when the head asks for volunteers; when silence falls, and eyes are carefully averted? At the heart of Lemov's discussion is the idea that everyone takes part, that the choice of hiding is simply not available.

If a pupil does not know the answer to a question or chooses not to answer, the teacher moves to a second pupil and asks again. Assuming that the answer is given correctly by the second, the teacher returns to the first, and asks the same question a third time. The option of hiding is no longer a possibility, and the pupil has learnt that work is expected in the class. If the pupil refuses to answer, actively refuses, then firmer and more direct action might be needed. Lemov (2015) suggests variations on this theme. The first is simple repetition:

What's the key of this piece Abhinav?

C major.

No, the key is B-flat major. Now, you tell me. What's the key?

DOI: 10.4324/9781003112402-6

B-flat major

Good, Abhinav, the key is B-flat major

A second student might be asked the question before returning to Abhinav for him to repeat. The second variation is where the teacher helps the pupil to correct the initial mistake:

What's the key of this piece Rela?

C major.

Look at the key signature at the beginning between clef and time signature; there are two flats there. Can you work out the key from that?

B-flat major.

Good Rela, the key is B-flat major.

(adapted from Lemov, 2015: 94–5)

The correction helps Rela to check her answer, to use her existing knowledge, and practise the calculation required. Other pupils might be involved in this process ('Where do we look to work out the key?'), or other tricks which pupils may have learnt by rote ('The penultimate flat of a key signature gives the major key.'). The increased richness of the second variation – that pupils are helped to practise the techniques of finding-out rather than just the knowledge – makes it a valuable part of teaching. Thinking is made visible ('Where in the music can we look to check that this actually is in B-flat major?') and principles established ('Yes, when working-out keys and harmony, the bass-note is always the first place to look.').

You can make Rela – whose head you've seen on the desk in other teachers' lessons – feel that she does understand music by gradually expecting more of her: 'Now that you know that the penultimate flat of a key signature gives the major key, tell me which is the penultimate flat in this key signature [writes on the board] ... That's right, a D flat, which means that the major key here is?' Rela's increasing confidence in her knowledge, the practice you have afforded her and the opportunity to explain her knowledge out loud, together give her a sense of agency and success. By believing in her, and by the simple craft of teaching done well, a lesson bigger than key signatures has been learnt.

This is a twofold belief: that every pupil should work, and that they can achieve great things. It also means that getting the answer wrong is an important part of learning.

Mistakes

Mistakes are wonderful things. One of my earliest pupils was Elizabeth. She was an accomplished player, with a well-trained ear and highly-developed musical sensibilities. It fell to me to teach her four-part harmony, and it was an unabashed disaster. For whatever work I set she completed it perfectly, without a note wrong, and she learnt nothing whatsoever from me. Making mistakes, the bigger the better, is one of the foundations of learning, especially learning about music. Action is inherent to making a mistake – if we don't do anything, nothing will go wrong – but the nature of that action matters, too; that it consists in experiment, trial, and, of course, error.

Music combines strong rules with great freedom. One of the wonders of Western notation is the way it embodies this truth, combining prescription with invitation – in the greatest performances you will hear every dot, line, and slash of a score, clearly and convincingly, but, because of the freedom inherent in notation, those details will be different every time, often radically so.

It's the same with the best teachers. It's a sign that a great teacher is working both that pupils are willing to make mistakes, and that each individual will take a slightly different approach to the task at hand. A great teacher will set parameters for an activity, and then within those bounds, the pupils can explore, can practise for themselves. Mistakes are celebrated as an opportunity to learn something new – here's why parallel intervals should be avoided, and how – mistakes can help teach pupils to respect and to learn from all work, irrespective of its source. That's another thing great teachers do – learn from their pupils.

Learning is hard, is often a struggle. Respecting the work of others, and learning from it, paints part of a bigger picture – what it is like to be a pupil in your classroom. Pupils come to our classrooms with different experiences, knowing different things, knowing how to do different things. It means that the skills of some pupils will seem like magic to others, often the same individuals who might easily be discouraged. If conditions are just so, then it's not what pupils can do that is important, it's how hard they are working – celebrating and enjoying the hard work seems implausible when it's put in a sentence, but is possible in a classroom.

It's possible to plan for mistakes. If you take a pinch of the highest expectations, and mix it with the knowledge that the optimal conditions for learning mean that pupils get the answer wrong about 15% of the time, then you can build something quite powerful (Leigh, 2020). Try teaching something to a class which is a very long way beyond the work with which they are familiar. This should be something about which the teacher themselves is excited, and something which can be portrayed as a treat for the pupils – the forbidden fruit they can taste only when they are in the sixth-form or at university. It's a tremendous exercise for teachers, too, working out the foundational knowledge which is required at each level, levels which slowly build into an impressive edifice of learning. The result of my teaching four-part harmony to year 7 was not that all the boys in my class were able to write a chorale; it was that many more than normal could read the bass clef, could identify triads, could understand that there is a hierarchy of chords.

It takes courage to admit mistakes, and teachers should show the way. To teach is to learn, as we've seen, and one of the joys of children is that they teach you so much. Teachers can be a model to their pupils in admitting fallibility – not too much mind – and in taking joy from working out and finding out new things. Our pupils should take intellectual risks, and should be encouraged to be courageous in their thinking. Even if a train of thought leads to a mistake, there is often great value in the way in which that thought is pursued. Explaining to a class why thinking is good, even if the conclusion is wrong, can teach a great deal. Because a pupil identifies Poulenc's *Concert champêtre* as a work by Bach is still correct in its deduction, still uses correct and well-attested knowledge, even if in its final conclusion is faulty.

But ultimately, we need our pupils to get the answer right, and for us to listen to them when they do.

Listening to pupils and the power of silence

We hear what we want to hear, hear it perhaps more often than we care to admit. When we ask a question of a pupil, we really want them to get it right. There's something fundamental here about the way we think, that we first tend to believe something, attempt to make the very best of it, before discounting it (Spinoza, cited in Kahneman, 2011: 80–1). Try:

> The gihelid is shining.

This is nonsense, invented to perplex, but we seek first to find the meaning in it, to catch sight of the gihelid. Daniel Kahneman (2011: 81) relates this to a 'general *confirmation bias*', and it's why we want the pupil to get it right.

We are pleased when the pupil answers correctly, feel the altruistic pleasure of a teacher seeing their pupil learn and thrive. The correct answer also confirms to us that we've taught well, it flatters our sense of self. It also means that the lesson can move on to the next thing, and we can experience once more that little frisson of the new.

But here's a danger: because we want the pupil to be right, we all-too-often accept from them as completely correct an answer which is only partially right. The flaw in the pupil's answer might be a lack of essential detail ('The piece is in D'), or a close and related misconception (when asked to identify chord V – 'It's a perfect chord.'), or an internal contradiction ('It's by Mozart and he was a baroque composer.'). So often in class, teachers will correct the mistake, and believe that all is well ('That's right, thank you; the piece is in D major').

If we are to maintain the highest expectations in our classrooms, it's essential that pupils' answers are completely correct. The error is first in ourselves, that we hear what we want to hear. It's important to return to the pupil with generosity, but with an insistence on obtaining a completely correct response.

The close misconception ('perfect chord') is the most interesting and tricky to address. The pupil has heard from you 'perfect' in at least two different contexts: as a description of an interval and as a species of cadence. Music is full of this sort of 'nested' information, in this case because the interval of a perfect fifth is quite so fundamental to our understanding of the Western canon. It's there in the harmonic series between the second and the third harmonics; it's there between the roots of the tonic and the dominant chords; and it's there again between the roots and the fifths within both tonic and dominant triads.

A possible exchange might go like this:

Please identify that chord, Tom.

It's a perfect chord.

Thank you, but perfect is not the name of a chord, it's the name of a particular pair of chords which are often found at the end of a phrase. What is that pair of chords called?

A cadence

Try again then, what is the name of that chord?

It's a dominant chord

Good, and it's the first chord in which cadence?

A perfect cadence.

And what's the purpose of a perfect cadence...

At some stage very soon thereafter, the teacher would need to drill perfect intervals, the four types of cadences, and chord identification – a neat piece of planning-by-pupil which would not have happened if the teacher had not listened completely to the pupil's response.

Lemov (2015: 100–1) calls this approach 'right is right'.

But the teacher is not just listening for answers which are completely correct; they are looking for opportunities to help every pupil learn. The next stage is obvious for Tom, who has had the chance to practise using the word 'perfect' in different contexts; harder for Ivy:

> Please identify that chord, Ivy.

> *It's a dominant seventh.*

Ivy is an instrumentalist, and a good one; this is a very easy question for her, she might well feel a glow of pride, and sit back and relax, having answered it correctly. That's a performance, and she's not learning.

> Thank you. What's the most common use of a dominant seventh?

> At the end of a phrase as part of a perfect cadence.

> And describe its resolution.

> The leading note rises, and the minor seventh falls.

This is going very well, but Ivy is still not working hard.

> You played that piece by Debussy very well in last night's concert. Could you come to the piano and show us the place where dominant-seventh chords are not resolved and teach us about parallel motion.

And that, hopefully will do it. The teacher has helped Ivy to use her knowledge in a new way, to make new links between items in her long-term memory.

By listening hard, by asking pupils to explain further, or to re-phrase their answers to give different emphasis; by asking why? and where else? every pupil, regardless of their level of experience, is being asked to work hard – to learn.

Little musical experts

One of the more engaging papers in the annals of the *Journal of Personality and Social Psychology* begins with this story:

> In 1995, McArthur Wheeler walked into two Pittsburgh banks and robbed them in broad daylight, with no visible attempt at disguise. He was arrested

later that night, less than an hour after videotapes of him taken from sur-veillance cameras were broadcast on the 11 o'clock news. When police later showed him the surveillance tapes, Mr. Wheeler stared in incredulity. "But I wore the juice," he mumbled. Apparently, Mr. Wheeler was under the impres-sion that rubbing one's face with lemon juice rendered it invisible to video-tape cameras.

(Dunning & Kruger, 1999: 1121)

The raid was justly awarded an Ig Nobel Prize in 2000, and the article is the source of the eponymous Dunning-Kruger Effect. It states that most people overestimate their abilities – the original study concerned telling jokes, logical reasoning, and grammar – and that the most telling over-estimation is associated with the most 'incompetent'. The more expert one becomes, the less the over-estimation becomes, and the truly expert – like 'the best' in Yeats's *The Second Coming* – 'lack all conviction' and are apt significantly to under-estimate their ability.

One of the jokes which participants had to tell as part of the study was:

Question: what's as big as a man, but weighs nothing?

Answer: his shadow.

(Dunning & Kruger, 1999: 1123)

Which makes one glad that Dunning and Kruger have secure employment at Cornell University.

But this effect is something we see everyday in our classrooms, in the ways our pupils behave as musicians. How often, when faced with a musical instrument, do we find a child performing their party-piece? In boys' schools, it's inevitably associated with James Bond: in my day the Monty Norman theme, more recently Adele's *Skyfall*. In youth orchestras, it's the 'cellists playing the first solo phrase of the Haydn C-major concerto or the first movement of the Elgar. It's nearly what the great Isaiah Berlin (1953) called the difference between the hedgehog and the fox – of which more anon.

To see an inexperienced musician perform is a joy, but to see incompetence celebrated whilst excellence sits by is something we should avoid. And whilst performance is a glory, seeking attention and approbation is not. This asks impor-tant questions of the culture we foster as music teachers in our classrooms, and in our rehearsal-rooms.

There are two immediate observations here. First, that in the spaces for which we are responsible, we should aspire to the impossible – that they become spaces in which every contribution is valued, in which all are treated equally, and that they are places every individual is vital to the whole. The collective 'we' is more important than the selfish 'I' (with apologies to Lord Sacks (2020)).

This observation leads into the second, which is that there is an appropriate behaviour for every moment. Thus, whilst it's important to warm-up before an orchestral rehearsal, the difficult passage in the symphony on the music stand is probably more becoming, less McArthur Wheeler-esque than the Elgar. That musical instruments are to be used is unarguable, but they are to be used with respect, and with due regard to the precious and tiny time we can afford them. The older we become, the more we appreciate what can be achieved in a few moments' truly attentive work, the more we regret time wasted in the past.

Dunning and Kruger (1999: 1131) describe the 'burden of experience' – the idea, commonly expressed, that a little knowledge is a dangerous thing. This 'illusion of knowledge', in American historian Daniel Boorstin's coinage, is a powerful effect in music (Hall *et al.*, 2007). It can go in one of two ways.

First, music requires some foundational specialist knowledge. Musical expertise is released only when the knowledge and experience accumulated in an individual reaches a metaphorical 'critical mass'. Every child is capable of seeing the long view, but can do so only once they've climbed to the first summit of the hill, only when they have that knowledge-endowed perspective available to them. On the slopes, whilst ascending, it's easy see only the paths to one side and the boulders at their feet. It's here that they mix their metaphors horribly, and can become hedgehogs. Berlin's (1953) hedgehog knows one big thing, and views all of humanity through its prism. This effect you see so often in the teaching of musical elements. Teach tempo, and tempo is the only prism available to a pupil, and for a long time thereafter; teach texture or imitation or form, and the single, first unthinking answer to any question will be an instantly recalled, teacher-pleasing form of words associated with what they have more recently in mind.

This can be avoided by skilful planning, by a strong technique in the teacher of questioning, and some old-fashioned robust humour – and for the pupils to become Berlin's foxes. The foxes value a breadth of experience, and keep an open mind about them all. The sequence of knowledge encountered by each pupil needs to be planned carefully, and the categories to which each piece of knowledge belongs should be drilled incessantly – the attribute *staccato* belongs to the category of articulation, the antonym of which is *legato*. Which brings us again to Nuthall (2007), his rule of three – that a pupil needs, before it is understood, to have encountered a particular piece of information on three different and separate occasions. On the march upwards, seeking the perspective which is the gift of knowledge, the teacher needs to leave caches of information and knowledge – the same sustaining treat should be available at least three times in three different caches. Low-stakes testing, as we shall see, is a vital part of this.

But the 'illusion of knowledge' can have a second effect in the classroom: some familiarity with a subject or a situation might actually constitute a barrier to learning (Hall *et al.*, 2007). In part it's what Dunning and Kruger (1999: 1123) describe as the 'inflated self-assessments' associated with the 'incompetent' individual. But it's also the over-confidence engendered by a little knowledge. The so-called 'topical knowledge', the categories which allow new knowledge to be organised, are themselves a danger (Pressley *et al.*, 1987). Think of a pupil revising for an examination. He has done two things against which you've advised: he has bought a revision guide, and has dutifully highlighted all of the material he thinks he needs. It's the night before the examination, and the final hours of preparation are spent flicking energetically through the revision guide. Gamelan is sure to be a topic on the paper, and he's confident, has coloured the page, has stared hard, thinks that he can tell his *kendang* from his *gendèr*. Cometh the examination, cometh the question, and comeuppance comes. Although the material seems familiar, the answers, the specific details to which marks are attached simply do not come – he has worked, but not in the right way, not by testing and properly diagnosing those things which he does not know.

There is a final aspect to the Dunning-Kruger effect, which is the propensity of truly expert individuals to doubt themselves.

This is a tale of boy whom I will call Aditya. He is a fine young string-player, pianist, composer, and an academic musician of great ability. He's in the sixth form now, but I tell of his end-of-year-7 experience. It was a great start at school for him, and he wanted the summer examination to validate all he had done. What actually happened in the examination is a question of perspective. This teacher was proud and a little amazed that a boy could achieve 99% on a test, yet the boy himself left in tears over the lost 1%. 'Such striving for perfection is all-too-common in the music classroom, particularly in the early years of senior school. If you are already an accomplished instrumentalist, then the self-imposed pressure of a subject you are supposed to be good at can be overwhelming.

What can the teacher do? To differentiate work is clearly part of the answer – choosing which question to ask which child. And many classroom tasks can and should be both sufficiently approachable for the least-experienced and sufficiently open-ended for those who need to fly. But I suspect that the true answer lies more in the teacher's attitudes and beliefs. If they truly welcome every contribution, know and model that mistakes are inevitable and desirable, truly value and learn from every pupil, then every pupil will feel that they are included.

This is part of the greatness and the impossibility of teaching – and part of the reason which its challenges and rewards never fade. Berlin's 'Hedgehog and the Fox' is an essay about Tolstoy, and it reaches much the same conclusion: that for the great Russian, there are limits to what can be known rationally, limits therefore to the explanatory power of science, but no limits, none whatsoever, to the value of humanity as expressed through art.

Exactly.

Teaching notation

Reading and writing music is a fundamental of Western music, and is something which is surprisingly difficult to teach well. Part of the problem is that reading music is something most musicians do automatically, without conscious thought. And those childhood half-remembered mnemonics about good boys and favour do us none.

We need to build in our pupils the automaticity we ourselves take for granted. As ever, this demands from us clarity in our explanations and worked examples, first directed and then independent practice.

Start with a stave, explaining that you can write musical notes using its five parallel lines, either on the line, or in the spaces. Notes, for these purposes, are semi-breves – simple circles. When they move by step, the notes alternate lines and spaces, circles on lines and circles in spaces. The spaces can be a problem – in handwriting class our pupils are drilled incessantly to write on a line, and not in a space. In this, as in so many things, musicians are different.

The stave is also a metaphor for up and down in music. Higher notes are found at the top of the stave, lower at the bottom. And it's possible to extend the line-space pattern above or below the stave using ledger lines.

Next comes the first seven letters of the alphabet, in their proper order:

A — B — C — D — E — F — G

Up and down happens here, too: D is a step higher than C, and F is lower than G. You can skip letters, too, so E leaps three notes higher than C (there is no zero, which fact becomes useful later when teaching intervals). The language here is really important, by saying step and leap, you lay the foundations of teaching the difference between conjunct and disjunct melodic movement. In the classroom this can easily become a rather-silly game, a line of seven children, 'played' when you point at each.

But there are 88 notes on the piano, and only seven letters, so some repetition is needed. Once you reach G, you start all over again at the beginning. This means that just above G is A, and three notes lower than A is F. The line-of-children game becomes very silly indeed.

But why not 88 different letter names?

This is a question often asked at this point, and one which it's quite fun and useful to answer, giving a chance to talk a little about the mind, and how best to learn. For the seven letter-names in music match neatly with 'The magical number seven, plus or minus two' in Miller's (1956) wonderful but optimistic characterisation of the limits of working memory. Asking children about their own experiences of memory is always a fascinating experience.

In illustration, I often ask children to memorise 12-letter groups. They will manage about five characters of the following:

HSBIBGNBCCAK

And they will manage most all of:

NHS BBC KGB CIA

An 88-character-long list of note names is analogous with the first; ABCDEFG the second. The first is an incomprehensible jumble; the second, letters of which we have some knowledge, of which we possess an extant mental schema. This is no mere digression, it's an opportunity to explain why music works practically as it does, to help your pupils to understand a little more about their own limitless capacities for learning. In talking around the musical alphabet, you are able covertly to repeat and practise with them the fundamental knowledge.

Clefs

Pupils now know how a stave works, that musical notes have one of seven letter names, and that those names are the first seven letters of the alphabet. The thing which joins together stave and names, unlocks them if you like (you may be fortunate and they might help with *la clef*), is the clef.

The treble clef is also known as the G-clef, and I ask my pupils always to learn both names. They practise drawing one, in sharp and precise pencil, using a three-stage method. In the first stage, pupils start from the G line, the second line up, drawing a clockwise spiral up to the middle line and down to the bottom. In the second stage, the line continues up above the stave in the shape of a flattened letter s. The final stage is a vertical line to beneath the stave, cutting in half the original spiral. This is easier to see on the board than it is to read in words:

That the G clef starts on the G line is tremendously important. Rather than mnemonics, the best way to teach and practise musical literacy is to use the clef as a starting-point, and then read the letter names up or down, line — space — line — space, until any given note is identified. This means that the bass clef becomes the F clef, and that the alto, tenor, and soprano clef are all C clefs. The second line up on any stave can represent the notes G, B, A, F, or middle C, and only the clef allows one to determine which.

Spelling

They are also firmly reminded that there is only one 'f' at the end of the word:

> At the end of 'clef'
> There is only one 'f'
> It's a common mistake
> You're likely to make.

There is a place for the ridiculous in the classroom, too.

Notes on the piano keyboard

The relationship between the written notes and the physical keyboard is important and useful. It gives practical value to the theory, and helps to encode the knowledge in a separate and different form.

Teaching music

For reference, it's good for pupils to have available in their books something which makes explicit the way in which notes map onto the keyboard. I print a keyboard onto a small sticker, and help my pupils to copy the following into their books:

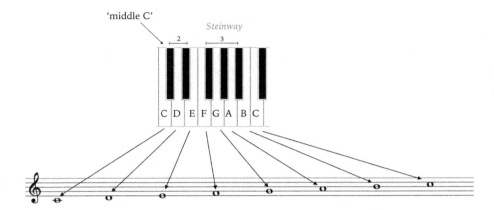

This reminds them how to find 'middle C' on the keyboard – maker's name, three black keys, two black keys – as well as the names of the notes. The only compromise here is the use of a scale which starts on C, when the alphabet starts with A. It's made because the introduction to a C-major scale is more valuable in the long term than to the natural minor, and its consequence is that the letter-name practice needs to be quite secure before moving on.

Sharps and flats come later, as part of the teaching of scales.

Teaching scales

Dry though they might be, scales are an essential part of both the understanding and the performance of music; they are impossible to escape. Fluency in performance comes from knowledge of scales – from the understanding that the sequence of notes F — G — A — Bb — C is likely to be the first five notes of an F-major scale, and that, on the piano, they are best played in this position using this fingering. Think of the fluency of a jazz performer, effortlessly mixing major, minor, Lydian, and Dorian; a wonderfully expressive combination, which comes only from a deep familiarity with scales.

Scales are the foundation of composition, too. A pair of notes in the context of a scale are the smallest comprehensible unit of a tune – morpheme of melody – as well as being the foundation of harmony. Whilst it's entirely possible to create really successful melodies using a given set of notes (for example pentatonic groups without semi-tones, such as C — D — E — G — A, F — G — A — C — D, or G — A — B — D — E), to compose with any understanding requires the use of a scale.

There are many different scales, but all share the same definition: a succession of unrepeated notes arranged in order of height within an octave. The intervals between every pair of notes in every scale are fixed – in a major scale, for instance, between the first and the second notes there is a tone, between the third and the fourth a semi-tone and so on; to change any interval is to change the scale.

It's best to teach scales from notation, using the piano keyboard as a metaphor for music.

It starts from tones and semitones, sharps and flats.

Start with the piano keyboard, real, printed, or drawn. Pupils find 'middle C' by looking for the maker's name, and the three black keys underneath it (3). They then move down (left) to the pair of black keys (2). 'Middle C' is the white key immediately to the left (1):

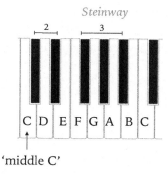

'middle C'

The seven letter-names of the C-major scale then unfold in alphabetical order from there (C — D — E — F — G | A — B). There are only seven letter names in music, the letter 'H' is only allowed in Germany.

Pupils then need to learn that the smallest distance on the piano is called a semi-tone. On the piano keyboard, this distance will either be from a white key to a black, from a back key to a white, or from one white key to another white key. It will never be from black to black.

The next smallest distance on the piano is a tone. This is the distance of one semi-tone followed by a second.

Because the black keys on the piano are raised above the white, in the classroom this needs a little careful drilling. Some pupils will be very confident, and others will need a little more help.

Next come sharps and flats. A sharp sign (#) in front of any given note raises it by one semi-tone, moving the note one semi-tone to the right on the keyboard;

a flat sign (b) lowers any given note by a semi-tone, moving one semi-tone to the left. This making-music-visible is why the piano keyboard is so valuable in the teaching of music.

As part of this process, there is a misconception and a caveat, one common, one less usual. The misconception is that sharps and flats mean black keys. Of course, this is often the case, but not invariably so, and pupils need to be sufficiently flexible in their understanding of the concept to avoid the mistake. Carefully introducing enharmonic equivalence can be useful at this stage; that on the keyboard C and B# are the same note is often one of those moments when you can see learning happening before your eyes.

The caveat will come from more-advanced instrumentalists, who will already know that not all semi-tones are equal; that pitch can be altered for both aesthetic and expressive effect as well as to adapt to the contingencies of the moment (your colleague in the clarinet section is playing flat, and you need to fit with them).

Then the pupils are ready for major scales.

This starts by introducing pupils to different major scales, helping them to understand that all major scales use the same pattern of tones and semi-tones:

T — T — S — T — T — T — S

Some learn this pattern by rote, but this often proves to be fallible. It's preferable to return to the white keys of the piano, from which it's very simple to find the notes of C major, and accordingly the pattern of tones and semi-tone which apply in every major key:

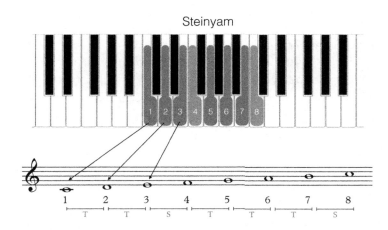

Steinyam

A brief digression on intervals

An interval is the distance between two notes. Measuring this distance is a simple yet powerful idea, which has the potential to make pupils better performers, more-perceptive listeners, and more-interesting composers. Why does Mozart include that huge leap downwards in the second movement of his Piano Concerto K467? How do you treat the melodic interval of a major sixth? What are the harmonic implications of the tritone?

Many pupils are familiar with the idea of an interval from ABRSM examinations; but it is a idea which often comes loaded with misconceptions. The most dangerous of which is associated with semi-tones. Pupils are often taught that there are six semi-tones in the interval of an augmented fourth, a fact both hard to remember, and misleading.

The missing foundational stage is to teach pupils that the letter names are essential to the meaning of any interval. The following interval might be a place to start:

Ignoring key signatures and accidentals, work out first that the bottom note is an A and the top a D. Then work out the letter names between the two:

A — B — C — D

There are four letter names here which means that the interval is a fourth. It's useful to develop in pupils the habit of saying whether a melodic interval is ascending or descending. Younger pupils may need help in their literacy here: to go from the cardinal to the ordinal, from two to second, from three to third, and so on.

Then pupils can compare the interval with the major scale from the bottom note (which generates major and perfect intervals), and work out whether it is major, minor, diminished, or augmented.

Working first with the letter names makes possible things in the future – the difference between dominant seventh and German sixths, for example – which the counting-semi-tone method denies pupils.

Writing scales

The same is true when writing scales. The daunting outline of an A-major scale can be made much more approachable if it starts like this:

Stage 1

A — B — C — D — E — F — G — A

When writing scales, pupils start from the letter names. They then write the corresponding notes onto a stave, labelling each note with its letter-name:

Stage 2

There are no accidentals here, neither a key-signature. Although semi-breves are the easiest rhythmic notation, it's a good idea to use minims here; it's an opportunity to teach pupils about the notation conventions of stems up and stems down.

The third stage is to add the pattern of tones and semitones which applies in every major scale to the pupils' own A-major scales. If pupils find this hard to remember, then it can easily be found from the C-major scale, the scale which uses the white notes from C to C. A completed stage 3 scale might look like this:

Stage 3

It's important to note that there are only two correct notes on this scale, the first and the last. Pupils celebrate this by marking the correct notes with a tick.

Stage 4

The fourth stage is to check and correct all of the other notes in turn. The distance from the first to the second note (from A to B) should, according to the pattern of tones and semi-tones, which applies in every major scale, be a tone. Using a real, drawn, or printed keyboard, it's easy for pupils to check:

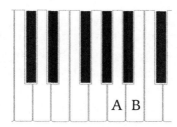

Because there is a black note between the two white notes, the distance is correct, a tone, and the note is ticked:

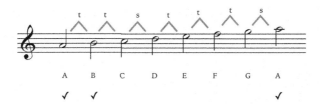

Between the second and the third notes (between B and C) should be a tone, but is, at present, a semi-tone.

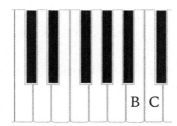

The presence of a tick is important: it means that the note has been checked and is correct. The B is now fixed, and it is the C which needs to change. A sharp is added before the note C, raising it by one semi-tone, and making the distance from B to C sharp a tone:

The third note is then ticked as correct.

This note-by-note checking means that the most difficult scale is possible for every pupil. The only problem is sometimes encountered by the very-experienced young musician, who knows already the key signature of A major, and rushes past the method.

Understanding scales, and the hierarchy of notes within them is essential to the understanding of music, particularly the understanding of structure and form.

Teaching form

Teaching form can seem a little daunting at first. Simultaneously, it brings to mind those somewhat arid charts of form which bedecked my childhood classrooms, and the fear-instilling difficulties of tracing a structure through tens of pages of orchestral score.

Accuracy of language is particularly important here: the words form and structure, as I've shown in the previous paragraph, can be used as near-synonyms; in some cases it may be wise to choose one or the other for a year-group, and stick to it. The definition of both form and structure is something like this:

> The basic plan of a composition.

The musical word form is straight out of Plato. It implies the use of an ideal formal archetype to shape an entire composition – verse/chorus, binary, ternary, sonata, rondo. Structure can work at different levels within a composition – a question-and-answer structure, the use of a small-scale ternary arch within a verse, for instance – as well as throughout.

It's often useful here to start beyond music, and then return to it. The form of a building, or the structure of a story – beginning, middle, and end – can help to introduce form as an idea.

This leads on to the form of a song. Your first aim is to teach that:

> the two essential ingredients of a complete and satisfying form are:
>
> 1. repetition
>
> 2. contrast

The repetitions within a strophic song are a really good way to show this. I've tried various examples here, my disastrous naïvety with *Lucy in the Sky with Diamonds* is painful to recall. Franz Schubert is somewhat safer, his song *Die Forelle* a powerful and effective instance.

Start with the Fischer-Dieskau recording, and a YouTube clip which projects with the audio file with both the German and English words. Tell your pupils that a *Lied* is a German art-song for voice and piano. Questioning can start with the story – a fish in the clear waters; the cunning fisherman; the fish caught. And immediately and easily there is a narrative structure to be found in the song.

Then the text, German on one side of the board, English on the other. The poetic form has three verses (stanzas) each with a rhyming pattern ABABCDCD. As you listen to each verse in turn, the pupils can be helped to observe that the last two lines of each verse are repeated three times in the song, identical music with different words at the end of each of the three verses. They will also hear that the music of the first two verses is identical, the third, despite the common ending, quite different. They will ideally be able to tell you what the differences are, and why they are there.

To explain this in words is possible; simultaneously to illustrate on the board is far more powerful. The finished board, and the accompanying handout, might look like this:

Die Forelle (Christian Schubart)   The trout

In einem Bächlein helle, Da schoß in froher Eil' Die launische Forelle Vorüber wie ein Pfeil. **A** Ich stand an dem Gestade Und sah in süßer Ruh Des muntern Fischleins Bade Im klaren Bächlein zu.	In a clear brook the vivacious trout in joyful haste shot past like an arrow. I stood on the bank in sweet peace, watching the jolly fish swim } in the clear brook. } **Z**
Ein Fischer mit der Rute Wohl an dem Ufer stand, Und sah's mit kaltem Blute, Wie sich das Fischlein wand. **A** So lang dem Wasser Helle, So dacht ich, nicht gebricht, So fängt er die Forelle Mit seiner Angel nicht.	An fisher with his rod stood on the bank watching with cold blood the fish's movements. So long as the water is clear, I thought, he won't catch the trout } with his rod. } **Z**
Doch endlich ward dem Diebe Die Zeit zu lang. Er macht Das Bächlein tückisch trübe, Und eh ich es gedacht, **B** So zuckte seine Rute, Das Fischlein zappelt dran, Und ich mit regem Blute Sah die Betrogene an.	But eventually the thief grew impatient. Cleverly he made the brook cloudy, and instantly his rod quivered, and the fish struggled on it. And I, my blood boiling, } looked on at the betrayed creature.} **Z**

The annotation of a different score, listening again to the Schubert and others, learning the key terms (strophic, repetition, contrast) can easily become homework or class activities.

We know that repetition is one ingredient in building complete and satisfying musical forms. The other is contrast.

Contrast

A composer can establish contrast in every musical element: in tempo (a fast or slow speed); in dynamics (loud or soft); in instrumentation (more instruments or fewer); or in key and mode. This last is by far the most important.

How far to go with key depends on the age group being taught. With a little practice, it's possible for less-experienced musicians to pick out a change of mode – where major contrasts with minor – but it's a little harder to talk about modulation.

Here are four ways to explore changes of key:

1. Because there is a hierarchy of notes in every scale, and because that hierarchy applies to the chords built on those notes, the most common notes in a melody will be those of the tonic triad, followed by those of the dominant. This ubiquity, combined with the presence of tonic or dominant notes at significant points – at the beginning and end of phrases, for instance – should give a good sense of where the key is.

2. The use of accidentals (sharps, flats, and naturals) in a score is a sure sign of something having happened. If you see a stray sharp or natural sign, it's rather likely that the altered note is the leading-note of the new key. Flats are often the seventh of a dominant-seventh chord. It's possible to be simpler still: two flats in a melody (say one in the key signature and the other an accidental) will strongly suggest B-flat major; two flats plus an accidental F sharp, G minor.

3. Cadences are musical endings, and you end on the prevailing key. If you find a perfect cadence, working from its distinctive bass-notes, then the chances are that you have found the key of the piece – whether a fleeting modulation or something more permanent.

4. The most long-lasting way to understand modulation is by teaching pupils what is most likely. A modulation onto the dominant is the driving force of a huge part of classical music, certainly since the Enlightenment. The principal contrasting key in the major mode is almost certain to be the dominant. In the minor, it's likely to be the relative major. Other possibilities include the subdominant, and the relative major (from a minor key). But the dominant is king, and by far the most likely. This is why it's so very important to teach form using key, as well as formal outline.

Form

The analysis of *Die Forelle* was quite a visual affair, coloured boxes projected onto a whiteboard. And although it was predicated on poetic structure – on words – a visual model is a good one to pursue further. Even if a young pupil's musical literacy is still developing, they can see shapes when drawn onto the board. Pick a short classical ternary-form piece, project it onto a white-board, take your coloured pens, and pretend for a moment that you are a geography teacher, mapping out the patterns within it. It's amusing to do, and the pupils can immediately track a rather dry formal-equation (A:||B:||A:||) onto a score. Play the piece several times, and point at the score to help them to follow it. A pupil might easily do this for you.

This should expand quite quickly to composition – the pupils will better understand the techniques, and have a greater appreciation of just how good is some of this simple music if they write versions of it for themselves. They may well fail to reach the level of Bach or Beethoven, but their knowledge will be immensely enhanced. One of the most powerful ways to teach this is to use a model, to take an existing piece, copy its gestures, its harmony, and (within reason) its ideas. This is explored further in chapter 8.

Teaching large-scale form

Large-scale form is quite daunting. A single movement of a large-scale work might be tens of pages long. The challenges recede for all of us, for the least-experienced musician as well as the expert, with familiarity. It's important to listen to any given work many times, to the point that you can imagine what a particular section sounds like – better still, to hear the sound of a particular page of the score – without recourse to a recording. It's the teacher's role in this to find the right recording, one which will appeal, and which will entice the pupils to listen still more.

But you can also teach large-scale form through composition. *Ritornello* is a useful vehicle for this – although you have to take care to avoid that most common of misconceptions about the difference between rondo form and *ritornello* (that, although both forms alternate returning sections and episodes, the rondo returns substantially the same whilst the *ritornello* is often shortened, and always appears on different keys).

The whole class learns a *ritornello*, become the *ripieno,* and learn to play it together. Depending on the class, this can be a single line, or two- or three-part writing. I've used both electronic keyboards or the pupils' own instruments; I've also seen this taught brilliantly with xylophones. Then in the episodes, each pupil takes their turn to be the soloist (*concertino*), and improvises on a given scale. This can range from a simple pentatonic selection (CDEGA, FGACD, GABDE), through a more complicated harmonic progression, to full-scale baroque pastiche. The form emerges through performance, and the pupils learn about the alternation of solo and *tutti* in the baroque concerto. It's useful to have done this exercise lower in the school if you are to teach the use of Vivaldi as a compositional model (see chapter 8).

So far we have talked about teaching as an activity based in the classroom; what happens if the world is turned upside-down, and we are forced to teach in all manner of different ways. Imagine what lessons might be learnt.

On-line teaching

Covid-19 has opened Pandora's box, and the snow-day may have melted away forever: new technologies, Zoom, Microsoft Teams, and Google Meet and Classroom are now permanent parts of teaching and should be celebrated with gratitude.

New technologies have always had the power to change the classroom, to bring glory to their inventors. 'The inventor or introducer of the system deserves to be ranked among the best contributors to learning and science, if not among the greatest benefactors of mankind'. The name of this particular inventor is unknown, but one of the great early enthusiasts for this technology was one Josiah F. Bumstead, in 1841 the author of *The Blackboard in the Primary School* (Krause, 2000: 11). The ability to teach large groups of children simultaneously made the work of a single teacher infinitely more efficient, if not necessarily more effective, and we have been dealing with the blackboard's ramifications ever since. In the following section, I will treat some of the ways in which synchronous on-line teaching (in which all pupils learn at the same time) can be made to work. Its antonym, asynchronous on-line teaching, is the subject thereafter.

Synchronous on-line music teaching

Synchronous teaching has distinct disadvantages over asynchronous, but you might be required to do it. Its advantages lie in the direct contact between teacher and pupil, in one-to-one interaction. Pupils feel connected to their school and to each other in a way which is limited, but which is nonetheless important.

The danger in this is that too much time is spent in pleasantries, and the teacher finds themselves at the end of a lesson without much having been achieved.

This section will consider the use of Zoom primarily, although the features described are, at time of writing, also part of Google Meet and Microsoft Teams. It assumes the use of Google Classroom. It also makes three assumptions: first, that the school's policy is for pupils' and teachers' cameras to be turned on; second, that as many of the technological issues have been solved – that, for instance, all pupils have internet access, and a device bigger than a smartphone on which to work, and; finally, that pupils have stationery to hand.

The more that an on-line lesson can be like an in-person lesson the better. Similar routines are useful and efficient in both; can help pupils to remember what it's like physically to be in their school, and make the eventual return easier. My pupils know that they are going to copy a definition from the board if it is in a yellow box; that they have instructions to follow in grey – both on-line and in real-ity. They will expect a crisp greeting and use of pupils' names as soon as the cam-era goes on, or a question if it does not. If the lesson is using a slide-presentation, then that first slide will display what the pupils need (in a grey box).

The great danger of this teaching is distraction. There's every chance that the pupils in your class will have a smartphone close at hand, other browser tabs in front of them, and be assailed by the in-pinging of alerts and notifications (Christodoulou, 2020). Even the very best and most-motivated students are tempted to flick from one thing to another with astonishing rapidity – studies found that laptop studying undergraduates switched windows on average every 19 seconds (Yeykelis *et al.*, 2014). If the pupils have not been actively engaged in the lesson within the first few minutes, then torpor and passivity are likely to be their lot for its duration, and it's hard to blame them for that. Brief questions at the beginning to which everyone responds are a very good way to start – an opportunity both for retrieval practice and for the teacher to set the lesson's agenda. It's nice for pupils to work away from their screens as much as possible, and writing answers using pen and paper is a good excuse for this.

Then things become a little tricky. The teacher's walk around the room, and the subtle glance over the shoulder are not available to us in the on-line world, but there are a few things it's possible to do to check that things are going in the right way. First, pupils' cameras are there to be used. The teacher can ask the pupils to show that there is a piece of paper, giving some small measure of accountability, as well as another opportunity for some sort of engagement. Second, pupils can be asked to respond verbally, the teacher calling on pupils nearly at random. Finally, the teacher can display a set of model answers, and the pupils can then correct their own work.

Two principles of good teaching are even more acutely felt on-line. First, explanations and instructions need to be very short and very clear – rehearsed in advance. It's good practice in the class to repeat them, using slightly different language the second time, as an internet glitch will inevitably mean that one pupil has missed the vital noun. It's a good idea, too, to ask a pupil to repeat back the instructions – by this the teacher can check that the pupils have understood, as well as that the technology has worked.

Teaching music

The second principle is to make sure that the pupils are participating actively. This is Lemov's double planning, that teachers plan both what they are going to say and do, and simultaneously determine how the pupils are going actively to participate (Lemov, 2015).

In music, this teaching lends itself best to listening, to history, and to theory and analysis. In the physical classroom, this would entail playing a musical extract, a recording or a video, to the class. Sharing audio or video directly from the teacher's computer is not going to work in a way that allows any great discernment. Assuming that the pupils' bandwidth is sufficient, then it's possible to share the link to a video with the class, and ask them to watch it independently. Keep the Zoom meeting open here, cameras on, but with every microphone muted; display on the teacher's screen the instructions ('listen only until time-code 4'33"', 'write your answers on paper; please use full sentences which include the question.') and the specific techniques and elements about which questions will be asked ('what melodic devices does Moby use?'; 'what is the dynamic here?'). Allocate only a little more time than the extract is long, and ask the pupils to make some physical gesture when they have finished (folding arms, for instance). Although Zoom and the other platforms offer pupils the chance virtually to raise their hands, make smiling faces and the like, it's another distracting interaction with a computer, and the old ways are the best.

Helping pupils actively to participate is harder. Asking for first responses on paper is effective, then calling on individuals to read their answers to the class. But you can check only so many responses that way. The next stage might be a more formally-submitted piece of work – an electronic file or a photograph of hand-written work uploaded to Google Classroom. The pupils' work can further be guided by a template, or a knowledge-organiser, or a list of starting-questions.

The teacher will be sharing their screen much of the lesson, and there should be a little caution about this. It's good practice to make sure that there is nothing else open on the teacher's internet browser, that short-cuts to websites are hidden, and that only the materials needed for the lesson are open in other pieces of software. Zoom does not always play nicely with full-screen presentations, and it's all-too-easy for a click in the wrong place to end up with the school's information-management system being enjoyed by the whole class.

Whilst audio recordings are difficult, is just possible to share enough of your computer's sound for notation-program music examples to be shared. And the teacher's home piano can be heard, within limits. But the most powerful thing you can do is using a stylus and a tablet. If you share a blank screen, or a page of manuscript, you can narrate, and ask questions, whilst writing on what is effectively a white-board. It's possible, too, this way to display and annotate scores.

If composition is taught remotely using computers, it can be very useful to make video screen recordings of your feedback. The pupil's composition is open on your screen, and you can suggest corrections, next steps, and improvements, whilst modelling them on-screen. Your recorded narration, your explanation of what you are doing, whilst the pupil can see the mouse moving, clicking, and working, is very powerful – an auditory stimulus combined with a visual one helps to pack a little more into the limited space afforded by working memory. Such recordings are practical only in quite small groups, or if you use a single composition to explore with a group things that have gone well, badly, and what comes next. Whole class feedback when directed so strongly on the work of an individual needs to be done with great care, both in the way it is presented, and the choice of pupil.

Asynchronous on-line music teaching

If teaching is to take place remotely, then it may not be the decision of the music teacher whether or not to teach live, or whether to set work which pupils can access in their own time. If autonomy is afforded within a school's culture, there are many ways in which asynchronous work is better suited to the teaching of music, and certainly it offers significant scope for future explorations. It also allows the production of teaching materials which are well-considered, the use of explanations which have been honed and practised before they are committed permanently to video, and the exploration of material in far greater depth, detail, and complexity (Lemov, 2020). It opens the possibility of a remarkable depth of materials for the more experienced and more curious musicians to explore, and allows the teacher's feedback to be much more nuanced, detailed, and careful.

The disadvantages of synchronous on-line music teaching

There are a number of difficulties associated with synchronous on-line teaching.

Managing several pieces of technology live and in public, systems which are apt to fail at any moment, adds significantly to the demands made on the teacher – to the cognitive load on them when teaching on-line. Attending to the craft of teaching, honing and adapting knowledge to the needs of a class are hard enough without being expected to provide technical support, or mouthing into a screen, silently and idiotically, with the 'mute' button turned on.

Long periods in front of a screen are as exhausting for the teachers as they are for the pupil, and technology is increasingly designed ruthlessly to harvest our attention (Wu, 2017; Williams, 2018). There is also the price in attention extracted by the devices themselves and the algorithms which invest them with their power. Many are the claims that young adults can 'multi-task' – can send a text message, read an article, and buy a t-shirt simultaneously; they are 'digital natives' and their brains are fast becoming wired another way (Christodoulou, 2020: 135–8). The wiring may well be changing, and that may or may not be a good thing, but it's certain that the ability to attend to several things at once, multi-tasking, is a pervasive and pernicious myth. What might appear to be doing several things at once is actually the rapid switching from one to the next – to the distinct and well-attested detriment of all (Willingham, 2010).

And some of this is the fault of the music teacher. Much as we want our pupils to listen to music, listening whilst studying, particularly listening to music with lyrics, has a distinctly damaging effect on homework and revision (Perham & Currie, 2014). It's the switching effect again. You learn what to attend to, remember what you think about, and the mind's capacity for both is limited. One thing at a time is always best when it really matters.

Synchronous on-line music teaching is also based on the assumption that pupils will have then-and-there access to devices, bandwidth, and a quiet and warm space in which to work; and it assumes the technology will work properly at that very moment. None of these things can confidently be expected, and all of them are directly related to the affluence or otherwise of the pupils concerned.

Lessons from a pandemic

For all its hazards and pitfalls, on-line teaching does open tremendous possibilities, and the lessons learnt from the pandemic are with us permanently. Or perhaps, to adopt a current truism, the paradigm has shifted and we have been caused to travel more quickly through the history of teaching to the place we were already going. Sudden and enforced adoption of technology has been an education for teachers, and a mass-experiment, albeit a haphazard one, in what works.

The foundations were there long ago, built by teachers who spent their evenings working out how best to use clunky 'virtual learning environments' to help their pupils to learn at home. They recorded their teaching, spliced together speech and music, laptops perched awkwardly on the piano. We would call these podcasts today, but they were just ways for pupils to learn set works, or music more generally, whilst sitting on the bus travelling to and from our schools.

The idea became more formalised in higher education, particularly in medical education. There was talk of 'flipped' classrooms, of students learning new material at home, and then using lesson-time to for practice, and for individual feedback and guidance from the teacher (Hamdan, 2013; Nouri, 2016).

The idea is a sound one. We know that pupils need to have engaged actively with knowledge something like three times before there's a chance of remembering it (Nuthall, 2007); we know that there needs to be time between those repetitions, time for the pupils to forget, at least a little (Brown, 2014). What if one or more of those repetitions could be made between classes, and what if the explanation of that new knowledge was as perfect as each teacher could make it, delivered when the pupil was receptive; what if the pupil could control the speed at which the explanation is delivered, pause, re-wind, and repeat the difficult bits?

And this is where it gets interesting for music teachers. We have as little as 40 minutes for a lesson on the six teeming minutes of *Bohemian Rhapsody*, or the 12 minutes of a Haydn op.76 string quartet, or a night-long *rāga*. What if we can expand the confines of a lesson so that everyone learns at least something about our topic, giving, at the same time, some the opportunity to learn a great deal?

This is where the asynchronous on-line lesson comes into its own. At the time of writing, technology is such that it's very simple to combine words with music, with illustrations, music examples, and embedded video; and the good news is that it's highly effective, too. When making a multi-media presentation like this there are a few principles to which it's wise to adhere.

Multi-media presentations

As ever, the starting-point is simplicity; the simpler a slide is, the more effective it will be. The temptation to add flounces and cleverness is great, but the more stuff there is, the longer it will take for the pupils to process and the less they will learn. It's amusing to add a photograph of a rubber duck dressed as Mozart to a slide, but it's likely that that the floating toy will be the only thing which pupils remember (and learning is memory). The slide will also need to be placed in a context, giving pupils some chance to activate their prior learning; the knowledge *of* and knowledge *how to* embedded in our long-term memories which is the basis for new learning (Kirschner *et al.*, 2006; Willingham, 2010).

The next principle is that combining words with images is a good idea (the multi-media principle) (Mayer, 1956). We process new material in our short-term memories, which are famously limited to the processing of but a few items (Miller, 1956). Teachers can help their pupils to cram just a little more material into their short-term memories by presenting it simultaneously in two different ways – as sounds and as images. A currently accepted metaphor for the workings of the mind suggest that, in the short-term memory, visual and auditory material are processed in slightly-different ways in slightly-different places, therefore, importantly, have the capacity to be processed simultaneously (Paivio, 1971; Baddeley & Hitch, 2000).

Delivery matters as well as content (Mayer, 2020). A friendly voice, in conversational style seems to work best; and it matters that pupils learn from their own teachers – even if the presentation is a little more ramshackle from us than from a sleek on-line video.

What does a good presentation or video look like? Or: What to write on a white-board

In a unit which teaches the rudiments and theory of music, let's assume some prior knowledge: that pupils have been taught rhythmic notation, and that articulation is familiar. Here's a still from a video which addresses a common misconception, the meaning of dots in notation:

Dots in music

1. Dots above the notes denote a *staccato* articulation.
2. Dots after a note extend that note by half as much again. They are called dots of addition. It's possible to have single or double dots of addition (3).

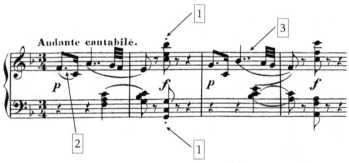

W.A. Mozart (1756-91): Symphony no.41 in C major KV550

On the audio track, the teacher will explain that this is a piano reduction of the second movement of Mozart's 'Jupiter' Symphony, and then the two uses of dots in notation. There is no reason why this slide should not be effective, but it needs to be streamlined somewhat. The problem is that the text explanations on the slide are divided from the music example: the pupil needs to listen to the teacher's explanation, to read the text, and must then look down the screen to find example(s) 1. This split-attention effect costs processing-time in the working memory (Mayer, 2020).

This might be better:

W.A. Mozart (1756-91): Symphony no.41 in C major KV550

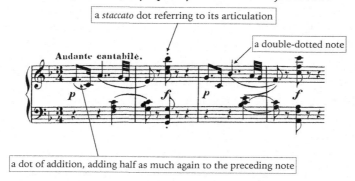

This is the final slide, fully revealed; each animated element appears in turn, at the same time as the teacher explains them: 'a dot of addition' and its arrow first; then the staccato dot; and finally the double-dot. This is much clearer, draws the pupils' attention to the relevant part of the example, and is a little more engaging.

But best of all would be this:

Dots in music

W.A. Mozart (1756-91): Symphony no.41 in C major KV550

This is a slide of radical simplicity, the appearance of each arrow showing the pupil where to look whilst the teacher explains. Omitting most of the text from the slide removes one last piece of distraction – when there's text present, pupils will expend their precious short-term memories trying to link the teacher's spoken words with the written text. Reading aloud the text of a slide is redundant, and will actively hinder the audience's listening (Mayer, 2020).

There is another cautionary tale here. The two 'components' of the short-term memory exist separately to process sense data from the ears and from the eyes.

Teaching music

Speech and music both come to us through the ears, and the effectiveness of the 'component' known as the auditory or phonological loop is this way easily overwhelmed. When we speak over any musical performance, however good our intentions, we also teach our pupils that music is not something to which we should attend, something we respect, and something we value. This requires great discipline, but our sometimes silence is at the heart of the craft of music teaching.

Before moving on, it's important to note that the three ideas explored here – Mayer's (2020) multi-media principle, the split-attention effect, the redundancy principle – are just as useful when planning presentations or teaching from the board in the physical classroom as they are on-line.

A new and fascinating alternative to a video-recorded presentation is to combine a video screen-recording (with audio narration), with a lesson delivered using a tablet and a stylus. The final frame of the video might look like this:

This is a lesson on the subject of composition, exploring three types of repetition: direct repetition; repetition by sequence; and repetition by motivic development. The subject of the previous lesson was contrast. The lesson unfolds as the material is drawn on the tablet – like an in-person lesson using a white-board. The difference here is that the pupil is asked to pause the video to write the answer to some questions: identifying and explaining clef, key signature, and time signature, and the pitch- and rhythmic-characteristics of motif x. Once the video resumes, new material is delivered, until x' is explored. Pupils pause once more, and then compare x with x', noting what has remained the same, and what has altered. The last part of the lesson is for pupils to take one of these melodic openings, and continue it as their own.

Making on-line learning active

Our next trick is to prevent pupils from becoming teenagers, staring glassy-eyed, slack-jawed at their screens. If the information they receive through their eyes and ears is to become knowledge, pupils need actively to be engaged with it. It's possible to embed activities within a video, and to ask pupils to pause the video to do them. Questions are quite an easy way to do this, particularly if you can build in your pupils good habits:

Learning is an active process.

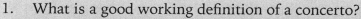

1. What is a good working definition of a concerto?
2. How many movements are there in a concerto?
3. What is the *tempo* of the first movement of concerto?
4. What is the *tempo* of the last movement of a concerto?
5. How many movements are there in a symphony?
6. In what year was Wolfgang Amadeus Mozart born and when did he die?

This is low-stakes testing (the brain-graphic a subtle reminder of a previous lesson on learning-how-to learn), practising both what the pupils have learnt from the previous slide (here about the baroque concerto), as well as contextual knowledge which was the subject of previous lessons (the symphony and something of Mozart's autobiography). When the video starts again, the teacher's feedback can be immediate, and there can be a moment for pupils to correct their answers. The teacher can check that this has been done by asking the pupils to photograph their work, and upload the pictures to Google Classroom.

Going further on-line

Producing on-line materials takes a great deal of time – somewhat less if the teacher uses the tablet-and-stylus method above, but still it's demanding – and it's important to use that time well, to do a single task but once.

If there are explanations involved in teaching – and there nearly always are – these can be recorded separately, and in such a way that they can be both long-lasting, and useful in several different settings. It might be possible, for example, to use a year 7 explanation as the starting-point in year 8 or beyond. To make this possible, in the recording, teachers should carefully omit any identifying material, reference to specific forms, years, or times of year. The explanations can then easily be added to any on-line lesson, and uploaded separately to the VLE or to Google Classroom. Pupils can use them for clarification at first and then later for revision.

We know the importance of practice and of low-stakes testing in teaching (Roediger & Marsh, 2005); building 'quizzes' on Google Classroom can help pupils to do exactly this. The examples here discuss Google Classroom, although many of the features are also part of other on-line learning platforms.

It's the facility to build multiple-choice questions in Google Classroom which is the most interesting – most especially the possibility of testing in which the pupils are given immediate feedback on work which is marked automatically. Multiple-choice questions have long been thought to be inferior to so-called 'cued-recall' questions. Giving the pupils the answer, rather than expecting them to recall it from their memories, seems instinctively to be a little too easy (Little & Bjork, 2015). But there's growing evidence that they are not inferior, merely different.

If the multiple-choice questions are designed carefully enough, there's a great deal they can do actively to promote learning. They need to be difficult enough to challenge pupils, but not so difficult that most pupils will get most of them right. An 80% success rate seems about right (Rosenshine, 2012). In their design, mixed with the correct answers should be incorrect 'lures' and 'distractors' (Brame, 2013).

These might be common misconceptions, or easy mistakes, but should not be too straightforward to spot. They need to be sufficiently plausible that the pupil is forced to stop and think, that the correct and incorrect compete with each other for primacy.

And, as ever, it is in the struggle and the hard work that learning is made possible. If the pupils are forced to use their prior knowledge to test the validity of each answer, irrespective of whether it is correct or incorrect, to engage in other words in retrieval practice, then the propositions tested are likely to be remembered and learnt (Little & Bjork, 2015).

An example might help to make this clear.

As a home-learning task associated with a series of lessons on notation, pupils are asked on Google Classroom to read a passage which contains information about the meaning of a number of easily confused symbols: dots, which might be of addition, *staccato*, or part of repeat signs; and curved lines, which are either ties or slurs. There follows the first multiple-choice question:

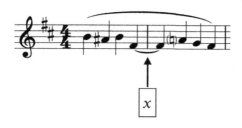

1. You see this curved line (x) which joins two notes of the same pitch either side of a bar line. Is it?

i. a slur

ii. a tie

iii. an instruction to play staccato

iv. an instruction to play legato

There are three types of answer here: the first is correct; the second plausible but incorrect; and the third less likely. The fourth is a 'distractor', there to make the pupil think hard about an abstract definition (Christodoulou, 2016: 164–9). The intention of the question itself is to make the pupil rehearse the difference between a tie and slur, to retrieve from memory definitions and explanations, and to test the present instance against them. The combination of music-example and question-text is a quite a deliberate piece of re-teaching, reminding pupils of one part of the definition of a tie.

Teaching music

The act of retrieving from memory, even retrieving from memory particulars of a plausible-but-incorrect answer, serve to strengthen the knowledge, and to make stronger links between its individual constituents. Even the two less-likely answers have the potential to build links and associations – that the articulations *staccato* and *legato* belong together in a single category.

As with any re-enforcement, there exists the danger that pupils are going to practise the wrong thing (Roediger & Marsh, 2005). Because there exists the perennial confusion between tie and slur, such risk is especially apparent here. There are two safeguards built into this exercise, albeit both somewhat imperfect. The first is in the question, in its juxtaposition of music example and text – the reminder about 'the same pitch'. The second is what happens next: after submission, the system provides immediate pre-programmed feedback, telling the pupil that their answers were either right and wrong, and offering, either way, an explanation of why. There are four possible pieces of feedback.

1. You are right. It's a tie because it links two notes of the same pitch either side of a bar line. Well done for seeing the difference between tie x and the slur. The slur above the stave indicates that all seven notes of the example should be played *legato*, smooth and bound.

2. You are wrong. It's a tie because it links two notes of the same pitch either side of a bar line. Because these two notes are the same pitch, it can't be a slur. There is also a slur over both bars. This indicates that all seven notes of the example should be played *legato*.

3. A *staccato* dot means that the notes should be played with detached articulation. The curved line x is a tie because it links two notes of the same pitch either side of a bar line.

4. A *legato* slur would be the instruction to play *legato*. The curved line here, however, is a tie because it links two notes of the same pitch either side of a bar line. There is also a slur over both bars. This indicates that all seven notes of the example should be played *legato*.

Attached to each piece of feedback is a link to a short explanatory video – students check again and revise.

The outcome of all of this should be a greater understanding of a tie. But there's every chance that by engaging in it, the pupil will also have learnt a related piece of information – that a curved line can also be a slur – as well as rehearsing the particulars of articulation (Little & Bjork, 2015). It's likely that a subsequent cued-recall test – asking, for instance, the question 'What are the two types of articulation?' – would be rather more of a success as a result.

Here are two more possible sets of multiple-choice questions which cover the same ground, attempt the same alchemy:

What does a tie do?

i. it instructs the player to play legato.
ii. it extends the note by half-as-much again.
iii. it extends a note by joining it together with the next note.
iv. it instructs the performer to repeat the preceding section.

What does a dot after a note mean?

i. it extends the preceding note by half-as-much again.
ii. it means to play the note with a staccato articulation.
iii. it means to repeat the previous section.
iv. it is a tie.

There is such potential here, and this way of thinking is really important. How learning works, and how best we might harness technology in its service is one of the last great mysteries. There is much talk of the use of machine learning, so-called artificial intelligence, in the classroom (Christodoulou, 2020). In music this is rudimentary, to say the least, but the foundations we lay in our experiments with on-line learning, the insights we bring to bear, and the deep thinking we do now will pay great dividends in the future. Certainly guiding our pupils' on-line explorations of our subjects is our duty as teachers.

This is the miracle of it, because pupils' enthusiasms can be followed almost without limit. There is no reason why a pupil cannot listen complete to *Bohemian Rhapsody*, or to all of Haydn's op.76 string quartets, or to a night-long *rāga*; or why they cannot explore the on-line wonders of *JSTOR* or *IMSLP* or *YouTube*. Whether posted on a school's VLE or in a Google Classroom, carefully-curated links to external resources can be a wonderful thing. When a Music Department's culture is right, when pupils share their enthusiasms with each other and with their teachers, it's sometimes quite hard to tell who is teaching whom.

References

Baddeley, A.D. & Hitch, G., 2000. Working Memory, in Bower, G.H. (ed.) *The Psychology of Learning and Motivation: Advances in Research and Theory* I, 8, 47–89, New York, Academic Press.

Berlin, I., 1953. *The Hedgehog and the Fox*. London, Weidenfeld & Nicolson.

Brame, C., 2013. *Writing Good Multiple Choice Test Questions*. Available at: https://cft.vanderbilt.edu/guides-sub-pages/writing-good-multiple-choice-test-questions [Accessed: 9 March 2021].

Brown, P.C., 2014. *Make It Stick: The Science of Successful Learning*. Cambridge, Massachusetts, The Belknap Press of Harvard University Press.

Christodoulou, D., 2016. *Making Good Progress*. Oxford, Oxford University Press.

Christodoulou, D., 2020. *Teachers vs Tech?: The Case for an Ed Tech Revolution.* Oxford, Oxford University Press.

Dunning, D. & Kruger, J., 1999. Unskilled and Unaware of It: How Difficulties in Recognizing One's Own Incompetence Lead to Inflated Self-Assessments. *Journal of Personality and Social Psychology*, 77(6 December), 1121–34.

Hall, C.C., Ariss, L., & Todorov, A., 2007. The Illusion of Knowledge: When More Information Reduces Accuracy and Increases Confidence. *Organizational Behavior and Human Decision Processes* 103(2007) 277–290. Available at: http://tlab.princeton.edu/publication_files/Hall_Ariss_Todorov%20OBHDP2007.pdf [Accessed: 10 November 2020].

Hamdan, N., McKnight, P., McKnight, K., & Arfstrom, K.M., 2013. *A Review of Flipped Learning*. Available at: http://www.flippedlearning.org/review [Accessed: 7 March 2021].

Kahneman, D., 2011. *Thinking Fast and Slow*. London, Penguin.

Kirschner, P.A., Sweller, J., & Clark, R.E., 2006. Why Minimal Guidance During Instruction Does Not Work: an Analysis of the Failure of Constructivist, Discovery, Problem-Based, Experiential, and Inquiry-Based Teaching. *Educational Psychologist*, 41(2), 75–86.

Krause, D.A., 2000. Among the Greatest Benefactors of mankind': What the Success of the Chalkboard Tells Us about the Future of Computers in the Classroom. *The Journal of Midwest Modern Language Association: Computers and the Future of the Humanities*, 33(2), 6–16. Available at: http://www.jstor.org/stable/1315198 [Accessed: 15 April 2020].

Leigh, M.D., 2020. How to Fail Perfectly, a Research Review. *TES*, 20 November 2020.

Lemov, D., 2015. *Teach Like a Champion 2.0: 62 Techniques That Put Students on the Path to College*. San Francisco, Jossey-Bass.

Lemov, D., 2020. *Teaching, Technology and the New Normal: A Short Guide to Surviving and Thriving in the World of Online Teaching*. New Jersey, Jossey-Bass.

Little, J.L. & Bjork, E.L., 2015. Optimizing Multiple-Choice Tests as Tools for Learning. *Memory & Cognition*, 43(1), 14–26.

Mayer, R.E., 2020. *Multimedia Learning*. Cambridge, Cambridge University Press.

Miller, G.A., 1956. The Magical Number Seven, Plus or Minus Two: Some Limits on Our Capacity for Processing Information. *Psychological Review*, 62(2), 81.

Nouri, J., 2016. The Flipped Classroom: For Active, Effective and Increased Learning – Especially for Low Achievers. *International Journal of Educational Technology in Higher Education*, 13, 33.

Nuthall, G 2007. *The Hidden Lives of Learners*. Wellington, Nzcer Press.

Paivio, A., 1971. *Imagery and Verbal Processes*. Oxford, Oxford University Press.

Perham, N. & Currie, H., 2014. Does Listening to Preferred Music Improve Reading Comprehension Performance? *Applied Cognitive Psychology*, 28(2), 279–284. Available at: https://doi.org/10.1002/acp.2994 [Accessed: 23 February 2021].

Pressley, M., McDaniel, M.A., Turner, J.E., Wood, E., & Ahmad, M., 1987. Generation and Precision of Elaboration: Effects on Intentional and Incidental Learning. *Journal of Experimental Psychology: Learning, Memory, and Cognition*, 13(2), 291–300. doi:10.1037/0278-7393.13.2.291.

Roediger, H.L. III & Marsh, E.J., 2005. The Positive and Negative Consequences of Multiple-Choice Testing. *Journal of Experimental Psychology: Learning, Memory, and Cognition*, 31, 1155–59.

Rosenshine, B., 2012. Principles of Instruction: Research-Based Strategies That All Teachers Should Know. *American Educator*, 36(1), 12.

Sacks, J., 2020. *Morality: Restoring the Common Good in Divided Times*. London, Hodder & Stoughton.

Williams, J., 2018. *Stand Out of Our Light: Freedom and Resistance in the Attention Economy*. Cambridge, Cambridge University Press.

Willingham, D., 2010. Have Technology and Multitasking Rewired How Students Learn. *The American Educator* 34:24–8. Available at: at https://www.aft.org/sites/default/files/periodicals/willingham-summer-10.pdf [Accessed: 23 February 2021].

Wu, T., 2017. *The Attention Merchants: The Epic Struggle to Get inside Our Heads*. London, Atlantic Books.

Yeykelis, L., Cummings, J.J., & Reeves, B., 2014. Multitasking on a Single Device: Arousal and the Frequency, Anticipation, and Prediction of Switching Between Media Content on a Computer. *Journal of Communication*, 64(1), 167–92. https://doi.org/10.1111/jcom.12070.

Chapter 7

Knowledge, assessment, and feedback

A hilarious shade of green

It was a piano painted the most hilarious shade of green, with faux Louis XV moulding rococoing around its case-work; but it was mine. That May, it had been moved into the local cathedral, a word conjuring mediaeval grandeur, but, in my friendly northern town, an appropriately friendly and approachable space – literally half a nineteenth-century building and half an optimistic modern space. The occasion for the move was a concerto, my first, organised by my school, as part of its annual choral jamboree.

It was my last year at school, and preparation of Mozart's G-major had been a constant part of my existence for months. The invitation came early in the academic year, but, what with university interviews, geography trips and projects, my youth orchestra, playing the organ at church, serious preparations began only after the Christmas vacation.

Looking back now, these preparations – learning the piece – were the best part of the experience.

At the beginning, I felt daunted by the scale of the thing. KV453 is a little concerto, as these things go, but there were still three movements, a cadenza to choose and learn in the first, ornamentation to add to that lovely second, and all those dashing variations in the last to overcome. It was so long and there were too many notes, as Emperor Joseph II maybe said to Mozart (Hampe, 2016).

But I started at the beginning, and, as I worked little-by-little, the task shrank, as it always does. There were tricks which helped. At the suggestion of my teacher, I divided the first movement into 52 sections, dug out a set of playing cards, and allowed chance to determine my practice.

A little clockwork metronome became my constant companion. My trick was to play each fifty-second of the movement very, very, slowly – 40 beats-per-minute – and then speed up by moving the weight two clicks down the metronome's arm – missing 42 and rushing to 44. Then down to 42, up to 46, down to 44. Up two,

DOI: 10.4324/9781003112402-7

down one. My teacher must have taught me this, although I have no recollection of his so doing, and I later found out that the method was a favourite of Dorothy DeLay, after Liszt, perhaps the greatest of all instrumental teachers.

I played short sections over and over. Mrs. Day, hanging-out her washing next door, spoke to my Mum over the side fence, said that it was getting a little dull. My parents went away for a few days, I stayed at home. Alone, somehow, I hefted that lumpen piano into the front room, so I could play for longer without Mrs. Day noticing.

The ace of diamonds meant that tricky bit in the development, all that intricate eighteenth-century figuration, those exposed and exposing broken chords. The metronome ticked, and I played the chords together, their individual notes in groups, in different orders, and with different rhythms – practising the triplets in groups of long-short-short, short-long-short, short-short-long – with dotted rhythms (forward and in reverse) and with different articulations.

And there were piano weekly lessons. I had a driving licence by now, and was allowed (carefully) to take the family car the four miles to my teacher's home – an adventure in itself. In his coffee-smelling studio, I was allowed (carefully) to play his Steinway, to show him what I had been doing. He played the orchestral part on his battered old upright, and I was the soloist. It was a chance to perform, find out whether the metronome's ticks had driven all of those notes into my fingers and into my brain. I desperately wanted to impress, and some bits worked, but some bits stubbornly did not. They seemed fine at home, I could reel them off effortlessly, but with my sometimes-despairing teacher, the too-many notes became all-too tangled, and any sense of line simply fell away.

But he persisted, showed me tricks and shortcuts, suggested practical and consistent fingerings, offered ideas about interpretation, corrected my mistakes. He wrote reminders in my music in confident pencil, found different ways to explain the things that I could not quite grasp.

Much to the ire of Mrs. Day, it was then back to the metronome, and even more time. At school, Mr. Taylor said he would be away for a double period, and I had done the work set – I went to the school hall with my metronome to practise; Mr. Edmonson was fearsome, but easily evaded, and games afternoons involved only the exercise of my fingers, hidden away in the recesses of the music block. There were times when I tried to perform sections of the work, short passages which I thought were close to being ready. I borrowed the school's cassette recorder and microphone, and made recordings. At school, I enlisted other Edmonson-evaders covertly to listen, to provide the sense of an audience. A risky strategy for our gang of wimps.

I had my treasured CD player, and Murray Perahia's performance of the concerto with the English Chamber Orchestra was one of the three discs in my library (the Grieg and Schumann piano concertos with Kovacevich and Mahler with Szell, since you ask). I listened and admired and wondered how such polish would ever be possible.

There were more lessons, more tearing of my teacher's hair; but it was slowly getting better. The crashes were no-longer fatal, and the hesitations fewer and of less note.

Then the day of the performance. The cathedral, the local instrumental teachers coming together in a small orchestra, the audience, and my green, over-ornate piano. I don't remember much of the evening, certainly not at this remove; but people seemed pleased. I do remember stumbling at the end of the first-movement cadenza, feeling doubt creep in; the sense that this was the moment when I had to take a grip on the performance, make sure that Mrs. Day's torture was not for nothing.

My teacher himself was playing that evening, could not be there. But another of his pupils, Eliot, trumpeter and sceptic, was clearly enlisted to report back. I was nervous in my next lesson, relieved beyond belief by his laconic 'I heard it went well'.

A model of learning

So many music teachers can draw on formative experiences like this, have been part of a major gig, sung a big part in the musical; sometimes it is hard to forget what powerful lessons these provide for us. It's another one of the ways in which music teachers are different.

The concerto was a goal, clearly defined, both in time and in the bounds of its knowledge. This is the first of Wiliam's principles of classroom assessment, 'Clarifying, understanding, and sharing learning intentions' (Wiliam, 2011). My teachers wanted me to learn from the opportunity of playing it, thought that it would be a valuable part of my preparations for university and of my development as a player.

The aim of all music teachers, always, is to produce interested and passionate listeners; members of musical society who have the life-long enthusiasm to explore music for themselves, and who possess sufficient knowledge successfully on a first hearing to understand enough of a work new to them. But that's not quite enough for success in the classroom. Any given goal needs to be broken down into its contributing parts, with the knowledge required for success in each carefully specified.

Part and whole

As Mrs. Day probably will still shudder to remember, the means of learning the concerto and the end performance were related but quite distinct one from the other. I did not learn to play Mozart's KV453 by sitting down at the piano and experimenting with the whole, I dealt the cards, and worked section by section.

It's all-too-easy for a pupil, even a pupil enthusiastic for music, to sit in front of a computer, wondering when creativity will strike, when they will be able to put something, anything down on paper. This is not how teaching works. Being asked to think like a composer does not teach composition any more than being asked to think like the next Niels Bohr (Willingham, 2007).

To give the pupil the tools to succeed, having first defined the composition task, we need to break down the domain of compositional knowledge into its component parts.

I divided the Mozart concerto into 52 pieces, practised each one in turn. The young composer, when asked to write a short piece, needs to know some key things, things which fall into three distinct categories.

First comes the knowledge which they need to have at their fingertips, the prior knowledge the absence of which will cause the whole project to fail. Pupils need to understand and be sufficiently well-versed in clefs and notation, in notes and their rhythms, in dynamics, articulation, and tempo. This knowledge includes the technical means the task requires – this might include skills with notation programmes, in exploiting keyboard instruments in composition and as compositional tools, in hand-written music-notation.

Then there is the knowledge which is specific to the task. This comprises the component parts of knowledge, which make it possible for a pupil to compose a technically convincing piano piece. It can be specified in quite precise and granular detail and is the bedrock of the abilities of our ideal listener.

When working out the reality of this knowledge in the classroom, a neat analogy to use is that of the cricket coach, devising drills and exercises which practise specific elements of the game. For batsmen these might include trigger movements, bat-lift, watching the ball. Working on these tiny parts of the game require focused attention, and have the proven effect of making batsmen more skilful more quickly than they would become by playing the game alone. Net practice means that batsmen can repeat the drill, can face hundreds of balls, can do the thing they are trying to improve far more often than they can in a match (Ericsson *et al.*, 1993). The unforced genius, the extra-ordinary talent, these things simply don't exist; it's all in the work and in the practice. If we return from cricket to our piano piece, drills might include how to treat conjunct and disjunct movement, how to begin and end phrases, how to build a pleasing and considered contour, what different registers and ranges of the piano mean and which are best avoided.

Knowledge specific to the task does not just include that which the teacher expects their pupil to learn; there is another type of knowledge here, too. This second related type is knowledge which is critical to the shorter-term moment-by-moment understanding of the task, but which is not essential for pupils to commit to long-term storage. In teaching a specific aspect of form, for example, it might be helpful for pupils fleetingly to understand the structures of a number of exemplar pieces, but not permanently to remember them. To learn permanently that the point of recapitulation in a movement written according to sonata principles will involve the return of the opening material, it's useful to be able to work on examples where the recapitulation is unequivocal as well as those examples where the composer breaks the rules and creates wonderful things (for instance, the point of recapitulation in the first movement of Brahms's Fourth Symphony with its timeless augmentations, or the first of Mahler's Fourth which says 'once upon a time' all over again). As we prepare our pupils to write for the piano, they might be shown and need to understand examples of and imitate examples of piano writing, but, to appropriate Daniel Willingham (2004), 'no great educational harm is done if the particular facts about the particular [pieces] are forgotten'.

Finally there comes the knowledge of what good looks like. Murray Perahia was and is a extraordinary example. In our composition an example might be the best work of pupils who tried this task in previous years. Displayed, analysed, and annotated, it helps children to know what's possible, gives then something to which they can aspire.

There is the closest relationship between this hard thinking about knowledge, this unpicking of the implications of a given task, and feedback and assessment. This is the necessary background to Wiliam's (2011) second principle of classroom assessment: 'Engineering effective classroom discussion, tasks and activities that elicit evidence of learning'.

Assessing musical domains

Yes, I played KV453, a concerto and it 'went well'. But that did not mean that I could now 'play piano concertos', did not mean that I could immediately perform KV466 or 595, let alone one of the Brahms concertos. Perhaps there were skills which transferred from one musical domain to another – some scale figurations, a cadential formula, a melodic gesture – but any new concerto would need to go through the same process as KV453 had done. I could reasonably expect my journey through the next one to be slightly smoother and slightly more direct (I had learnt something about efficient work, after all), but its final success was dependent on still more hours spent driving Mrs. Day to distraction.

There are quite significant pitfalls in the teaching of such generic skills ('play piano concertos'), however self-evident they might seem, or well-intentioned their proponents. Common examples of this are critical thinking or managing information (Willingham, 2007); particular examples in music might be the skills of listening, or analysis. A pupil might be able very successfully to unpick the intricacies of a string-quartet minuet by Haydn, understand rounded-binary form and motivic development, but be quite lost when presented with Bach's *Art of Fugue* arranged for string quartet, or Elliott Carter's second. To improve, the pupil needs more knowledge which is specific to the case, not more help with analysis in general – in this instance they need to know about fugal forms and about the methods and brilliance of Carter.

Music departments are busy and complicated places, and it's sometimes easier for each component part to work in ignorance of the others. How frequently do music teachers complain that children learn scales with their instrumental teachers, yet don't understand them in the classroom? How often do pupils perform a work brilliantly, yet when asked to talk or write about it, struggle to find the words? This is partly an example of the same thing – that skills are not automatically transferred from one domain to another (Hirsch, 1987: 61) – and partly the responsibility of the leader to keep each part of the music family talking. In utopia, the classroom teachers know what and how the instrumental teachers are teaching and vice versa, and the performances planned by the department are relevant to the classroom. That this is impossible should not make the best the enemy of the good, and what can be done to break down barriers, should be done.

Deliberate practice

'How do you get to Carnegie Hall?', so the old joke goes. It's said that Jack Benny's answer was 'Practise, practise, practise'. Mrs. Day would say the same, albeit through hard-gritted teeth.

I broke down the Mozart into sections, practised each by repetition; practised by altering the tempo, and by making the difficulties of each into a technical exercise. This is a useful model of good teaching and good learning, but not quite sufficient.

Wiliam returns to bat-and-ball sports when he talks about what a coach does. Their role is to 'have a clear notion of quality' but also to understand the

> anatomy of quality; he is able to see high-quality performance as being composed of a series of elements that can be broken down into a developmental sequence for the athlete
>
> (Wiliam, 2011: 120)

The task of writing a short composition for piano is the goal, and we know already what a good one would look like ('notion of quality'). We also know some of the 'series of elements' which the pupils need to understand. To complete the picture, we need to turn these into a 'developmental sequence' for our pupils. In theory, it's obvious that this entails laying out the elements in order of difficulty, and in such a way that each follows-on from the last. In practice, this involves both hard thinking and a little compromise. Do you teach first the use of conjunct and disjunct movement? The importance of repetition and contrast in a melody? How to start and finish a phrase or a piece? The answers to these questions depend on the pupils and their prior experience, but it's thinking which needs to be done.

The way this material is delivered – how each element is practised in the classroom – is also central to successful teaching. 'In a nutshell':

> The teacher decides the learning intentions and success criteria, makes them transparent to the students, demonstrates them by modelling, evaluates if they have understood what they have been told by checking for understanding, and re-telling them what they have told by tying it all together with closure.
>
> (Hattie, 2012: 206)

For deliberate practice, the key word here is 'modelling'. Pupils, particularly inexperienced pupils, learn new material best when they are guided through it for the first time; expecting them to discover it for themselves – the pupil sitting in front of a computer, being asked to compose, for instance – will almost always lead to worse outcomes (Clark *et al.*, 2012). A 'worked example' helps pupils to learn by simplifying and streamlining their first encounters with a problem, alleviating the cognitive load placed on them (Sweller & Cooper, 1985; Carroll, 1994). This finding comes from the solving of algebra problems; it's not too big a leap to go from mathematics in the calculations required to write music.

In music, a worked example of our melody means that the teacher does the exercise themselves. Moving between the piano and the board, narrating all-the-while the choices they are making, the possibilities they are considering, and the pattern of their thoughts. The level of support (and consequent reassurance) which is needed by inexperienced musicians is immense, the skills of teaching it painstaking, almost pedantic. Greg Ashman calls this the 'attention to picky, picky detail', and he's right (Christodoulou, 2014: 48). Insisting that pupils call the note which helps them to find their place on the keyboard 'middle' C, not just C; that, in answers, the names of every accidental is correctly annunciated – F sharp, not F; that the treble clef is the G clef – these all have their parts to play in deliberate practice: each of these individual pieces of knowledge lead to another, and then another. This relates to Lemov's 'right is right' (2015: 100–1).

After watching the worked example, the pupils are asked to do part of the exercise themselves – complete a half-completed melody, or write a complete melody to a pre-ordained rhythmic-pattern. With each iteration – the metronome weight clicks up two steps – the task becomes a little more difficult; but not too difficult – down one. Too much difficulty can overwhelm, just enough to be 'Germane' is a very good thing (Sweller *et al.*, 1998: 259).

This works very well indeed with inexperienced musicians; is potentially of less value with those who have been musicians for longer (Leslie *et al.*, 2012). The reason for this seems intuitive: the more-experienced musicians have built stronger schemas of learning, can rely on more experience and knowledge. With them, the scaffolding is redundant.

To take the next step, we turn to Wiliam's fifth principle of classroom assessment; that teachers provide 'feedback that moves learners forward' (Wiliam, 2011).

Feedback

Without my teacher, the Mozart would have been impossible. I did not know KV453 before he suggested it, knew not that the work was written for Mozart's pupil Barbara Ployer (neither had heard the story telling how the last-movement theme was sung to the composer by a pet starling), and that it was cleverly written to be simultaneously impressive and relatively easy to play. But most of all, it was the way he worked with me in lessons that opened the possibility that I would become a better pianist. He would listen to a section, stop me, suggest corrections and improvements, then ask me to play again, with those improvements incorporated. He suggested, I did, he told me what to do to reach the next stage. Instrumental teachers' work is the very model of responsive teaching (Leigh, 2021).

Responsive teaching is what Dylan Wiliam at first called *Assessment for Learning* (Christodoulou, 2016: 21), and it's what great teachers do. Teachers attend to pupils' work, and then they respond to it, suggesting actions the pupils can take to make it better.

I listened to my piano teacher because I respect him immensely as player and as a man, because of the record of his former pupils, and because my instinct told me how much he had to offer. It was only in hindsight and with experience that I realise what a wonderful teacher he is. This is the prerequisite of feedback, that 'In the end, it all comes down to the relationship between the teacher and the student' (Wiliam, 2016: 15).

Responding to pupils' work, and helping them to make it better is what we seek to do, and there are some useful principles to keep in mind. First, the feedback needs to be 'specific and clear' (Didau & Rose, 2016: 86). This might seem obvious, but it's worth a little thought. It's not the egregious examples which are the problems ('Use the correct chords'; 'Make it more beautiful.'); these are the example which Wiliam says are

> rather like telling an unsuccessful comedian to be funnier — accurate but not particularly helpful
>
> (Wiliam, 2011: 120)

The real problem is with feedback which seems to be both specific and clear, but which is not: for instance, that a pupil's minor-key composition needs to use the correct accidentals. This is true but not useful, neither is the teacher's suggestion that they need to add A sharps. Far better is to ask the pupil to listen hard and then to say why a particular note sounds strange, then make sure that their understanding of the leading note is secure, and finally to ask them to find another, say, six examples in their piece – at least one in the bass clef. This looks cumbersome in print, and certainly is a model of feedback which needs to be practised by the teacher to make it efficient in the classroom; but it can become an easy part of classroom conversation, and the teacher can make the content their own. Note that this explains the immediate and detailed ways in which the pupil's work can be improved – this is the problem; you now understand the mistake which you have made; these are the things you need to do right now to improve (Didau & Rose, 2016: 86).

Second, good feedback 'refers to the task and not to the person, and it aims to increase the pupil's commitment to the work' (Didau & Rose, 2016: 86). This raises the ugly spectre of talent. Telling a child they are not talented is both wrong and counterproductive; it's equally dangerous to say that they are gifted. The first is dismissive of an individual and the second encourages complacency. There's nothing wrong with courtesy, thanking pupils for their work and saying that you enjoyed it; but the most effective feedback commends effort, and celebrates the process and strategies which the pupil has adopted (Gunderson *et al.*, 2013).

Third, feedback needs to help pupils to understand that it is in their power to improve (Kluger & DeNisi, 1996: 254). How often do you hear a pupil say that they are rubbish at music? This is especially true when there are a few high-performing children in the class. Good feedback needs to help pupils understand that knowledge – both knowledge of and knowledge how to – is mutable, that it is subject to change over time, both for good and ill. Knowledge is not a monolithic 'can-do-music', nor its opposite; you are only momentarily a success, you have only momentarily failed, the result is provisional, a direct result of how hard you've worked, and how much attention you've paid to the task in hand. In other words, the pupil has the power to improve (Didau & Rose, 2016: 83). The building of knowledge is a patient thing, and each step leads to the next. I had played the Mozart, and it 'went well', but there was more work to do if I wanted to become a better pianist, and Beethoven was next.

Finally, feedback needs to make pupils think or at least act. This is perhaps the hardest and most important part of all:

> The only thing that matters is what the student does with the feedback. If the feedback you're giving your students is producing more of what you want, it's probably good feedback. But if your feedback is getting your less of what you want, it probably needs to change.
>
> (Wiliam, 2016: 10–15)

It was relatively easier for my piano teacher: there was a passage to practise, and this was how to do it. In the classroom there is also much to be said for asking pupils to repeat and refine. A piece of analytical writing can itself be analysed – for content, clarity, strength of argument – then its weaknesses addressed and practised. The skill of writing is both vested in and practised by re-writing, and a paragraph repeated, to the satisfaction of both pupil and teacher, is time well spent. In a composition project, imagining an exercise away from the main work might help to address a weakness or a misconception in it. With the leading-note problem, for example, the student could be asked to write three short melodic snippets – each four- or five-notes long – making prominent use of the sixth and seventh degrees of the minor scale. This is feedback leading to more work from the student, often work which does not look very much like the final outcome (a paragraph within an essay; a melodic fragment within a composition).

Responsive teaching in the classroom

The most important feedback is that which happens minute-by-minute in the classroom (Wiliam, 2016). Within every task set there should be the opportunity for feedback, the chance for the teacher to check what has been mastered, and what still needs to be clarified. This way the teacher also monitors their own practice, seeking to improve and refine what they do themselves.

Giving moment-to-moment feedback in the classroom seems so very simple. At the end of an explanation, you check for understanding. But it's absolutely not sufficient to ask, 'is that clear?'. An affirmative answer to that question could mean anything from, 'I understand completely and am ready to use my understanding in practice' to 'I haven't a clue and I truly wish you would leave me alone'.

Knowledge, assessment, and feedback

In checking for understanding, a teacher is doing just that, but they are also giving all students an opportunity to practise and make memorable that particular piece of knowledge. Once the question is asked, this is why it's important to give the whole class sufficient time for every pupil to consider an answer before asking anyone to speak. This feels uncomfortable at first, hard to measure, and it needs to be done explicitly – you tell the pupils that you are giving them time to think for themselves (Lemov, 2015: 244–8). The teacher is silent, thinks with the pupils, showing them what to do.

Here, for instance, is a definition of sequence:

> In a melody, the immediate repetition of a motif in the same part but at a different pitch

Like Matryoshka dolls, nested together, within it is an array of foundational information, each part of which is necessary to the whole. From the definition of pitch, melody, and repetition, through motif, to that key word, 'immediate'.

A teacher can, first, ask students to repeat what has just been explained, but using their own words. This is a useful exercise for more-experienced pupils, or when working through material taught in a previous lesson. Pupils can respond verbally, or with quick answers in rough work, or on individual white-boards.

But it's important to check that every component part of the definition is clearly understood; which takes a series of pre-planned (and rehearsed) quick questions:

> 'Using the musical elements, tell me where you will hear a sequence, John? [melody] … Good, and what is another word for pitch, Pratush? [notes] … and a synonym for melody, Shreyas? [tune] … And what are the two parts of a motif, Henry? [pitch and rhythm] … And how long is a motif, Enoch? [short] … What is special about the repetition of a motif in a sequence, Nehemiah? [each repetition is at a different pitch] … And what is the second thing, Dare? [the repetition is immediate] … Thank you.'

This is both checking for understanding and rehearsal of knowledge, an opportunity for the teacher to find out what the pupils know, and to teach again those things which are not yet clear or have been forgotten.

The concept of a sequence can then be expanded and related to other devices:

> 'If you hear the immediate repetition of a motif at the same pitch but in a different part, what's that called?' [imitation]

'And what's the particular type of imitation called when the first part stops whilst the second part is copying?' [antiphony]

'In world music, what is call-and-response?' [when one voice or instrument plays, and a group answers]

And then the concept can be deepened further, to concede that there might be such a thing as an imitative sequence, where a motif is passed between two parts.

It's important for the questions to be pre-planned because the teacher should be doing lots of things at the same time: choosing carefully who answers which question; scanning eyes to insist on attention and concentration; and looking for physical cues that a pupil or group of pupils have not understood. You are trying to make sure that every pupil has understood, and by asking a mixture of the more- and less-experienced pupils, you should be able quickly to ascertain whether it's time to move on or not.

And if something goes wrong, is not clear, then it could be a fault with the teacher's explanation. This needs to be addressed immediately with the class – re-teaching in a slightly different way, perhaps with a different example – and in private as the teacher reflects on what was not quite clear, and how it could be better next time.

Testing in the classroom

Every piano lesson began with a performance of the Mozart. Sometimes it was a whole movement, sometimes just the last section learnt. The coffee-smelling studio was not the cathedral, but the sense of performance was real, a chance to practise for the real thing. I would not have called it a test, but this is exactly what it was, a short, relatively low-stakes assessment of how my preparations were going, and diagnosing what was next. This is formative assessment.

It seems that this sort of testing is a very good thing. A short test at the beginning of a lesson sets the tone, helps pupils to engage with work immediately, and helps the teacher to find out how much the pupils have remembered and know. It's a flexing of the intellectual muscles before the new content begins. The act of answering questions, of thinking hard and trying to remember may itself help knowledge to become permanent in the memory (Carrier & Pashler, 1992). For their efficiency in the classroom, multiple-choice questions are the medium, and, as we saw in chapter 5, there is a little art in their construction.

These tests are designed to provide information to the teacher, but it's not necessary for the teacher laboriously to mark every paper. In fact, it's probably best if the pupils mark their own or each other's work. This involvement, this 'Activating students as owners of their own learning', can be quite powerful (Wiliam, 2011) and it's an important step towards intellectual maturity:

> Being able to tell the difference between competence and incompetence is actually an aspect of developing competence. Developing our pupils' ability involves developing their ability to perceive quality.
>
> (Christodoulou, 2016: 48)

Written feedback and marking

To the doctor the stethoscope, to my piano teacher the soft blunt pencil, to the teacher the red pen; these are the adornments of our calling, of our office. The marked book is teaching's shibboleth, something to which we cling, but is something which is becoming increasingly hard to justify. Marking makes teachers' (considerable) efforts visible but does not always constitute useful feedback – we need to think again.

It's especially hard in music, where the pupils compose and write about music, where they listen and perform, where they learn about the cultures and times from which a piece originates. The richness and variety of our subject are themselves problems.

When marking books, there is the 'proofreading trap', where spelling and grammar are corrected, but more fundamental problems of knowledge or reason are ignored (Cogie, 1999). In concert season, it's very hard to find time to mark a set of books in a timely fashion, and the longer the interval between the work and its feedback, the more meaningless the feedback becomes. And it looks increasingly as if marking, assigning work to categories or giving raw marks, does little to help our students to improve (Elliott *et al.*, 2016).

One of the neatest solutions is to make feedback on a piece of work the substance of the next lesson. It's relatively quick to scan a set of books, to read their essays on Beethoven's Seventh Symphony, and privately to record a mark. Then the teacher can extract and share examples of the very best work ('A knight returning from a long and tedious quest and how glad he is.'), work which goes above and beyond ('premiered in Vienna on 8th December 1813 at a charity concert for soldiers wounded in the Battle of Hanau. It was also conduced [sic] by Beethoven himself.'), and examples of common misconceptions ('The Tempo – at first, it starts quite [sic] and suddenly loud in between.'). The lesson then demonstrates to the pupils what matters to you – a spelling test (homophones like 'peace', and easy mistakes like 'quite', 'stagato', 'cleff'), work on the musical elements, the worth and dangers of Wikipedia – as well as saving considerable time. And the pupils, having first engaged with the symphony at home, are now more receptive for the next part of the lesson – ready to learn how to listen with more discernment and insight.

Written feedback on compositions is much harder. Particularly for coursework compositions produced under timed conditions, many teachers make extensive notes about the feedback given. This is often highly effective but time consuming, and the Goldilocks amount of time with each pupil – not too much, not too little – is highly elusive. A useful shortcut is to print the composition, highlight the section to be improved, and ask the pupil to make notes of what's next. This builds into an interesting and satisfying portfolio, demonstrating to both pupil and teacher how the composition has developed over time.

What music teachers know already

Many music teachers have had that formative experience of a major performance, hilarious green instruments notwithstanding. And it's important to remember what a valuable experience that is for our work now, that instrumental teaching is a near-perfect model for learning in the classroom.

Dylan Wiliam puts it succinctly:

> … I think that there's a lot we can learn from music teachers. Music teachers know that in the 20 or 30 minutes that the teacher gets with a student every week, progress is going to be very small. In that 30 minutes, not much improvement is going to happen. If students do get better at playing a musical instrument, it is because they have been practising productively at home. That is why music teachers spend a lot of time making sure that students know what they need to be doing when they're practising alone.
>
> (Hendrick & Macpherson, 2017: 39)

Of this directed practice, knowledge, assessment, and feedback, we know a lot already.

References

Carrier, M. & Pashler, H., 1992. The Influence of Retrieval on Retention. *Memory & Cognition*, 20(6), 633–42.

Carroll, W., 1994. Using Worked Examples as an Instructional Support in the Algebra Classroom. *Journal of Educational Psychology*, 86(3), 360–67.

Knowledge, assessment, and feedback

Christodoulou, D., 2014. *Seven Myths About Education*. London, Routledge.

Christodoulou, D., 2016. *Making Good Progress*. Oxford, Oxford University Press.

Clark, R.E., Kirschner, P.A., & Sweller, J., 2012. Putting Students on the Path to Learning: The Case for Fully Guided Instruction'. *American Educator*, 36(1), 6–11.

Cogie, J., 1999. Avoiding the Proofreading Trap: The Value of the Error Correction Process. *The Writing Center Journal*, 19(2), 7–32.

Didau, D. & Rose, N., 2016. *What Every Teacher Needs to Know About Psychology*. Woodbridge, John Catt.

Elliot, V., Baird J.A., Coleman, R., Hopfenbeck, T., Richardson, J., Ingram, J., Thompson, I., Usher, N., & Zantout, M. 2016. A Marked Improvement? A Review of the Evidence on Written Marking. *Education Endowment Foundation*. Available at: https://educationendowmentfoundation.org.uk/public/files/Presentations/Publications/EEF_Marking_Review_April_2016.pdf [Accessed: 16 March 2021].

Ericsson, K.A., Krampe, R.T., & Tesch-Römer, C., 1993. The Role of Deliberate Practice in the Acquisition of Expert Performance. *Psychological Review*, 100(3), 363–406.

Gunderson, E.A., Gripshover, S.J., Romero, C., Dweck, C.S., Goldin-Meadow, S., & Levine, S.C., 2013. Parent Praise to 1- to 3-Year-Olds Predicts Children's Motivational Frameworks 5 Years Later. *Child Development*, 84(5), 1526–41.

Hampe, M., 2016. Too Many Notes. In Walton. C. (Trans.). *The Crafty Art of Opera* (99–106). London, Boydell & Brewer.

Hattie, J., 2012. *Visible Learning for Teachers: Maximising Impact on Learning*. London, Routledge.

Hendrick, C. & Macpherson, R., 2017. *What Does This look Like in the Classroom: Bridging the Gap between Research and Practice?* London, Routledge.

Hirsch, E.D., 1987. *Cultural Literacy: What Every American Needs to Know*. Boston, Houghton Mifflin.

Kluger, A.N. & DeNisi, A., 1996. The Effects of Feedback Interventions on Performance: A Historical Review, a Meta-Analysis, and a Preliminary Feedback Intervention Theory. *Psychological Bulletin*, 119(2), 254–84.

Leigh, M.D., 2021. There's a Lot We can Learn from Instrumental Music Teachers. *Impact, Journal of the Chartered College of Teaching*. May 2021.

Lemov, D., 2015. *Teach Like a Champion 2.0: 62 Techniques That Put Students on the Path to College*. San Francisco, Jossey-Bass.

Leslie, K., Low, R., Jin, P., & Sweller, J., 2012. Redundancy and Expertise Reversal Effects When Using Educational Technology to Learn Primary School Science. *Educational Technology Research and Development*, 60(1), 1–13.

Sweller, J. & Cooper, G.A., 1985. The Use of Worked Examples as a Substitute for Problem Solving in Learning Algebra. *Cognition and Instruction*, 2(1), 59–89.

Sweller, J., van Merrienboer, J., & Paas, F., 1998. Cognitive Architecture and Instructional Design. *Educational Psychology Review*, 10(3), 251–96.

Wiliam, D., 2011. *Embedded Formative Assessment*. London, Solution Tree Press.

Wiliam, D., 2016. Looking at Student Work. *ASCD Education Leadership*, 73(7), 10–15.

Willingham, D.T., 2004. Practice Makes Perfect—But Only If You Practice Beyond the Point of Perfection. *American Educator*, Spring 2004.

Willingham, D.T., 2007. Critical Thinking; Why Is It so Hard to Teach? *American Educator*, Summer 2007.

Chapter 8

Composing in the lower school

A talent for composition

We've all heard it, 'she has no talent for composition'. And it's both pernicious and untrue. The premise of these chapters is that everyone can be taught to compose. These next two chapters explore the ways composition can be taught through the secondary school. Although the models provided have designated years – the twelve-note string quartet in Chapter 9 is taught in year 10, for example – their principles can be adapted to the particular needs of the school and of the pupils, and be taught wherever they fit into the curriculum.

Year 7 – melodic composition

This is one of the very first projects taught in year 7, and it develops into a strain which runs throughout the year. It combines note-reading and simple keyboard-playing skills, with the rudiments of composition. It is taught in a room where all pupils have access to keyboards, shared one-between-two. Two pairs of headphones are attached to each keyboard, meaning that, when the pupils are playing, the room is orderly. Two children working together like this is a really powerful private space for them, and it needs to be used well. Wherever possible, the seating-plan should place experienced musicians next to those who are new to the subject, and they should be encouraged, at least some of the time, to teach each other.

Stage 1 – five fingers

Pupils are taught how to find 'middle C' on the keyboard – 'maker's name, 3, 2, 1' – and then encouraged to play a five-note five-finger C-major scale. For later

DOI: 10.4324/9781003112402-8

reference, it's useful for them to have neatly drawn in their exercise books the following:

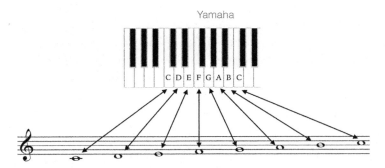

Pupils then play their five-note scales. A good scale will be accurate in its notes and fingering, but, more importantly, steady and even in its tempo. Those who seek to flash through at high speed do no service to the class.

It's really important that everybody plays. By carefully selecting whom to call it's easy to differentiate. Every performer needs to succeed publicly, whatever their prior experience. The more experienced can then be helped to improvise short melodic fragments, using only the five notes. Everyone listens, explains, and evaluates.

Stage 2 – conjunct and disjunct

Next teach the difference between melodic movement which is conjunct (by step) or disjunct (by leap). Again this is done through performance. First, pupils learn groups of notes, of steady, equal rhythm:

Melody 1 — using exclusively disjunct (leaping) movement.

Melody 2 — using exclusively conjunct (step-wise) movement

Melody 3 — using both conjunct and disjunct movement

The less experienced musicians will use the piano fingering to read these, rather than the notes. This is no bad thing, building their confidence in stave notation; the fingering-scaffolding can be later removed, after all, and it's useful for every pupil to begin to think about degrees of the scale, and their relative importance. The evaluation of their playing starts by praising slow, steady performances; then questions might draw out why some cells sound complete and others incomplete (ending on 1 or 5 respectively), what proportion of disjunct and conjunct movement is good (more conjunct than disjunct, because too much conjunct is dull and too many leaps are unsettling), and how disjunct movement should be used (leap up – step down).

It's possible to introduce articulation here, too: *legato* is joined and *staccato* is detached. A pupil can perform for the class the difference between the two. About this, there is a misconception which needs to be addressed very early: that *staccato* is 'jumpy'. For young players this lacks sophistication, and causes children to confuse disjunct movement with *staccato* articulation. A drilled association between the category of articulation and its two possible types, *legato* and *staccato*, should begin early. Teach them how to spell *staccato*, too (nearly a palindrome):

Melodies can be introduced very early:

This melody is copied into the exercise books, practising musical knowledge all the while. Stave, clef, lines, and spaces should be part of the classroom conversation as they write (see Chapter 6). The pupils learn and play the melody. This comes early in year 7, and not every pupil will read rhythm confidently, nor be familiar with notation. Depending on the class, it can become an exercise which teaches how to draw the treble clef and other notation, what 3/4 is called and what it means (and, importantly, why it's neither the same as a fraction, nor notated in the same way). I teach then the rhythm, call-and-response, clapping one bar, then gesturing that the pupils are to respond immediately. Then the second, and finally both. Don't explain, just expect – if you believe, it will work. It's also an early chance to teach that repetition is a musical device not to be overlooked.

Stage 3 – modelled examples and simple techniques

Pupils next compose, notate, and play an eight-note collection of notes, starting on 1 or 3 and finishing on 2 or 5. They can use only the first five notes of the C-major scale, and can repeat and omit degrees as they wish. A finished collection might look like this:

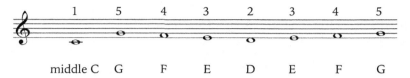

Pupils write in the piano fingering for utility, and the names of the notes for practice. Pupils play their note-groups, slowly and steadily, to the class; everyone listens for musical features (conjunct and disjunct) and evaluates. This example starts on 1 and finishes on 5, sounds incomplete as a result. The movement is mostly conjunct, and the opening leap (1 to 5) has step-wise movement afterwards.

We then return to the brief 3/4 melody and turn it into a phrase. This last is very hard to define, and it's easy to flounder, talking about singing and breath. A definition which works well is:

A phrase is a division of a melody which belongs together

The exercise aims to teach the importance of repetition, and that four-bar periodicity is one of the standard units of music. First, the brief melody is sawn in half, each severed unit placed at opposite ends of a four-bar phrase:

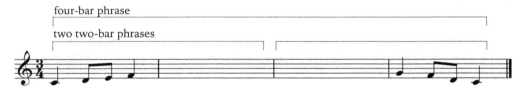

Within a four-bar phrase like this it's quite likely that there will be nested two, two-bar phrases. Pupils listen to this, and are asked why the fourth bar sounds finished.

Pupils are then asked how to complete the second bar. It should use the material of the last bar, but needs to sounds unfinished. The last bar sounds finished because it ends on 1; the second bar needs to end on 5 or 2. Only one note needs to be changed, the final C to a G or to a D:

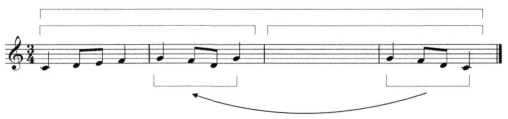

Composing in the lower school

This is the first time some pupils will have come across the operating idea of a motif – that short musical fragments can be closely related, can sound very similar yet not be exactly the same. It's worth showing them this, a principle for the future.

The final step is to repeat the first bar in the third:

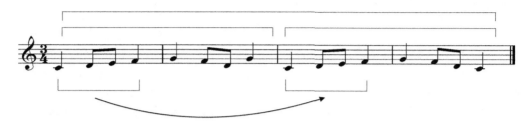

Next, pupils take this rhythm and the eight-note group they invented earlier, and turn it into a phrase. They first feed their notes into the first two bars:

This pair of bars sounds unfinished because it finished on 5. The next bar to add is the last one, altering it in order that it finishes on 1:

The leap from F to C in the last bar is not elegant, and a more sophisticated approach might be found here; but this is effective and easy.

Some simple copying, and the four-bar melody is complete:

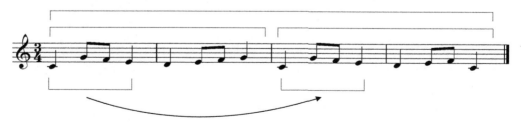

A pupil's completed example should be performed by its composer and should look like this:

But this is not the end. It has taught the importance of the four-bar phrase, which notes can be used to create a half and a full close, and most significantly, the primacy of repetition as a compositional device. But there is a little more still to extract – motif and sequence.

A motif is a short musical building-block consisting of pitch and a rhythm. The first bar of the pupil's melody might be treated as such:

Motif x, as it's nattily been named, consists in a four-note group (C — G — F — E) and a rhythmic group (crotchet — quaver — quaver — crotchet).

This is an important part of repetition, that the entire piece can be explained using this single musical building-block:

KEY:

x' = the rhythm of x; pitches altered to consist in ascending conjunct movement from D to G

x" = x' with the last note altered from G to C.

How much of this to share depends on the predilections of the pupils in the class. Children of a mathematical bent often enjoy the rigour of this approach.

Once a motif has been identified, it can be used to create a melodic sequence. A sequence is the immediate repetition of a melodic pattern (motif) a little higher or a little lower.

Motif x can be used to create and play an ascending sequence:

Or a descending one:

Playing a sequence on the piano involves a repeating pattern of fingering – teaching that the thumb need not be fixed on middle C. If pupils stay on the white notes, and keep a hand-position and their patience, it's not an impossible thing to play. Thus:

A sequence is a very useful way of starting a piece – especially for the less-experienced and less-confident composer. Its very facility tells us something of its character: a sequence fills space between more-substantial musical moments.

The two experiments can be the start of a composition. Pupils can be asked to listen hard to the implications of their sequences, and then compose what comes next. The sequence might be a single repetition of the original, or might be several – the potential to shape the task to pupil is significant here.

Equipped with a little experience, a little knowledge, then the composition becomes much freer.

Testing knowledge

At some stage during the process, it's useful to review the knowledge used with the pupils. Adapted slightly, the following might become part of a short, low-stakes test, or part of a class discussion. There are at least 12 pieces of knowledge which pupils should practise, and teachers need to ask of themselves the following questions:

a. what is conjunct movement?

b. what is disjunct movement?

c. what balance between conjunct and disjunct is best in a melody, and why?

d. at the end of a melody, which note(s) of the scale sound unfinished. Which finished?

e. why might the opening of Beethoven's *Sonatine* op.79 be a good example to show pupils as part of this sequence of lessons?

f. what misconceptions might be associated with conjunct and disjunct movement and articulation? A clue: do you need to explain dotted rhythms here, too?

g. how many bars long is a typical melody?

h. how does that divide?

i. what is a phrase?

j. what is a sequence?

k. what is a motif?

l. what is the most important compositional technique by far?

Year 9 – theme and variations

This is one of the most important means by which pupils can be taught composition, and, of those means, one of the most widely taught. The aim of this section is to show how it's possible to make a variation project open to everyone, yet simultaneously valuable for the most-experienced musician.

There are probably seven or eight different species of variation form, of which we will be mostly (but not exclusively) concerned with the melodic-outline variation. In this a melody is adorned with ever-greater decorations or replaced by a paraphrase of itself. It's a tradition, near mandatory, that teachers refer to Mozart's KV265, his twelve variations on 'Ah! vous dirai-je, Maman', which has been twinkling in classrooms for decades now. It's a wonderful piece of music through which you can teach the playfulness and knowingness of Mozart – his humanity as well as his mastery. As an aside, I cannot recommend highly enough Dohnányi's *Variations on a Nursery Tune* (op.25). It's a great work, and an immense contrast with the Mozart.

But there are other sorts of variations worth considering in the classroom. The fixed-bass species allows us to teach chaconne, passacaglia, and ground bass. The *Passacaglia* of Handel's Suite in G minor, HWV 432, is a very good example, one which teaches both variation technique and circle-of-fifths harmony. It leads perfectly into the sublime and inevitable 'Dido's Lament' by Henry Purcell.

There is also the fixed-harmony type of variation, best exemplified by the ancient and mysterious *La Folia*. This pervasive and ancient chord-pattern is the subject of wonderful sets of variations by Corelli and Rakhmaninov, amongst many others. Give the chord-sequence to an experienced young musician, and great things can result.

La Folia, and working from a harmonic outline

The method is a standard one for composing from chords. Using only the notes of the chord, it involves first inventing a melodic framework. This is then elaborated. In the elaboration of the framework, there are only four rules:

1. use mainly conjunct movement (in the melody, steps are better than leaps);

2. only rarely will you use a note which is not part of the underlying harmony;

3. when you leap (disjunct movement), leap from and to notes which are in the chord(s);

4. except when following rule 3, leaps should be followed by steps in the opposite direction (if you leap up you step down; if you leap down, you step up).

A pupil who has chosen, for instance, to write their *Folia* variations for unaccompanied violin would use two staves, the upper for their own composition, the lower for the chords in root position. The chords support the process and are not part of the final composition.

The compositions should start very simply:

This pupil has invented a melody consisting in two broken chords forming a pleasing, up-and-down contour. This broken-chord pattern is ripe for elaboration. It could itself be the basis of further broken-chord figuration:

For the purposes of illustration, the pupil's composition appears on the middle stave, the original framework, the broken-chord pattern on the top, and the root-position block-chords on the bottom. In the composition, the pitch-skeleton, D — F — A, has been retained, but its octave has been changed, and it is filled-out with semi-quaver broken chords. This pupil has made the composition a little more convincing both by instructing the violinist to use an open A, and by altering slightly the second group of four semi-quavers to avoid excessive string-crossing.

This example occasions two general ideas about composition. The first is that the pupils are themselves splendid resources for teaching. In an ideal world every pupil would have their own instrument, their own computer or notation device (if needed), and they would enjoy infinite access to the guiding teacher. In reality, it saves immense amounts of time if most pupils do much the same thing at the same time – by paying the toll of a certain degree of homogeneity, the whole class has more time collectively to go further. That having been said, it's important not to neglect the resources of the room. The broken-chord variation for unaccompanied violin seen above assumes some knowledge of the violin, and no teacher is an expert in every instrument. If you have a string-player in the room, use that pupil to help with bowing, to check for practicality, for advice about how best to exploit the instrument. Both pupils will learn, one by helping and the other by being helped.

Composing in the lower school

The second idea is about range. Save in my wildest dreams, I've never seen a school computer-suite equipped with 88-key controller-keyboards. We are lucky, enjoying the relative luxury of 49. But the missing 39 constitute a physical and psychological barrier to pupils, prevent them from writing music which goes above and beyond the limits they have before them. It takes a conscious effort on the part of the teacher to overcome this limitation. It is preposterously easy, using a notation program, to move music one octave higher or lower, and that program will also go some way to warn when you have gone too far. Pupils should be encouraged to explore higher and lower ranges, to evaluate the results and the possibilities, and not to be too hidebound by the 49 keys before them.

There is a different direction possible for a pupil's *La Folia* variation, which explores conjunct rather than disjunct movement. It starts from the same broken-chord crotchet pattern, to which conjunct quaver movement is then added:

Here, the framework crotchet outline (top stave) is filled-in with quaver movement (middle stave). The tempting gaps in the first bar are plugged with passing-notes; there are passing notes, too, in the second bar. The F on the second crotchet beat is an accented passing-note (because the gap to be plugged is a fourth, and not a third).

This is quite satisfying, but the most-experienced musician will probably want to go further. With these pupils, there is a balancing act to be performed by the teacher. It's important to celebrate and to encourage all they can do; but there's also a distinct danger that they will rush through the early stages of any project unthinkingly, assuming that they know what to do because they have seen something like it before. They call this the 'Illusion of knowledge' (Hall *et al.*, 2007), that some familiarity with a subject of a situation might actually constitute a barrier to learning. It's important that the most-experienced musicians commit to even the most simple exercises – it's often there that they will find the most fruitful way to become better musicians. Semi-quavers are the next stage for them and for the whole class:

This example shows the whole progression. It starts with the top and bottom staves, from a root-position chord in the bass, and the three-crotchet framework selection at the top. The second stave down shows the elaboration of those crotchets, the addition of quaver passing-notes. The third and final stave shows the final composition, a further elaboration of those quavers. The semi-quaver movement here uses two lower-auxiliary notes (lower neighbour-notes) – the C sharp and the second E – and a leap at the end of the bar (disjunct movement). This is a legal leap, as it moves from and to a note in the chord.

Melodic variations

But by far the most common type of variation-structure in education is the melodic-variation type. We've seen that this is where a melody is decorated with ever-greater complexity and ingenuity, or where the original melody is replaced by a paraphrase of itself.

There is a rigour in this type of variation which pupils are apt to ignore: that the first bar of the theme and every subsequent variation are clearly related; the second bars are equally of a family; and every subsequent bar likewise relates forward and backwards. Notation programmes, where you can temporarily keep the original melody above the variation as it is composed, are very useful in keeping the work disciplined.

In this project we are writing for solo piano.

First, of course, comes a melody. This might be something familiar to the pupils – recent examples which have come my way include *Michael Finnegan,* the evocative and numinous theme to *Postman Pat,* and something about a Baby Shark. It might also be melodies of the students' own composition. Which chosen option depends on the age and experience of the children, and on whether the work is to be submitted for public examination. In the latter case, take great pains to check your board's requirements and regulations.

If the whole class is to work on a single melody, then a little analysis comes first. Here's *Polly Put the Kettle On*:

In its harmony, this is immensely simple: a regular two-bar-changing harmonic-rhythm using only the primary chords. It is eight bars long, divided into two four-bar units, which themselves divide into two-bar groups. Bars 1 and 2 are the same as bars 5 and 6 (marked x); in bars 3 and 4 appears the same material but this time on the dominant chord (x'). The dotted rhythm gives a little interest to the first, third, and fifth bars, and the melody mixes conjunct and disjunct melody rather charmingly. The whole has a range of about an octave (itself a good sign), its lowest note is D above middle C, and, save an upper-auxiliary E, its highest the D one octave higher. The outline of each two-bar unit is a descending perfect fifth (decorated by an upper-auxiliary), and the final crotchet scalic ascent its inevitable conclusion.

If the pupils are to compose their own theme, it's wise for them to aim for the same degree of simplicity. Many will find this restricting, but simplicity will make the variations much, much easier to produce – and the final outcome will be far more satisfying as a result.

For the rest of this project, acknowledgment should be given to the influence of Aaron Copland, especially his delightful little book, *What to listen for in Music* (1957). His appendix I contains a set of model variations on *Ach! du lieber Augustin*, from which the best of the following ideas are taken (164ff).

The first stage is to add notes to the melody, thus:

In the second bar, the gap between B and G is plugged with a passing-note, and the effect is sufficiently pleasing that the anapaestic three-note unit is repeated in the second half of the bar. The presentation of this example is important: when developing melodic-outline variations, pupils need to remember that their variation should have a close relationship with the original; when working, keeping the original melody, sound muted, in view (as on the topmost stave) is a very good idea.

The relationship with the original melody should be close, but that relationship need not be restricting. The next variation might be a paraphrase of the original:

Here, the broken-chord structure of the melody stands as a symbol for the whole – the quaver passing-note is removed at the end of the first bar, and the second bar is also simplified.

Pupils need to explore range and register including wider ranges and the expressive possibilities of different registers. The next variation might swap the hands:

Here the left-hand takes the melody, unchanged save for the octave, whilst the right-hand plays an off-beat chordal accompaniment.

Attention might next be paid to the metre:

Composing in the lower school

The outer vestments of the waltz – time-signature and characteristic accompaniment – make it hugely versatile when writing variations. Here, the melody and accompaniment pattern both easily become a waltz.

Mode comes next, G major becoming G minor:

There is a misconception here, which teachers need to work hard to overcome. It's that minor-key variations should use the relative minor. In this simple form of melodic-outline variations, it's much more appropriate to use the tonic minor, sometimes called the parallel minor. Only the most-experienced musicians will be able to attempt a set of variations which explore different keys – which possibility the relative minor opens up – and in almost every case, it's best avoided.

The *Polly* variation here is simple, but quite effective. That minor-key music is slow and quiet is a cliché, but there is no reason why pupils should not, just this once, submit to the predictable. The registral changes in the left-hand here – moving the first note one octave lower, and the second note one octave higher – are very simple indeed, but add a great deal to the character of the moment. Pupils should here begin to explore piano pedalling, both its possibilities, and its notation.

Most often, melodic-outline variations start simply, and with time become more complex with each subsequent variation. For teachers, this is a very helpful feature of a set of variations. Many pupils will be able to reach this stage – five variations in – and have produced a simple and convincing piece. Many more will go much further.

They might try a little counter-point:

The simple harmony – the first two bars use chord I – makes this possible. The first stage is to copy the first two bars of the right-hand melody into the second bar of the left-hand part. Pupils should then listen, slowly and with great attention, to the result. If they listen, they will hear the limitations, be able to move the unit around sufficiently to discover something rather lovely, rather strong.

Pupils might play with texture and counter-melody:

Here the melody is played in octaves in the right-hand, and the bass becomes a tonic pedal. In the tenor line, a descending chromatic counter-melody fits rather beautifully.

This next is Copland's finest idea, although I suspect that he himself was copying it from Stravinsky:

Parallel root-position triads in the right-hand and off-beat octaves in the left-hand are very effective, and surprisingly-easy to apply in many melodies.

Composing in the lower school

When attempting variations, it is natural to want gradually to increase their complexity, but there's often a moment when a composer draws back within themself, enjoying a moment of repose before the steady forward march begins again. This repose might be achieved using simple chords:

The art here is to use the register and the voicing of the chords to make a satisfying piece of work. Pupils will need to be encouraged to explore a wider range, especially to use the lowest reaches of the instrument; they will also need to be taught to check carefully for the practicality of their plans.

Although we are concerned here with melodic-outline variations, there is no reason why some fixed-harmony work should not be part of it. Note that, as a result, the method of working for the pupils changes a little, with the chord-pattern guiding from underneath in this first example:

This variation uses a simple arpeggio pattern laid out in triplets.

This also lends itself to explorations more-generally of piano technique. One of the easiest to manufacture is where the left-hand crosses the right:

The final suggestion is both particular and more general. Which is to trust the children. With respect to you, reader, they are always going to be more imaginative and creative than we are, and sometimes it's best to let them free. This idea, basing a variation on a whole-tone scale, comes from a GCSE composition by my pupil Gabriel:

As with everything in teaching, there is a balance to be struck. The pupils need to work through the first stages of every project, to master the basics, and the very simple ideas, before they are allowed to fly. And choosing the precise moment to unleash them is a matter of experience, of trial and error, and of confidence in what they might achieve – what they might teach you.

References

Copland, A., 1957. *What to Listen for in Music.* London, McGraw Hill.

Hall, C.C., Ariss, L., & Todorov, A., 2007. The Illusion of Knowledge: When More Information Reduces Accuracy and Increases Confidence. *Organizational Behavior and Human Decision Processes* 103(2007), 277–90. Available at: http://tlab.princeton.edu/publication_files/Hall_Ariss_Todorov%20OBHDP2007.pdf. [Accessed: 10 November 2020].

Chapter 9

Composing in the upper school

Year 10 – MINUET MODEL

This chapter concerns four composing projects for use in the upper school: a minuet model; a concerto in the style of Vivaldi (page 175); a twelve-note string quartet (page 193); and a method for teaching harmony (page 206).

Johann Sebastian Bach married the singer Anna Magdalena Wilcke in 1721, and clearly thought a great deal of her. For, in 1725, he presented her with a handsomely-bound manuscript-collection of music, songs and keyboard pieces – works of his own but also the music of his sons and his contemporaries. One of them is a little *Minuet* (BWV Anhang 116) by an unknown composer; the basis of this project.

It is taught as part of a module on music of the baroque period, and explores baroque style, binary-form dances, texture, harmonic rhythm, and rounded binary form.

Part 1 – analysis

The module starts with analysis.

The first task is for the pupils to listen to and annotate the score of the minuet. We discuss the definitions of the following terms and I ask them to add to the score the following labels:

> motif built on two ascending broken chords
> imitation of the opening motif
> repetition of the opening two bars
> imperfect cadence (here, I - V)
> perfect cadence (V - I)
> triplet rhythm
> relative minor
> perfect cadence (V - I) on the relative minor
> descending melodic sequence
> dominant pedal on G major

DOI: 10.4324/9781003112402-9

return of the opening four-bar unit
return (slightly-altered) of bars 9-16
perfect cadence (V - I)

A successful annotation might look like this:

From J.S. Bach (1685-1750): *Notenbüchlein für Anna Magdalena Bach*
Menuet by an unknown composer, BWV Anhang 116

Composing in the upper school

In order to be successful in the project, pupils need to have this knowledge at their fingertips. And it's another example of the importance of practice. They should be able to return, verbally as call and response, that musical imitation is copying: that a motif is a short musical building-block; that you can find the relative minor of any given major key by going down 0,1,2,3 semitones; that a stray accidental sharp will likely be the leading-note of a new key. You can also teach here about form.

This minuet is a good example of a binary form – two parts, A and B, divided by a double bar and repeat signs – and also of a species of binary form sometimes called rounded binary:

A :||: B (A) :||

I   VI I

In rounded binary, the return of the opening material (here a near-exact repeat of bars 9 to 16) balances the whole, and provides a satisfying outline. In teaching, it's a plausible model for the explanation of hundreds of baroque, binary-form dances. To be a more-perfect model still, representative of even more such works, the A section would end on the dominant, thus:

A   :||: B (A):||

I – V   ?   I

Part 2 – harmonic analysis

The next stage is to produce a harmonic analysis of the minuet. This sounds rather daunting but really isn't. I assume that simple scales and keys are relatively fluent, that the definition of a chord (two or more notes sounded together) is understood. The following order of teaching has worked well for me:

i.

Explain that there is a hierarchy of chords, that the primary chords (I, IV, and V) are the most important, and the most common. A plausible hierarchy is this:

I – V – IV – II – VI

The primary chords, I, V, and IV, are the most common, and it's unlikely that III and VII will be seen. Drill your pupils in the letter names of each triad; in them they need to be rather fluent. The exercise works more quickly if at this stage you ask the pupils to omit the sharps and the flats.

ii.

Taking up the music, explain that harmonic rhythm is the speed at which chords change. In a 3/4 time signature of moderate tempo, there are four likely possibilities:

1. a single chord in each bar;

2. two chords, the first of minim duration then a crotchet;

3. two chords, crotchet followed by a minim (this most likely at cadences), and;

4. three chords, each one crotchet long.

iii.

Whenever working with harmony, always and unfailingly start from the bass note. Work out the letter names, first of the bass note, then of the notes vertically above it, and try to (re-)arrange them into a root-position chord. Sight of a keyboard, whether projected or drawn on the board or physically in front of the pupils, makes this far easier. They are looking for the pattern, you can explain, in which the notes are as close together as possible; in the root position, there is just one letter name between each component, not two.

iv.

The pupils now know that tonic chords are more common than dominant, dominant than subdominant, and so on. It's the same with inversions: root-position chords are more common than first inversions, and second-inversion chords are rather scarce.

v.

Pupils should identify the chords, and present them using whatever notation software comes to hand. Like this:

Part 3 – presenting the harmonic analysis in practice

I ask the pupils to produce a harmonic reduction using bald and rather ugly root-position triads. The exception to this in the minuet is in bar 30, where it's useful to maintain the second-inversion triad.

Composing in the upper school

There are some bars, bars 1 and 2 for instance, in which the reduction merely involves conjoining broken chords:

Others where passing notes can be found, taught and understood, then removed:

KEY: - = passing note

Others again where the passing notes are accented:

KEY: - = passing note

The final harmonic reduction will have two staves free for the pupils' own minuets, and a third stave with their harmonic reduction. It will begin like this:

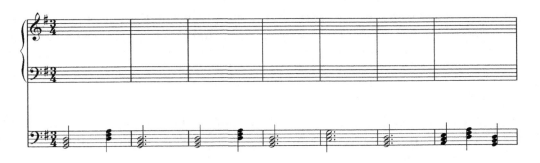

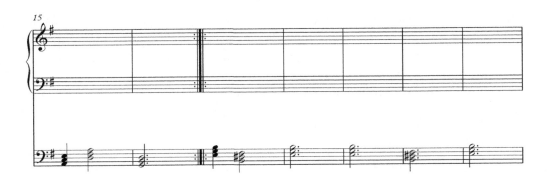

You can differentiate here by asking all pupils to try the exercise, expecting that most will be able to work out the first eight bars. It will take a little longer with others, and you can eventually help them with the hardest chords (those in the B section).

Part 4 – composition

The teaching of composition is, in some ways, the same process in reverse. There are two strands here: first, to teach that a good way to start a composition is with a harmonic model; second, to learn about the techniques and features of baroque music by using them as a composer – to do as Bach does.

i. Using a harmonic model

The first strand, working with a harmonic model, might look like this.

Ask the pupils to choose one note from each chord, and input it as the melody line of their compositions. At this stage an arbitrary choice is as good as any, although the more-experienced musician will want to begin to consider where the highest and lowest notes will come in the phrase (and that those extremes of range, should in some way, be associated with either the tonic or the dominant).

In the first bar, this pupil has put one note against each chord, in the second, they have decided to change the rhythm a little by choosing two notes from the chord:

Both of these decisions are good. It's really important that experiment and play are part of this whole process; that the pupils listen critically to their work, and come to an aesthetic opinion about it. A useful mantra is, 'If it sounds good, it probably is'. Unfortunately the opposite is also true.

The next part of writing a melody (or thematic material) to a harmonic model involves five rules – the first four of which are already familiar – which pupils should understand, learn, and live by:

1. use mainly conjunct movement (in melody, steps are better than leaps);

2. only rarely will you use a note which is not part of the underlying harmony;

3. when you leap (using disjunct movement), leap from and to notes which are in the chord(s);

4. except when following rule 3, leaps should be followed by steps in the opposite direction (if you leap up, you step down; if you leap down, you step up);

5. when one part is boring, the other part should be interesting.

These rules can result in slightly pedestrian pieces, but the exercise is powerful in enhancing an understanding of baroque music and beyond. Pupils should understand that, although these are called rules, this handful will speed the process of composition – acting as a catalyst on the imagination, not as an inhibitor.

The experiments should proceed step-by-step, pupils gradually adding shorter note-values, listening and evaluating all the while. There will always be demi-semi-quaver splurges at this stage, examples of musically-incontinent enthusiasm. You should value and enjoy the enthusiasm, delete the rest.

The pupil's next move might be this:

Disjunct movement has been added in the first bar, leaping from and to a note in the chord. An evaluation of this would be rather positive, the upwards leap in the first bar balancing the downwards leap in the second.

Next, in the first bar there is a gap between B and D. This is too good to waste, and deserves a passing note:

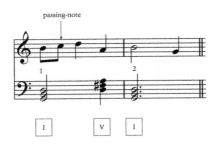

Composing in the upper school

This can go further still, adding step-wise (conjunct) movement throughout the first bar in the form of another passing note, and then an accented passing note:

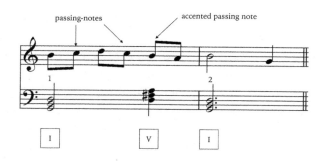

I've suggested that pupils should listen to and evaluate their work at each stage. In practice, this depends on the size and nature of the class and the space in which you are working. There are three parts of an evaluation. First, when you are using Sibelius, Musescore, or another notation package as your teaching platform, it's a good idea for the pupils to reduce the tempo, to explore how their compositions sound when played very slowly. They will perceive dissonance differently this way, and your job is to teach them to distinguish between sounds which are ugly and poorly executed, and those which add a necessary seasoning to the dish. Try this with a piece of minor-key chromatic contrapuntal work in Bach, and you will be surprised by what you hear. You can also ask them to play their compositions with and without the chords, checking the shape of the melody.

The second part of evaluation is to teach them how to listen. It's powerful to use a headphone splitter, and listen privately to a pupil's work with them. Your immediate reactions provide powerful and instant feedback to them – the very best kind.

The third is to play pupils' work to the class, explaining to all what they hear. In each group you will find some compositions which have not quite worked, some which are exemplary, and some which show just a touch of genius. There is real power in showing how improvements might be made to the former; in explaining how the textbook has been followed in the second; and by teaching everyone that with chance, good luck, and some experimenting, everyone can also come up with something (in the last) which is surprising, unexpected, and wonderful.

Back, then, to work, and the final lesson is knowing when to stop. This next figure takes the passing-notes of the previous example, and allows semi-quavers to dance around them.

upper auxiliary-note (upper neighbour-note)

In the baroque period, the technique used here in the first bar, namely anchoring a melody to a single returning note (here a G in the first two crotchet beats, and a D in the third) is rather idiomatic. It's something you can teach. And the second bar's conjunct movement has been generated precisely using the techniques we are exploring – first adding quaver movement based on the underlying chord, and then adding semi-quaver passing-notes. The pupil here has gone a little further, and added an upper auxiliary-note (in American English an upper neighbour-note (neighbor-notes?)).

This is by no means a demi-semi-quaver splurge, is actually a rather attractive starting-point. But you have to decide in this case whether to allow the pupil to pursue what is becoming a contrapuntal work, resembling one of Bach's two-part inventions, or whether to ask them to make it more like a minuet: in other words, to return to the relative simplicity of the minuet example. Your decision in this depends on the pupil and their context.

The next step is to return to Bach's minuet model, and do what he does. His work begins with a broken-chord pattern in the right hand of bar 1, against a simple single-note left-hand. Rule 5 is in action here – the right-hand is interesting, the left-hand is boring. The opposite is true in the second bar, when the right-hand's opening material is repeated in the left-hand, albeit slightly altered to fit with the prevailing chord.

Composing in the upper school

It's worth saying that, for the less-experienced musician, the broken-chord model is a very good one, and that it's relatively easy for them to produce something which is quite similar to Bach's original.

Doing what Bach does is easier for us, with our computers, than it was for him: our first step is to copy the right-hand part in the first bar into the left-hand of the second. The music will need to be moved one octave lower, but that's the job of a second (and an opportunity to teach the requisite keyboard short-cut). The next step is to simplify the bass line of the first bar:

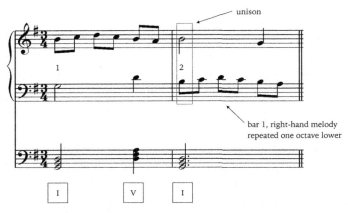

The evaluation of this should be quite positive: the canon in the second bar is pleasing, its outline both plausible and attractive. But there is one problem – the unison B at the beginning of bar 2. Unisons can be difficult. They are a strong statement, and need to be used sparingly and deliberately.

The first possible solution to the unison problem is to move the left-hand part in bar 2 down again (teaching selecting areas in a notation programme and the use of the arrow keys), in order that it starts on the root of the chord, and not the third:

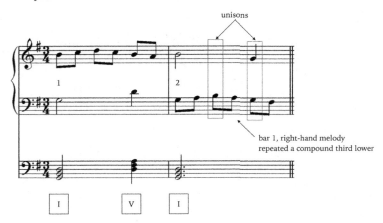

But this also causes problems, unison Bs and unison Gs, as well as similar motion which is, at best, distinctly weak, at worst, parallel octaves (you can teach this very successfully without reference to the technicality). Similar motion is often bad, contrary motion is nearly always better. But how to change, whilst doing as Bach does, which is to say whilst still imitating (copying) the right hand's part in bar 1? The final stage is composition – that sublime combination of knowledge, of boundaries and rules set, with experiment, good luck, and sheer chance. Here's one solution, there are many, many more which every child can easily achieve.

This combines imitation with pleasing harmonic movement. It also assumes that bar 3 will be the same as bar 1 – doing again as Bach does. But using Bach as a model goes beyond the harmonic dimension.

ii. Doing as Bach does

Working with the harmonic model is the heavy-lifting of this task, and it's the most wonderful practice for pupils. They are forced to engage with, repeat, and use their understanding of keys and chords, and if nothing else comes from the project for them, then this reinforcement of prior knowledge is a powerful and long-lasting outcome.

The next stage is to compose a minuet. This really is the simple bit. For you do as Bach does. In his Minuet, Bach repeats the opening two-bar unit in bars 3 and 4, in 9 and 10, in 11 and 12, in 33 and 34, in 35 and 36. Repetition is the first thing which young composers, with all their enthusiasm and their fantasy, forget to do. There is nothing wrong with copy and paste – and our only hesitation should be the sadness of great music denied us: had Bach possessed our facility, what might he have produced after the 1164th work in his catalogue, the Motet BWV1164?

Where Bach reaches an imperfect cadence, so should the pupil; where a sequence, a sequence; where relative simplicity (bar 18), then simplicity; where a dominant pedal, and on and on. The use of a model is how generations of composers have learnt, combining creativity with analysis, expression with knowledge.

Part 5 – extension work

There are going to be pupils who work through this with great ease (particularly if you use this project in year 12 or year 13), and with them you should seek to add a little finesse.

The composition so far has been quite intricate, pupils working on pairs and small groups of notes, thinking about single chords. This is important but tends slightly towards myopia: in building on this, the next stage involves taking a slightly wider view of each phrase, and of the shape it produces.

Here's one possibility for expanding experienced composers' horizons:

The lower two staves here represent the original minuet, the upper two a plausible reduction showing its contrapuntal derivation, a skeleton without its flesh. That sounds complicated, but is not: the first four bars show the outline of a pair of perfect cadences; the underlying structure of the melody in the fifth to the eighth bars is a scalic descent from E to A. The bass moves in parallel tenths (compound thirds). This structure (plus the figured bass in bars 6 and 7) gives an alternative far-seeing pattern to that given by the triadic reduction, a contrapuntal structure, the use of which ultimately has the power to be much more satisfying.

Part 6 – knowledge

You can make this quite a rich experience for the pupils, drawing in listening examples from Bach, and from other baroque composers. But it's also very useful to be able to represent the content quickly.

Knowledge organisers have their limitations – not least the inference inherent in them that they must be comprehensive and complete, that there is nothing to know save what is contained on them. But, sometimes, they have their place.

The following would be typical of the material which accompanies the project, a source for homework, for regular low-stakes testing, and as an *aide-mémoire* for later revision. It's drawn from a larger document, which builds through the year.

	preliminaries	
1	minuet	a dance in 3/4 time
2.	J.S. Bach (1684-1750)	a composer of the baroque period
3.	baroque period	a period of music from about 1600 until 1750
4	chord	two or more notes played simultaneously
5	harmonic rhythm	the rate at which the chords change
5	binary form	A form consisting in two parts separated by a double bar [A:||:B||]
6	rounded binary form	A binary form in which music from the A section returns at the end of the B [A:||:B (A)||]
K	**melody**	**tune**
1	conjunct	movement by step
2	disjunct	movement by leap
3	motif	a musical building-block, consisting of notes and a rhythm
4	sequence	in a melody, the immediate repetition of a **motif** in the same part put at a different pitch
L	**The names of the notes**	
1	Tonic	Tonic is the name of the first note of every scale and the chord built on that note
2	Super-tonic	Super-tonic is the name of the second note of every scale and the chord built on that note
3	Mediant	Mediant is the name of the third note of every scale and the chord built on that note
4	Sub-dominant	Sub-dominant is the same of the fourth note of every scale and the chord built on that note
5	Dominant	Dominant is the name of the fifth note of the scale and the chord built on that note
6	Sub-mediant	Sub-mediant is the name of the sixth note of the scale and the chord built on that note
7	Leading Note	Leading Note is the name of the seventh note of the scale and the chord built on that note
M	**Hierarchy of chords**	
1	The **tonic** chord is the most important in any key	
2	Dominant	
3	Sub-dominant	
4	Sub-mediant	
5	Super-tonic	
5	Leading Note	
7	Mediant	
O	**Compositional devices**	
1	repetition	what King Edward's boys forget to do in their pieces
2	imitation	where one part copies another
3	canon	where one part copies another exactly
6	tonic pedal	a long-held tonic note, often in the bass
7	dominant pedal	a long-held dominant note, often in the bass
9	contrary motion	the parts move in opposite directions — one goes up and the other down, or *vice versa*

Part 7 – conclusions

This has been quite a detailed explanation of a task which I teach in year 10; but its principles can be adapted to anything from a four-chord year 7 'Axis of Awesome' composition, through simple, eight-bar compositions, to more ambitious works. How to understand chords, and how to write music from them is a skill which all musicians have always needed, will always need.

Summary and review

It's useful for both teachers and pupils to ask themselves these questions.

1. How will you explain and drill these pieces of knowledge?

   Melody:

   a. conjunct

   b. disjunct

   c. passing note

   d. auxiliary note

   e. motif

   Texture:

   a. imitation

   b. similar motion

   c. contrary motion

   Form:

   a. binary form

   Harmony:

   a. harmonic rhythm

   b. inversion of chords

2. Where do you look first when you want to identify a chord?

3. How do you find the relative minor?

4. If you see an accidental, what does it mean?

5. Which chords are most likely in any given key? Which chords are seldom seen?

6. What are the five rules when writing melodies from a harmonic model?

7. What useful shortcuts can you teach in your music-notation software? How permanently are your pupils' pieces of work stored on your school's network?

8. How might this project lead on from the year 7 harmony and melody work?

9. What role do chance, good luck, and experiment play in your teaching of composition?

10. How can you give feedback in composition which engages the pupils, helps them to focus on the task and not on their own performance, and clearly shows them the next step? (Hattie & Yates 2014)

Year 10 – A CONCERTO IN THE STYLE OF VIVALDI

This is a year 10 project, taught often as a GCSE coursework composition. It builds on the lower-school teaching of *ritornello* form discussed in chapter 6.

Definitions

Ritornello form is characteristic of the baroque period, alternating ritornellos with episodes. Thus:

Ritornello — Episode — Ritornello — Episode — Ritornello

The *ritornellos* are played by the whole ensemble (*concertino*, *ripieno*, and continuo); the episodes by the soloist(s) (*concertino* and continuo). The first and last *ritornellos* are in the tonic key, the middle one(s) will be on a different key(s).

It is often easy to spot where a *ritornello* ends and an episode begins: the soloist starts to play, accompanied by only a few instruments; the texture thins, suddenly and dramatically. Solo accompaniments are often played by the continuo section (most often a 'cello and the harpsichord).

Ritornello form is used in the first and last movements of baroque concertos. There are hundreds of these concertos – a wave of Italian music which washes over Europe in the eighteenth century (1700s) – almost all with three movements, in the order fast—slow—fast.

Rondo and ritornello share a formal outline (A-B-A-C-A), but are rather different beasts. Rondo is a classical form, *ritornello* is of the baroque (and neo-classical); in rondo, A-sections return in the tonic key, nearly unchanged; in *ritornello*, they change keys and are often shortened dramatically; the essence of *ritornello* is the contrasting textures which alternate solo and *tutti*.

Starting points

Start with an analysis of a simple baroque concerto. It's surprisingly hard to find one which fits the textbook (meaning that it's wise to stay well away from Bach). Vivaldi's RV443 for recorder and strings is the clearest I have found. The pupils should listen to the chosen work, with and without a score, as many times as it takes for them to become quite familiar with the idiom.

The first stage in the analysis should be a formal outline, identifying the episodes and the *ritornellos*. Within each *ritornello* are typically three sections – the *Vordersatz*, the *Fortspinnung*, and the *Epilog*. Part 1 (*Vordersatz*) introduces the key; part 2 (*Fortspinnung*) is a continuation and extension, typically sequential; part 3 (*Epilog*) is the formal cadence. The German terms have no useful English equivalent that I know.

The harmonic idiom of Vivaldi's concertos is often very simple indeed, a series of conventions and devices which make them a very good model (stay away from Bach). The pupils can either prepare a harmonic outline, rather as they did with the minuet model, or can be given a chord sequence. The following is a typical sequence:

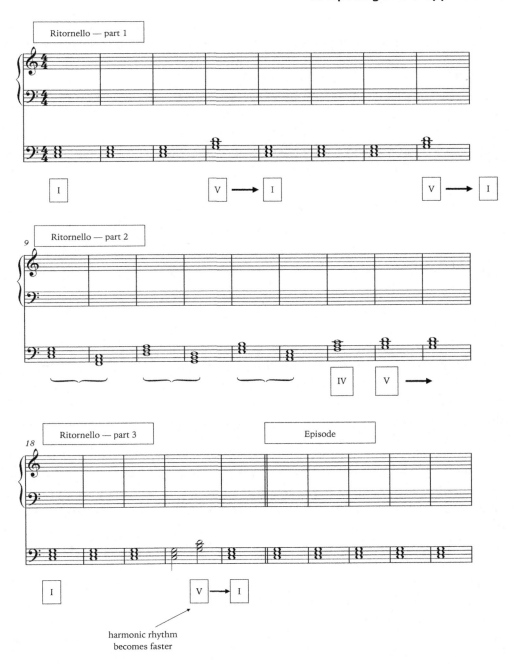

Composing in the upper school

Part 1 introduces the key. The first four bars use only V and I; the second four are identical to the first, but played as an echo, at a *piano* dynamic. Part 3 (18 to 21) is the formal cadence, where the harmonic rhythm typically becomes a little faster. Part 2 (bb. 9-17) is a little more complicated.

The harmony here might be addressed conventionally, showing how each chord relates to the home key: but the results quickly become meaningless (I — IV — II — V — III — VI). It's far better to cultivate in your pupils the habit of thinking about pairs of chords as perfect cadences, each on a different key, here forming a diatonic ascending sequence. Thus:

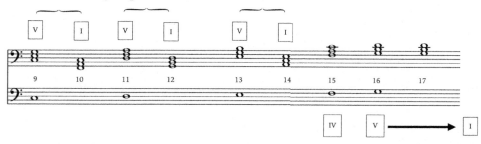

Two chords, one after another, will form a strong relationship, will sound good together, if the roots of those chords stand a perfect fifth apart. This immutable fact of music means that if you think in terms of perfect cadences – ignoring the prevailing key – then you will produce strong harmony. Where those perfect cadences are nested (overlapping at each stage, as each successive I becomes the next V), then you produce a circle-of-fifths; where the cadences are discrete, as here, a pleasing and strong harmonic sequence is the result.

There is a question of propriety in using a clichéd chord-sequence, which I think is easily answered. The C-major prelude from Bach's '48' starts with I-II-V-I over a tonic pedal; the first movement of Brahms's Fourth Symphony starts with an analogous progression (I-IV-V-I over a tonic pedal). This is a gesture common to hundreds of baroque pieces, hundreds of later pieces, too. There are only three primary chords in diatonic harmony, and there is no licence required to drive a perfect cadence, no copyright on its use.

Equipped with a chord sequence, pupils pick a key, major or minor, with a maximum of three sharps or three flats. Too free a choice here means that someone will try to work in B-sharp minor, with predictably disastrous results. Pupils then produce a harmonic scheme of their own: a bottom stave for the harmonic analysis, the upper two staves, treble and bass, for their own compositions. Some pupils might choose to work in 3/4 time – let them; others might halve the harmonic rhythm from bb.9-17, changing chord each minim rather than each semi-breve. This is also good.

Once the harmonic scheme is in place, it needs to be turned into music.

Elaborating a harmonic model

The elaboration of a harmonic model starts systematically. It might look like this:

Stage 1 is to put in a bass line in crotchets, using only the notes of the chord. Start with the root, and put it at the beginning of both the first and second bars. An arbitrary choice works as well as any, although it's best to avoid the same note either side of the bar-line.

The upper part is added in stage 2. The same note should be at the beginning of both first and second bars. This voice should move in contrary motion with the given bass, and the same note should not appear either side of the bar-line.

In stage 3, the parts are elaborated slightly using quaver passing-notes. This stage would make a perfectly acceptable concerto grosso, but it's possible to go further.

Semi-quavers are permitted for the first time in stage 4. Their sparing addition has made a significant difference. The pupils should be encouraged to listen to their compositions at an unbearably-slow speed and carefully apply the rule 'if it sounds good...'. This stage 4 is good, even though the pupil has chosen not to use stage 3 exactly; repetition of the anapaestic (short, short, long) rhythm is suggestive, implies that this motif will have a rich later life in the composition.

Here is a second possible elaboration:

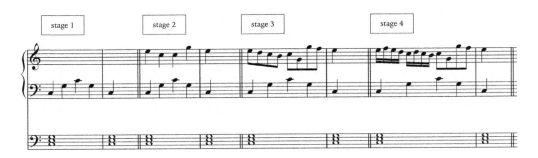

Composing in the upper school

In stage 1, a crotchet bass-line is first devised, the root of the chord at the beginning of bars 1 and 2; in contrary motion with the bass, the upper-voice is added at stage 2, the same note at the beginning of bars 1 and 2; in stage 3, quavers are added, mixing two passing-notes, one lower-auxiliary, and broken chords (leaping from and to notes in the chord). The octave leap is strong, and will be useful later. Note that the bass-line remains very simple, balancing the relative complexity of the upper-voice. Semi-quavers are added at stage 4, here upper- and lower-auxiliary notes (neighbour-notes). Elaborating a descending scale with auxiliary-notes as seen in stage 4, is a very useful trick.

Pupils may choose minor keys for this exercise, as the results can be very good, but they should take great care that every leading-note is preceded by the proper accidental. The exception to this is where they are trying to avoid the melodic interval of an augmented second. This will inevitably occur. They should listen more slowly, and with greater attention even than normal – the augmented interval is a powerful sound which can only sometimes be used. The melodic form of the minor scale can be taught, and can be used here.

Once the first bar is devised, the first eight come very quickly:

The second and the third bars are the same as the first – repetition is a feature both of good composition as well as of music of the baroque period. The fourth bar could have been exactly the same as the first, albeit transposed to fit with the dominant chord. The solution presented here, however, is more interesting. It allows the melody to return as before to the note G on the second beat, and then moving the anapaestic motif to outline the dominant seventh. The bass is altered to make a clear root-position perfect cadence from the fourth beat of the fourth bar onto the first beat of the fifth. This result might be the result of an experienced pupil's calculation; it might equally be the product of hard and attentive listening at a very slow speed, of experiment and chance.

Bars 5 to 8 are a *piano* echo of 1 to 4, an opportunity to teach and enact terraced dynamics.

The second part of the *ritornello*, the *Fortspinnung*, comes quickly, too:

Because the music is entirely based on the notes of the prevailing chords, it can easily be changed (copied in a notation programme, pasted, and moved as a unit). The result is simply achieved, effective, but perhaps a little bland. The unisons at the beginning of each bar are potentially a weakness, particularly if both are approached from the same direction. The movement between the second and third bars of the above example is an instance of such a weakness (unison A, however fleeting, to unison D).

And the anapaestic rhythm might suggest something a little more. Here's one solution:

The second half of the first bar is raised by an octave, and the second bar is substantially altered; the exposed octave D at the beginning of the third bar here is neatly avoided by means of changing the exposed interval to a tenth.

Composing in the upper school

The third part of the *ritornello* is the simplest of all, its idiomatic starting-point semi-quaver broken-chords and the anapaestic rhythm:

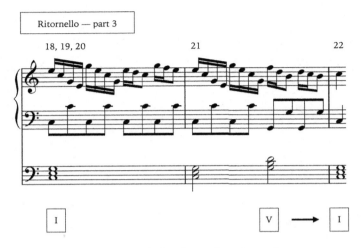

Bars 18, 19, and 20 are identical, broken chords and anapaestic passing-note figures above a tonic pedal; bar 21 only slightly altered.

A magical explosion

By this stage, pupils should have a complete, three-part *ritornello*. It's written on three staves, on the lowest the harmonic basis, on the remaining two their compositions. When pupils play this in their music-notation software, the volume of the chords turned-down using the mixer feature, the sound is likely synthesised piano, the compositions a little limp as a result. The pupils are learning about music of the baroque period; surely their works should sound at least a little like music of the eighteenth-century?

It's remarkably easy and satisfying to do this. With but a few mouse clicks, you can go from:

To this:

The procedure is this:

1. the bass-line becomes the 'cello and double bass parts, as well as the left-hand part of the harpsichord. Either remember that the double bass sounds one octave lower than written (and that its lowest note is either E or sometimes C), or trust your notation programme to tell you;

2. the upper-voice is the solo violin's music. It plays the same as the *tutti* first violins;

3. the upper-voice also becomes the second-violin's imitative part. As with all composition, luck and experimentation combine with a few well-considered rules to produce a good result. Because the notes of the chord fall on each main beat of the bar, there is every chance that you can build this way a pleasing contrapuntal structure (canonic to start);

4. in bar 4 of the second-violin part there is a little composition. It uses two rules: the first two crotchets use the anapaestic motif, based on notes of the chord

which move in contrary motion with the bass; the second two crotchets move in parallel thirds (parallel sixths also work), with the first violins' part;

5. many baroque-period string-orchestras omit the violas. Adding a viola part can be a useful extension for the more-experienced composers;

6. The root-position chord-pattern becomes the right-hand part of the harpsichord. In the third bar the ugly root-position dominant-chord is altered into a pleasing inversion. This can be taught in two ways: either, by asking the more-experienced musicians to change the inversion of the right-hand chord; or, by asking the pupil to experiment, moving each note of the triad up or down by one octave (using a keyboard short-cut) until there is as little movement between chords as possible;

7. The first four bars are repeated as the next four, as a *piano* echo (terraced dynamics).

Building the structure

The finished movement might have a five-part structure:

Ritornello — Episode — Ritornello — Episode — Ritornello

A more-experienced musician might well attempt a seven-part structure. Whether five- or seven-part, the pupils all now have complete the first and the last *ritornellos* – the final *ritornello* can be identical with the first.

The middle *ritornello*(s) will be on a different key(s), either the dominant (V) or the relative minor or relative major (depending on whether the pupil is working in a major or a minor key, VI or III). These are two possible major-key outlines:

Outline I

Ritornello(I) — Episode — Ritornello(V) — Episode — Ritornello(I)

Outline II

Ritornello(I) — Episode — Ritornello(VI) — Episode — Ritornello(I)

Pupils should note from this that the modulation is confirmed only in the *ritornellos*; that the role of each episode is to move from one key to the next. This inherent tonal instability makes them very easy to write, gives the pupils licence to use the two fundamental musical processes associated with instability – sequence and circle-of-fifths.

The first episode might indeed use both. The first stage is to work out the solo violinist's figuration.

This example shows the very first note of the first episode, which is played by the entire ensemble. Thereafter, the episodes are all played by the solo violinist, accompanied by 'cello and harpsichord – the continuo section. The soloist's figuration here has been derived from the prevailing harmony, adding first crotchets, then quavers, and then semi-quavers (lower-auxiliary notes in the first bar of the example). Faster movement is appropriate and idiomatic for a soloist's part, but needs not to be too unremitting. The second bar of the example, then, uses quavers, broken-chord movement, and the return of the anapaestic rhythm of the opening.

The purpose of this episode is to move from the tonic onto the relative minor. Here Vivaldi might use a sequence and a short circle-of-fifths. A sequence is merely an exercise in copy-and-paste and some nifty work with the down-arrow button:

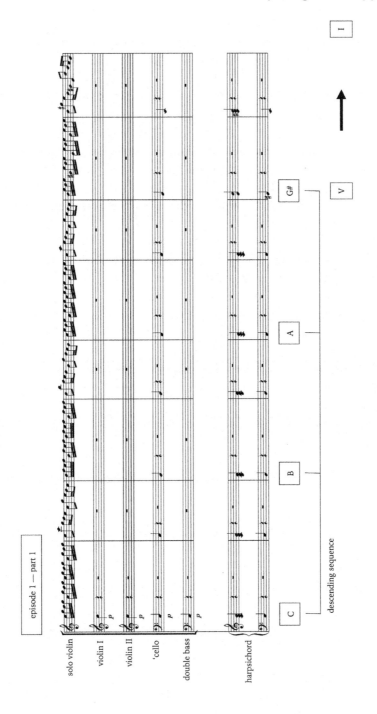

Composing in the upper school

The first bar becomes the third bar, the second, the fourth. There are no alterations necessary in most notation packages, but in others, where the arrow keys move a unit by one semi-tone rather than through the diatonic scale, a little more care may be needed.

Because through this descending sequence (Vivaldi would possibly know it as a *passus duriusculus*) we are moving onto the relative minor, its last two bars are altered: the diatonic G, upon which the penultimate bar is based, is altered to a G sharp; and the disposition of the chord in the last bar is changed from first inversion to root position. These last two bars become the dominant chord (V) of the perfect cadence which will establish the new key. It's possible to describe this as a chromatic pivot chord, but a pupil needs only to understand that by treating the chord as the dominant, it becomes one.

It would be quite possible for the *ritornello* (on A minor, the relative minor) to return in the next bar. But it's more interesting to extend the episode a little. We have reached the new key, and would like to confirm it, fill a little time. This is what a circle-of-fifths lives for.

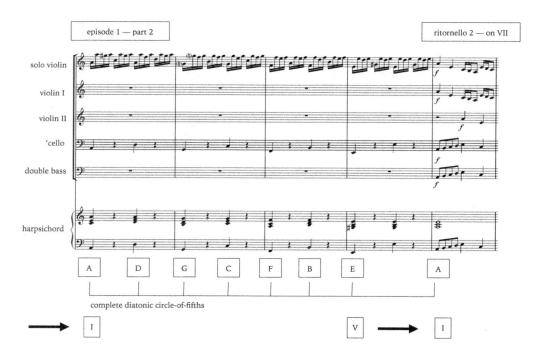

This example takes up where the last one finished. Whereas the descending sequence used a two-bar unit, this reduces the repeating unit to the length of a minim. The harmonic rhythm speeds-up considerably, changing chords at the beginning and in the middle of each bar. Note that this is a diatonic circle-of-fifths (the interval from F to B in the example's third bar is augmented); use of a chromatic circle-of-fifths would by the end of this little passage land us on A-flat major, with no possible hope of escape.

The last bar of this example again extends the dominant (V), and the *ritornello* returns (copy, paste, arrow keys) once more. In this, most pupils will forget to raise the leading note. It's a moment when individual feedback is necessary.

Completing the structure

If a five-part structure is the aim, then the last episode will need to move from the relative minor (VI) back to the tonic. Some possibilities for this movement in the key of C major are explored in the example below.

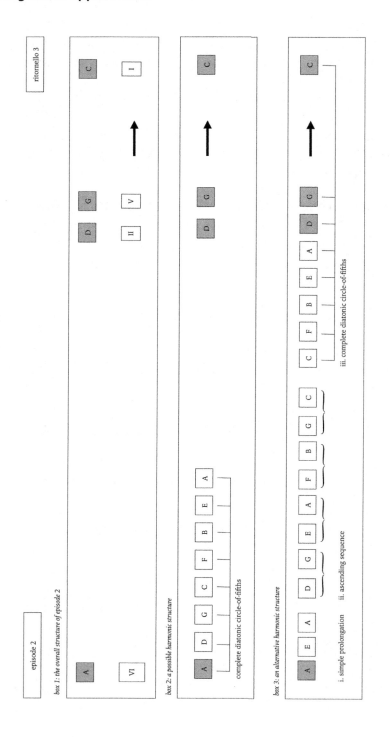

episode 2 | ritornello 3

box 1: the overall structure of episode 2

A | D | G | C

VI | II | V | I

box 2: a possible harmonic structure

A | D | G | C | F | B | E | A

complete diatonic circle-of-fifths

A | D | G | C

box 3: an alternative harmonic structure

A | E | A | D | G | E | A | F | B | G | C | C | F | B | E | A | D | G | C

i. simple prolongation   ii. ascending sequence   iii. complete diatonic circle-of-fifths

Box 1 shows the large-scale harmonic structure of the episode. It starts on A minor, which is established by the perfect cadence at the end of *ritornello* 2. The A minor chord, I in A minor, becomes VI in C major, which is followed by II, then V, and then I – the perfect cadence which leads back into the final *ritornello*. It's the strongest of progressions, with a perfect fifth between each of the roots (VI to II, II to V, V to I). The other two boxes show possible ways to spin-out the episode a little.

In Box 2, the influence of the A minor chord is extended by means of a complete diatonic circle-of-fifths. Depending on the music, it's possible to put one chord in each bar, or two.

Box 3 shows an even-more extensive episode, this in three parts: the first part is a simple I — V — I prolongation; the second is an ascending sequence, built on the same principles as part 2 of the *ritornello*; the third part is a complete diatonic circle-of-fifths moving from C to C.

In all three cases, Vivaldi would customarily make the G chord (V of the perfect cadence at the end of the episode) last a little longer – sometimes quite a lot longer. A dominant pedal, possibly with a more-virtuosic solo violin part above, should be seriously considered at the end of the episode.

In this way, you can differentiate this task in at least four different ways. The less-experienced musician, first, can use just the three chords of Box 1 to build a short episode; Box 3 is more extended than 2, and can be extended further still, secondly and thirdly; or, finally, the most-ambitious composer can write their own harmonic pattern.

In explaining this project here, the intention was to model how it might be presented to pupils: with a great deal of guidance at the beginning, leading to quite ambitious goals. By the end, the material is significantly more open-ended, encouraging musical and intellectual autonomy, hopefully sending the enthusiastic student (or teacher) to the scores of Vivaldi in order to find out for themselves.

Trust

This whole project looks daunting, but it's not. These are procedures which Vivaldi uses repeatedly, and are all fundamentally based on chord-progression patterns. Once pupils understand that they start simply from the chords, and only then elaborate, they will very often create highly-convincing work.

It cannot be stated often enough that it's not necessary for the teacher to be a composer – with a few rules, and some simple models, everyone can teach composition. And the key to this is trust.

This is a project to explore in stages and slowly, at each moment trusting the pupils. Children have the most extraordinary capacities, and trust in them is the biggest part of making a success of this. The pupils will also teach the teacher what comes next, and their work should, and often will, far outstrip the teacher's own capabilities.

And it's possible for the project to fail. But in failing, the worst that can happen is that the pupils gain a better understanding of the baroque concerto, a stronger grasp of harmony, knowledge of imitation, sequence, circle-of-fifths, who plays in a continuo group, and the beginnings of *ritornello* form. These are very big and very useful things.

The same concerto again?

There's a famous trope which consists in people being quite rude about Vivaldi. The accusation of 'writing the same concerto 500 times over' is said to have been levelled by Igor Stravinsky, Luigi Dallapiccola, Charles Rosen, and many, many others. Our use of Vivaldi's methods is rather more sophisticated, reflecting a truth about his music, that:

> Vivaldi likes to compose in a modular fashion: that is small flexible units are juxtaposed to create large units … The detachability of these units and their normally rather simple substructure (permitting elaboration in an infinite number of alternative ways) enables him to recycle them from work to work, crossing boundaries of genre or of mode (major/minor) without hinderance.
>
> (Talbot, 2013: 56)

Setting rules when composing from a given chord-pattern makes music possible. The results are not necessarily for the ages, but they most certainly give pupils the experience and the basic tools to become composers themselves; it helps them to practise those skills and habits which will make them into composers.

Summary and review

1. How will you explain and drill these pieces of knowledge?

   Melody:

   a. passing note

   b. auxiliary note (neighbour note)

   c. sequence

Harmony:

    a. circle of fifths

    b. modulation

2. What is the difference between rondo and *ritornello* forms?

3. What would be the formal outline of a five-part *ritornello* form? What keys might each section plausibly be in or on? Where might you find a dominant pedal?

4. Baroque pieces often start with a four-chord opening gesture. Give two different chord patterns which may be used here.

5. How might you best explain the following chord-sequence?

    I – IV – II – V – III – VI

6. What are the four stages of composing from a chord-pattern?

7. What are the two pitfalls when pupils use a minor key (one is melodic and the other harmonic)?

8. Where might repetition be used in this Vivaldi project? What different things are repeated?

9. What is the purpose, some might say the identity, of circles-of-fifths, and sequences? Where might they be found in *ritornello* form?

10. Think of a time when you trusted a pupil, and they exceeded your expectations.

Year 10 – TWELVE-TONE MUSIC

This is a composition project either for year 10, or for the sixth-form. Twelve-note music is also known as serial music (it uses a series) or dodecaphonic music. All three terms are interchangeable, although, for the sake of clarity in the classroom, it's best to settle on one.

Introducing twelve-tone music

Tonal harmony, we have seen, is intensely functional. The sub-mediant chord moves to the super-tonic, the super-tonic to the dominant, the dominant finally, home, to the tonic. Those compelling relationships of chords, whose roots are a perfect fifth apart, are the basis for centuries of music.

But those adamantine relationships, the dominant chord especially, become extended over time, further and further. By the break of the twentieth-century, dominant sevenths, ninths, elevenths, and beyond had become commonplace, their implications increasingly complex and, at times, self-contradictory. The 'added notes' took on a life of their own, deriving harmonies from their own internal chromatic implications, rather than from the necessities of their roots. This sounds complicated, but think of the way in which a diminished seventh simultaneously heightens the implications of its implied and missing dominant root, and allows resolution in completely contradictory ways. This deserves an explanation.

Take a four-note diminished chord consisting of the notes B — D — F — A-flat. It can legitimately be resolved in eight different ways. Here's the first:

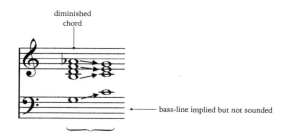

The upper stave here shows the first possible resolution onto a C-major triad. This is in accordance with the implied bass-line, shown on the lower stave but not sounded, which demonstrates how this might be construed a perfect cadence in C major, the dominant chord extended with a seventh and a flattened ninth. According to principles of good voice-leading in the key of C major, the leading-note rises by semi-tone step to the tonic, the minor seventh falls to the sixth, and the minor ninth falls by a semi-tone to the sixth.

But the exact same notes (albeit spelt a little differently) can be resolved in three further ways:

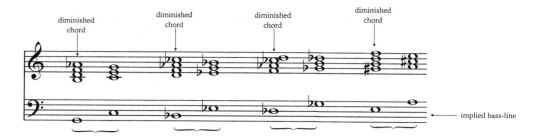

By treating each of the chord's four notes in turn as leading notes, the same four-note chord can plausibly move onto E-flat major, G-flat major, and A major, as well as C major. And the parallel minors (C minor, E-flat minor, F-sharp minor, and

A minor) are equally possible. Such wonderful freedom is a recipe for harmonic chaos.

Chords, then, can move either by the obligations of their roots, or by other, equally-plausible and compelling internal reasons – move often to sharply different destinations. This is the first part of the twelve-tone story.

It's useful to start teaching of the twelve-tone method this way: it anchors the pupils' knowledge in conventional harmony, allows the teacher to extend and deepen that knowledge a little further, and encourages big conversations about order, freedom, and rules in music and in art more generally.

The next stage is just a little history. It's often told that Schoenberg's innovative composition method – like many inventions its time had come, and others came to it at much the same time – is a consequence of increased tonal complexity. That it's an inevitable consequence of the motivic saturation of Brahms and the chromatic glories of Wagner is a creation myth which is simultaneously true, and simultaneously helpful propaganda put about by Schoenberg himself and his disciples. As teachers, we should tell the story – it helps to understand the composers' thinking – but we should also help our pupils think about truth and fabrication, about the foundations of knowledge in musical history.

The final part of this introduction is about musical dimensions. With due respect to the ingenuity of J.S. Bach – and not just him – music tends to work in a single direction: forwards through time. In order fully to understand a piece, a listener needs to remember what has come before. This is hard because we can no more reverse music, re-winding it to hear the salient moment again, than we can reverse time. A strong harmonic progression, especially, is robbed of all significance if it is played backwards.

But Schoenberg's twelve-tone method takes that method and turns it, literally, backwards. And upside-down, sideways, and whichever way too. In this new utopian musical dimension, a melody can become a chord and vice versa, there is no longer consonance or dissonance, progressions are robbed of their meaning (a perfect cadence no longer means the end, stops being a full stop) and can simultaneously mean everything and nothing. It's a remarkable and thoroughgoing musical vision, transcendent and luminous. It's very, very hard fully to comprehend and possibly just a little hard to love.

The value of twelve-tone composition in the classroom

The value of this type of project is immense, however, in ways which are all about the confidence of children. Four effects are commonly associated with it: first, although there are formal constraints in the twelve-tone method, rules which must be followed, pupils find them nothing like as prescriptive as those imposed by conventional harmony. Secondly, that the final result can and possibly should sound dissonant seems invariably to liberate the imagination. Third, some of the composition here is pattern-spotting and pattern-making, a process which seems to inspire pupils who are interested in things numerical.

Finally, it has the capacity to build confidence in writing for unfamiliar groups of instruments. The final piece of work associated with this module is a twelve-tone string quartet, and young composers can not only have the experience of working with the instruments, but can also be encouraged to dangle their toes in the world of string playing and extended twentieth-century techniques.

In an ideal world, the young composers will have their works played twice by professional musicians: first in a workshop in which the pupils are helped to correct, improve, and develop their works by the players; and secondly, as a recorded performance. This opportunity invariably means a great deal to the young people lucky enough to enjoy it; the moment when their music is transformed from a computer-realised sound-file is one of those rare instances when you see a young person's appreciation of themselves change. If circumstances permit, try it and you will see.

Preparing to compose

Fortunately, this music is far easier to write than it is to understand. Twelve-note music starts from a tone-row, which is an ordering of all 12 notes of the chromatic scale, each one used only once. From this source is drawn all of the pitch-based material in a piece. Composers after Schoenberg have used similar generative processes to derive rhythm, dynamics, and other elements, but we are here concerned only with pitch.

The notes themselves are initially unimportant, it's the intervals between each pair which give the music character and identity. Pupils start by understanding that in the row, each note of the chromatic scale is to be used once, and then that the notes are identified by the distance in semi-tones from the first note. The first note of a chromatic scale is 0 semi-tones from its starting-point, the second 1 semi-tone higher, and so on. The chromatic scale starting on C has been chosen as the starting-point, and is therefore labeled 0, its last note, B, is 11. Thus:

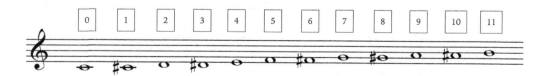

Pupils should understand that twelve-tone rows are conventionally notated from middle-C to the C one octave higher. It's irrelevant whether a note is spelt as a sharp or a flat, the chosen notation should merely be as convenient as possible for the player. The chromatic scale exemplified above uses sharps throughout. The presence of C natural and C sharp in a row can cause confusion in a software notation-programme, and great care should be taken that every note is correctly identified.

The next stage is a short-cut. It starts with a hexachord – a group of six notes, exactly half of the twelve-tone row. The short-cut involves one of the combinatorial sets developed by Milton Babbitt. The word 'combinatorial' should be used often in conversation, so pleasing is its rhythm and heft, but need not be defined. Suffice to say, that a row using Babbitt's hexachord [0 1 2 6 7 8] is going to yield good things.

If the original chromatic scale starts on C, then the notes which a pupil may choose from are:

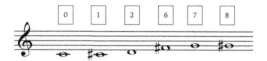

It's best if the order is then considered carefully in some way, that the young composers listen and imagine hard. Some pupils will want to find interesting repeating patterns in the row; others will choose quite at random – both work.

The re-ordering of following hexachord exploits the possibility of interesting disjunct movement, two perfect intervals around a central tritone [2 — 8]:

From the original chromatic scale, six unused notes remain. The beauty of Babbitt's combinatoriality is that those remaining notes, the second hexachord, will be related to the first in some way. The set [3 4 5 9 10 11] gives these remaining notes:

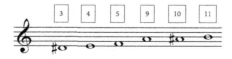

Composing in the upper school

Sure enough this can be used to produce a plausible second hexachord:

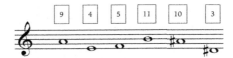

This second half of the row demonstrates exactly the same pattern of intervals as in the first, forming a promising and suggestive whole.

The first and second hexachords, first followed by second, become the starting row, known as the prime (P0):

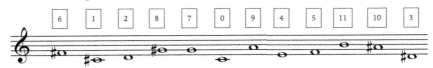

In twelve-tone technique there are three different transformations which can be performed on the prime, giving four possible rows, four different dimensions of musical space.

The first transformation uses the row backwards, last-note first, first-note last. This is called the retrograde (R0):

The second transformation is the prime inverted. There is always a misconception here in pupils, which it's best to treat immediately. When an interval is inverted, it becomes its corresponding pair, and that pair always 'adds up' to an octave. A perfect fifth inverted becomes a perfect fourth. In twelve-tone technique it is only the direction of the interval which is changed: the inversion of an ascending perfect fourth is a descending perfect fourth. Of course, and confusingly, the inversions of chords are something entirely different.

In twelve-tone technique, inversion is the prime with the intervals turned upside-down and is called the inversion. The first interval in the prime (P0) is a descending perfect fourth, the first interval in the inversion (I0) is an ascending perfect fourth.

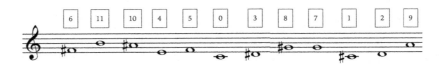

The third transformation is the inversion backwards, called the retrograde inversion (RI0).

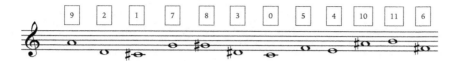

Teachers of a certain age remember the next stage with a certain frisson of pain. In our day, this involved graph paper, pencils, and many, many mistakes. It is to generate a complete matrix of 48 possible rows. The prime form of the twelve-tone interval-row starting on every remaining note of the chromatic scale, and the twelve inversions. The retrogrades and the retrograde inversions are, at least, generated for you.

Fortunately, technology comes to the rescue, with several on-line matrix-generating machines. Putting in the row, automatically (and correctly) generates all 47 other possibilities, and presents them on a table:

	I_0	I_7	I_8	I_2	I_1	I_6	I_3	I_{10}	I_{11}	I_5	I_4	I_9	
P_0	F#	C#	D	G#	G	C	A	E	F	B	A#	D#	R_0
P_5	B	F#	G	C#	C	F	D	A	A#	E	D#	G#	R_5
P_4	A#	F	F#	C	B	E	C#	G#	A	D#	D	G	R_4
P_{10}	E	B	C	F#	F	A#	G	D	D#	A	G#	C#	R_{10}
P_{11}	F	C	C#	G	F#	B	G#	D#	E	A#	A	D	R_{11}
P_6	C	G	G#	D	C#	F#	D#	A#	B	F	E	A	R_6
P_9	D#	A#	B	F	E	A	F#	C#	D	G#	G	C	R_9
P_2	G#	D#	E	A#	A	D	B	F#	G	C#	C	F	R_2
P_1	G	D	D#	A	G#	C#	A#	F	F#	C	B	E	R_1
P_7	C#	G#	A	D#	D	G	E	B	C	F#	F	A#	R_7
P_8	D	A	A#	E	D#	G#	F	C	C#	G	F#	B	R_8
P_3	A	E	F	B	A#	D#	C	G	G#	D	C#	F#	R_3
	RI_0	RI_7	RI_8	RI_2	RI_1	RI_6	RI_3	RI_{10}	RI_{11}	RI_5	RI_4	RI_9	

The prime forms start on the left-hand side of the table and are read from left to right. Starting top left, P0 is the original from; nearer the bottom, P1 the transposed version of the interval-row starting one semi-tone higher than P0, on the note G instead of the note F-sharp. The interval between each element of the row is retained, although the pitches differ.

Retrograde forms are read from right to left, starting top right with R0; R5 starts on G sharp, 5 semi-tones higher (0, 1, 2, 3, 4, 5) than R0.

Inversions start top left with I0 and are read from top to bottom; retrograde inversions are read bottom up, starting bottom left.

Composing in the upper school

How much of this a teacher explains to any given class depends on the class itself, the year group, and the amount of time available. If you practise your explanations — and it's desperately easy when explaining this to be unclear or misleading — then many pupils will be fascinated by the process, by the possible relationships, and by the sheer strangeness of it. If time is short, then on-line matrix generators are invaluable, explanations can be truncated, and composition can start almost immediately.

Starting to compose

The matrix having been generated, the ideal next step is to consider the rows carefully. The greatest twelve-tone composers start by exploiting some property of their row, some commonality of pitch or interval, some quality seemingly inherent in the rows and their combinations. Babbitt's combinatoriality method makes such coincidences almost inevitable.

The row can be used in three different ways.

1. A simple melody

In the first, it becomes a simple melody:

The upper stave shows the prime (P0) in its original form, distributed into three bars. The lower stave is a simple melody constructed from it. In the twelve-tone method, every note of the interval-row must be used in its given order, and no note may be repeated until the whole row has been used. Individual notes may be repeated, but only in their proper place in the row: that is, once you've moved on to the next note in the row, there's no going back.

Octaves are another thing, as are enharmonic equivalents. Each pitch can appear in any octave — in the example, the middle C in the second bar is raised by an octave, giving the melody a quirky range of a diminished octave. In the twelve-tone method, accidentals are pure information, they don't carry the level of meaning and implication found in diatonic harmony. This means that they should freely be altered for the player's convenience. In the third bar, for example, the descending interval from A sharp to D sharp is probably easier to read if altered to its enharmonic equivalent, B flat to E flat. Most notation software has a convenient code to effect the change, and this should be taught early.

The melody is well constructed – the first and the third bar use the same rhythm. It also shows the properties of segmentation, which is a good habit of thinking. There are twelve notes in the row. When fitting this into a rhythmic pattern, you can save some time by thinking in terms of its factors – 1, 2, 3, 4, 6, 12. The middle two of these, 3 and 4, are the most useful. The example allocated the first three notes to the first bar, then six (twice three) in the second, and three again in the third. For this reason, in the twelve-tone method pupils find compound time very profitable – it's a useful and subtle means of adaptive teaching.

Pupils should habitually label every row in their score. It makes it simple for the teacher to check that the twelve-tone technique has been understood and correctly implemented; and for the composer, it's desperately easy to forget which row is used where. The tiny text 'P0' just above the melody is clear and simply avoids these dangers.

2. As counterpoint

A single row can also be used to create counterpoint.

Here, the row (shown on the upper stave) is split in two, with eight notes in the first bar, and four in the second. But this is far less important than the separate split in the row between left- and right-hand parts. The first note of P0 appears in the right hand, but the second, third, fourth, and fifth are in the left. The right-hand resumes its melody at the end of the bar. This is completely in accord with the twelve-tone technique, as each note of the row (here, P0) is used once only and in its correct order.

This example shows three further things. The first is a facet of good composition, irrespective of style or genre: that the interest is distributed thoughtfully between the parts. In its texture, this example looks a little like a baroque piece: where the right-hand melody is less interesting, the left-hand part shines, and *vice versa*.

Composing in the upper school

Its second attribute is a question of notation. Twelve-tone scores, and, indeed, scores from the twentieth century, often contain rich and detailed performance-instructions. This is easy for pupils to imitate, at least in its outward signs. Here, in the space of not quite two-bars, there are slurs, *staccato* markings, and a pair of accents. Pupils should make their twentieth-century work at the very least look the part.

Third, this example shows a little of the magic of this method, of the combinatorial trick especially. It was produced without a great deal of prior consideration, using an almost random distribution of notes (albeit one informed by some degree of musical experience). And yet this is an interesting and suggestive opening to a piece. The quirky range, from F sharp down to F natural, tells us what comes next, begs to be repeated. The pairs of semitones in the left-hand are a figure which needs to return throughout the piece. At the end, the nearly-a-perfect cadence, B flat — E flat, is humorous enough to lighten the mood. Twelve-tone music can tend towards darkness, and it's good sometimes to sparkle.

What's true for this teacher is true for every pupil: the terror of the blank piece of paper, with this twelve-tone technique, is no more.

3. As chords

A single row can also produce chords.

This splits the row into four groups of three, and then conjoins each group into a chord. The principle that each note is used only once is maintained, but a very different result has been obtained. The only artifice here is that the voicing of each chord is quite carefully considered – the ear deals better with dissonance when there is space between each clashing element – and a pleasing ascending-scale melody (F sharp — G sharp — A — A sharp) has been derived.

Once more the mood is different: it's a pompous, lurching thing, which could easily turn into a character-piece of great distinction. To expand it is the next thing.

What comes next?

Having invented an opening, pupils can begin their pieces. As we have seen, looking and listening with attention to what's there will often be highly suggestive. And the very least pupils should do is to repeat what they've done, either using the same row, or a different one.

A contrapuntal texture is a possible realisation of the row, as we have seen, but it's also a possible continuation between rows. The simple melody seen earlier very easily becomes a little invention:

The balance of interest between the hands is rather attractive, where one hand has more movement, the other is simpler.

The same melody, with chords beneath, effortlessly changes century, and becomes an unfinished waltz:

The chords are three-note aggregates of I0, arranged in the characteristic accompaniment pattern of a waltz. Showing pupils this option is also an opportunity to re-visit the waltz as a topic, to revise and deepen pupils' understanding of and appreciation for the dance.

The choice of I0 is where the twelve-tone method starts to show its richness and depth – as well as its utility in the classroom. It's worth spending a moment thinking about this.

The first thing to say is that every pupil can achieve something really quite convincing here. The waltz example illustrates a good way to think about the twelve-tone method, which is to separate pitch from all of the other dimensions of music – from rhythm, register and range, contour, texture, and all of the generic signifiers. This sounds like a little waltz for the piano, written by a minor composer of the 19th century – but with all of the wrong notes. (At this moment teachers will immediately mark their generation, either by thinking of Morecambe and Wise, or of Les Dawson. The younger reader has simply missed out.) A waggish friend once described the Schoenberg piano concerto to me as 'Brahms with wrong notes', which is both funny and true. A pupil can take a tonal model – minuet or gigue, waltz or invention – alter every one of the notes in accord with the twelve-tone method and produce a new work which is both convincing in itself, and which results in a greater understanding in them of the original.

Pupils should use a variety of row-forms in their pieces, but the choice of which does not matter one iota. This is a horrible travesty of the twelve-tone method, but is hugely-effective in the classroom.

But the choice of row can matter, perhaps should matter, and is a source of great artistry in the master-composer. The first step towards mastery is to select combinations of rows because of their relationship one with another. In the waltz example, I0 is a good choice because it starts on F sharp, the same note as P0. But it goes further, reaching a common pitch, C, in the second bar. This is the opportunity which would form the crux of the 'tonal' argument in a piece by Schoenberg, Berg, or Webern. But our waltz shows a different possibility: it has been engineered to play with an alternation of highly-dissonant material (the closely-spaced clusters in the tenor register in the first bar) with the quasi-tonal (the suggestion of E major/minor and then F major chords in the second). This play goes further with a step-wise descending bass-line on the first beat of each bar (F sharp — E — D sharp — C sharp) which then suggests a perfect cadence, albeit a very strange one, from bar 4 into 5 (the bass-line C sharp to F sharp).

It needs to be stressed that none of this is in any way necessary for pupils to gain a great deal from this method, although many will explore and play and listen in ways which – if permitted and celebrated – will teach the teacher a great deal.

Final touches

Schoenberg's op.25 Suite has in it a Gavotte, a Musette, a Minuet, and a Gigue; which my cynical friend would describe as Bach with 'wrong notes'. Berg's master-piece, *Wozzeck*, contains waltzes and *Ländler*. What we are asking pupils to do is a simplified version of what these great composers have themselves done – pupils can listen for themselves if they don't believe us (hopefully).

But if it's valuable for pupils to imitate earlier forms of music on their own, then it's equally important to make their scores look right. Copyright makes it hard to distribute examples, but, if budgets allow, then pupils learn a great deal from seeing the scores of early-twentieth-century composers. There are increasing numbers of good YouTube videos which show the correct page of a score with a simultaneous audio file. Pupils should learn the meaning of the notations, the dynamics, accents, instructions (*Hauptstimme* and *Nebenstimme* are very useful) and should then litter their scores with them.

But it's even possible to expand this still further. Writing for string quartet is quite difficult for many pupils. It involves a knowledge of the instruments and their possibilities, the capacity to work in four staves simultaneously, as well as to read the alto and bass clefs. But asking pupils to compose for string quartet using the twelve-tone method, with the obligations of harmony and voice-leading, as it were, set aside, can give access to, and a first taste of confidence in working within the medium. The alto clef can be the biggest sticking point, easily overcome by asking the pupils to start their scores with a treble clef, and only then 'translating' it. As part of the teacher's early feedback they will need to be encouraged to use the bottom string of the instrument, but this is easily achieved.

And the string quartet offers a great deal of possibility. Say an opening section in a ternary structure looks like this:

Presto

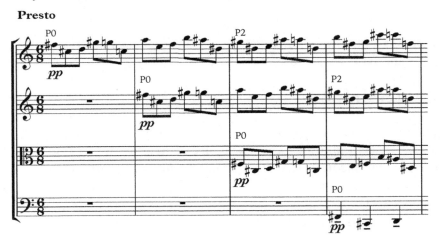

Because it trades in nice factors of 12, compound-time compositions work very well in twelve-tone music, and this is an example of one which has been put together with only very little thought and care. A contrapuntal texture is easily achieved using copy and paste; the first violin's first two-bar phrase is repeated by the second violin and then the viola. An ascending sequence is engineered in the third bar of the first violin's part by the use of P2 (the original (P0) transposed to start two semi-tones higher). The only hint of interest is in the 'cello part, which begins in bar 4 with a rhythmic augmentation in hemiola of the first violin's music. The ambiguity between 6/8 and 3/4 here might lead somewhere. A more thoughtful composer might exploit the parallel movement in what we hear as thirds between the first and second violins in the second bar.

The contrasting middle section of our string quartet might be truly strange, and might well exploit as many twentieth-century playing-techniques as we can squeeze into it.

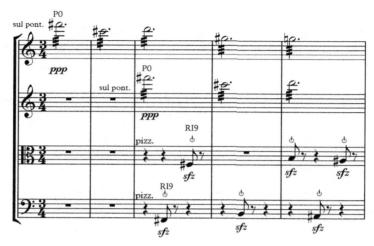

Here, there is a little *sul ponticello* tremolo canon between the two violins, whilst the 'cello and viola trade 'Bartók' pizzicatos.

Writing harmony

Composition starts rightly with melody, but, in our Western tradition, harmony is never very far behind. In the lower school, harmony is, at first, implicit – if your melody ends on this note, then it will sound complete. Later, compositions, even quite involved structures, can be built on simple given chord-patterns (and so much music can be explained by chord progressions whose roots are a perfect fifth apart – in effect, perfect cadences).

But there comes a moment where pupils need a little more knowledge about harmony, and it's good to have a method for teaching it. This is mine.

a. Scales and triads

i. Degrees of the scale

Each note, and the chord based on it has a name.

In any given diatonic scale, the first note is called the tonic, the second, the supertonic, and then the mediant, the sub-dominant, the dominant, sub-mediant, and leading note. Pupils should learn these, and begin to use them with ease.

The three-note chord on each note, called a triad, is given the same name.

In a major scale, the tonic, sub-dominant, and dominant triads are major and are called the primary chords – the four other chords are called the secondary chords; the super-tonic, mediant, and sub-mediant are minor; and the triad on the leading note is diminished.

ii. Inversions

Each three-note chord (triad) can exist in three different forms, three inversions:

The arrows show a way to calculate inversion, the lowest note of one moving up to become the highest note of the next.

Each is identified by its lowest note, the note in its bass. Thus, any chord, of however many doubled notes, with the root in the bass is a root position chord; any chord with the third in the bass is a first inversion; with the fifth in the bass is a second inversion. Individual notes identified as root, third, and fifth, in my nomenclature, refer always to the position of the notes in the original root position triad.

There are practical things which should be introduced at this moment. Music is written in pencil, and one which is sharp enough to wound if necessary (generations of my pupils will chorus 'murderously-sharp' at this moment). Rubbers are essential, too. This is because mistakes are important. Pupils should experiment, and be prepared to get lots of things wrong. They should work carefully, but without inhibition – if they never make mistakes, they will never learn. The more different and exciting errors a pupil makes, the more quickly they will learn. And for the record, pens erasable by friction, however remarkable the technology, will still leave more of an indentation on paper than will a soft pencil (a 2B pencil, kept sharp, is the measure of a true musician).

b. Doubling, spacing, ranges, and notation

i. Doubling

Pupils are writing chorales in four parts named after the four voices in a choir – soprano, alto, tenor, bass (SATB). Harmony is mostly based on triads, on three-note chords. One of the three notes has to appear twice, and the use of a single note twice is known as doubling, a note is doubled.

When I talk about the root, the third, and the fifth notes of a triad, I refer to the triad in its root position, not to the inversion in question. Thus, when I instruct pupils not to double the third in a second inversion C-major triad, I am asking them to remove the second E. This is quite important.

There are three rules for this doubling, important but simple ones:

1. In a major triad, it is preferable to double the root, and you may double the fifth, but you must not, under pain of hideous reproach, double the third. Actually, there are times when you may double the third (when the third is in both soprano and bass parts, for instance), but the richness of this sound is something you should treat with great care.

   Why? Because the third can quite often be the leading note, and leading notes must rise by semitone step to the tonic (this fact is so important that pupils should repeat it ('leading notes rise by semi-tone step to the tonic') as a mantra – all together now). If two such notes rise, then the cardinal sin of parallel octaves is committed. The root and the fifth are tones of more stability – the third less so; by doubling, you give a note emphasis, and you probably want to make the harmony stronger (=stable), not weaker (=unstable).

2. In a minor triad, you can double whatever you like.

3. In a diminished triad (chord VII), it is best not to double the root (which is the leading note – and, all together …).

There are times when only two notes are used. It takes only two notes to identify a chord, the root and the third. The fifth makes the sound fuller and stronger, but you do not need it. This is useful when pupils are in voice-leading trouble – a way out can be to omit the fifth.

ii. Spacing

Pupils also need to think about the spacing of their chords. There should be a gap of no more than an octave between soprano and alto, and between alto and tenor; the gap between bass and tenor can be as large as the pupil wishes.

iii. Ranges

Pupils need to consider the capabilities of singers – even if the chorale is to be played on a piano or an organ. Below are suggested ranges for the voices:

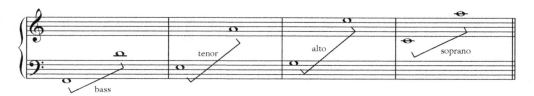

These are suggestions and are not binding. It is, however, a good idea to make the tenor sing quite high, most often in the range above middle C. For two reasons: first, it makes the part writing easier; second, it makes them go red in an amusing fashion, and is fun to watch.

iv. Notation

The soprano and alto are written using the treble clef. The soprano line is distinguished by stems which go up, alto by stems which go down. The tenor and the bass are written using the bass clef. The tenors' part may be identified by upward-facing stems, the basses' stems go down. Thus:

Pupils should do their best to maintain the voices in their proper order – SATB. The soprano should be higher than that alto; the alto higher than the tenor; the tenor than the bass. To infringe this is called crossing, and should be avoided.

c. Cadences

There are four types of cadences:

Perfect	V-I	finished	The most common cadence.
Plagal	IV-I	finished	Traditionally the 'Amen' cadence; both in use and in meaning.
Imperfect	?-V	unfinished	Analogous with a comma, a half-way cadence.
Interrupted	V-VI	unfinished, a surprise	Gives the impression of a perfect cadence, and then a huge surprise. In a major key, chord VI is minor

Composing in the upper school

Here is the perfect-cadence method I use with pupils from year 10 upwards:

1. Whenever chords are involved, whether you are writing, or trying to identify them, always start with the bass. Write in first the bass notes of V and I.

Note that the perfect cadences tend to move from a weak to a strong beat; the half-empty bar at the beginning is left deliberately vacant.

2. Work out the notes for each chord, and write their letter names, starting with the root at the bottom, and ascending. Cross off the notes you have already used.

3. Identify the leading note of the key and write it in. In a single part, this must, all together now, rise by semitone step to the tonic. Put it in any of the parts where it falls in an appropriate range. Cross off the notes you have used.

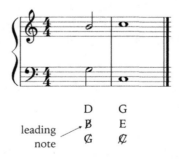

4. Put in the remaining notes using good part writing. Good part writing means that except for the falling perfect fifth or rising perfect fourth in the bass, neither the soprano, nor the alto, nor the tenor moves more than a step or so. Cross off the

notes you have used. You will need to double one note in the chord. Best to double the root, fine to double the fifth, do not (no, no, never) double the third of a major triad. It sounds really bad. If you have problems with a chord, the root and the third are enough to give it identity; you can omit the fifth.

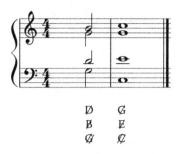

6. Try to give the each voice a note easily in its range; and try to avoid consecutive fifths and consecutive octaves (these are sometimes called parallel fifths and parallel octaves). Check for these bass against tenor; bass against tenor and so on:

B - T A S

T - A S

A - S

In writing the tenor part, it is likely, and normal, that you will have to re-consider the alto line. You are still writing in pencil, aren't you?

d. Before the perfect cadence

There are two chords you can use to precede a perfect cadence: II7b and Ic.

II7b is by far the more colourful of the two (especially in the minor), is used by Bach almost invariably, and is your default:

ii7b   V ⟶ I

Composing in the upper school

Note the obligations here: the seventh (C) must fall by step, resolving to the third of the next chord. The tenor part is both dull and high (in chorale work these are both very good things). In this progression, because the parts move so often by step, it is easy here to put in lots of juicy suspensions:

ii7b   V ⟶ I

A suspension is where one note, having been part of a chord, continues to sound in the next chord, creating a dissonance. There are three parts to a suspension: the suspended must be prepared (P), sounded (S), and resolved (R). It's conventional that all three of these component parts use the same note-value (in this case, all three are crotchets).

II7b is strong because its root is a perfect fifth higher than V; the progression II — V — I is a very small portion of the circle-of-fifths.

Here is the less-interesting Ic (in figured bass, a 6/4 chord):

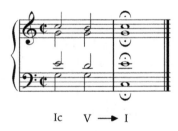

Ic   V ⟶ I

It's usually best to double the fifth in Ic, treating it as a double suspension of V:

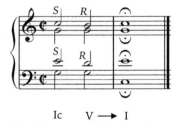

Ic   V ⟶ I

There is a sixth between the two sounding notes (E and C), which moves in parallel to the sixth between D and B. The inversion of the movement will also work, a different distribution of the parts changing the parallel-sixth movement to parallel-thirds.

e. *Figured bass*

Some think that figured bass is too old-fashioned to be of any great use, desiccated and dull. They are wrong. It's a really powerful way to teach pupils that all harmony comes from the bass note, a set of short-cuts which pay huge dividends quite quickly. It can make pupils better scholars and players, and save them a great deal of time.

At first, it's daunting, but there are two rules:

1. there is no zero, and;

2. the numbers are used to count up the prevailing scale from the bass note.

A root position chord looks like this:

Because there is no zero and the piece is in the key of G minor, the given note is 1; the chord is calculated by counting up the prevailing scale:

The given note is 1; then 3 is Bb, 5 is D, and 8 is G. Because root-position chords are those which are the most commonly-used, composers often omit the figures: if there are no figures, then it's a root-position chord.

First-inversion chords are written like this:

Which takes the F sharp as 1, and counts up this prevailing scale, three notes and then six:

A first-inversion chord is sometimes abbreviated to just 6. There is no 8 in a first-inversion chord, in this one in particular, because the doubled note would be both the third of the chord and the leading-note – the doubling of which would be a very bad idea.

Pupils should at least have encountered figured bass, have some of the basic tools to unravel it. The most experienced should have had the opportunity to try some at the keyboard – it is sometimes part of Oxbridge admissions tests.

f. *Voice leading*

There are some basic errors which it's best to avoid: namely, consecutive fifths and consecutive octaves. Later pupils should learn a more sophisticated solecism, exposed fifths and octave. But for now, this is really nasty:

Consecutive intervals are the interval of an octave or a perfect fifth between the same two voices in two consecutive notes. In the first full bar, here are consecutive octaves between S and T (Bb — C); here are consecutive perfect fifths between B and T (Eb/Bb — F/C). Octaves and fifths are the most powerful of intervals, intervals upon which one can build chords, places to finish pieces. Such power is to be used rather judiciously, and certainly not all at once, in one chord and the next. Their use is also very dull, reducing the independence of the voices, and the play of their interrelationships.

Exposed intervals (octaves and fifths) occur where the soprano and the bass voice both move in the same direction to an octave. The octave Bb in the following is exposed;

Again it's about the power of an octave, in this case drawing too much attention to its strength.

g. 'Three Blind Mice'

Most melodies move by step, and it's useful to think about ways to put chords to the first three notes of 'Three Blind Mice'. This repertoire of chords works both forwards and backwards – meaning that the progression associated with 'Mice Blind Three' is equally effective.

Putting harmony to a given melody means first adding a bass-line. The strongest and most secure bass-lines move in contrary motion to the melody. Which means that the best bass-line for 'Three Blind Mice' is 'Mice Blind Three':

The opposite is also true.

There are two harmonic possibilities here. The best and most interesting is VIIb:

I VIIb Ib

VIIb is both a colourful diminished triad, close relative of the dominant seventh (it can be thought of as V7 without the root).

Vc is a far-less interesting alternative:

I Vc Ib

215

Note that both of these outlines move in slightly different ways from tonic to dominant and then back to the tonic. The third possibility is to make this move more explicit:

I Vb I

h. Something upbeat

Bach's chorales often start with an upbeat, and there are two ways to deal with this. The first is simply to set the same chord either side of the bar-line:

There is seldom anything wrong with the simplest of solutions. The second possibility is to begin with the national anthem:

I   VI

The move from I to VI, in the major key from a major triad to a minor, is highly attractive and interesting. There are many occasions when VI substitutes for I, of which the interrupted cadence is but one.

Between the bass-notes of I and VI is the interval of a descending third, a tempting space into which a passing-note might be inserted. If that passing note is itself harmonised, then another version of 'Three Blind Mice' becomes available:

I Vb VI

There's a delicate balance to be struck in the teaching of harmony, especially in the teaching of harmony using the model of Bach's chorales. Clichés and conventions are a place to start, to give pupils a quick start and the confidence in their first interactions with harmony, but they are not everything. Too many rules, especially if they are presented as dry abstractions, can interfere one with another, and be somewhat dispiriting. Attaching names – 'Three Blind Mice', National Anthem – can help a great deal, to make progressions memorable, and promote pupils' recall. It helps, too, if pupils understand the thinking behind the cliché, why II7b is the chord which most happily sits in front of V.

And pupils need two more things: the confidence to work out harmony for themselves where no guidance exists; and the understanding of the importance of the bass melody.

i. Choosing chords

Maybe it's here that harmony and the teaching of harmony has acquired such a bad name: it's dry and mathematical, at one stage removed from music. And with all pervasive untruths, there is just enough about this which is plausible for it to survive. But not quite enough.

These rules and conventions are powerful knowledge, knowledge which makes it possible for pupils to produce convincing and strong harmony and to understand more about the work of other composers; it also elevates their own composition from imaginative flailing in the dark, to an imagination which is informed by a little knowledge. In their own works, they may – possibly should – break all the rules, but their work will be the more powerful for knowing them intimately.

Away from the freedom of cliché and convention, once the bass-line of the beginning and the end of the phrases is in place, there are three more things which will help.

The first is that the melody is full of information. The majority of notes in a chorale will belong to one of three different possible chords. Which of those three to choose comes down to their place in the hierarchy of chords: the more important the chord, the more likely it is to be used. A plausible hierarchy in a major key might look like this:

I — V — IV — II — VI — III — VII

This hierarchy is generated from the diatonic circle of fifths, like this:

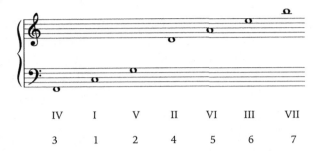

IV	I	V	II	VI	III	VII
3	1	2	4	5	6	7

Which can be laid out like this:

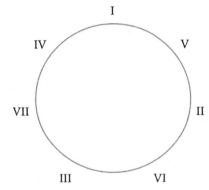

The second consideration when choosing chords is related: that a pair of chords whose roots are a fifth apart will sound good one after another. Pairs of chords whose roots are too close, especially whose roots are only a step apart, sound at best dull and weak, at worst, really bad.

The third thing is where to change chord. In many chorales, there is a new chord with each crotchet beat, a steady and unremitting harmonic rhythm. The exceptions to this are chorales which are in 3/4 time, where the first and second beats of which often use the same chord. A new chord, or a new inversion of the same chord, on every crotchet beat, then. Save at the beginning, using the same chord either side of a bar-line is quite dull.

j. Melody and harmony

The final part of this introduction to harmonic thinking involves melody, specifically the injunction to consider the bass-line itself as a melody. Just as good melodies move more often by step than they do by leap, so a bass-line. There are two constraints on this: first, that the cadence at the end of the phrase will necessitate a leap in the bass-line, and; secondly, that the bass-line has to respond to the given melody.

An example, worked with pupils, might help to make this clearer. Let's take a chorale harmonisation by Bach, *Du Lebensfürst, Herr Jesu Christ* (Riemenschneider no. 361). The first phrase looks like this:

The teacher can expect their pupils already to know quite a lot about this melody:

Look at the melody. What does the C sharp tell you about the movement of this melody?

That there has been a modulation from G major to D major; from the tonic to the dominant.

Given that there has been a modulation, what, then, is the cadence?

A perfect cadence on D major.

And the chord before the cadence?

How about II7b?

Pupils should always start at the end of a given phrase, always put in the bass-line of the cadence first:

There needs to be some care about the relationship between the given melody and bass-line, even here:

Check that you use contrary motion between your melody and your bass-line and that there are neither consecutive fifths nor consecutive octaves.

Composing in the upper school

It is and there are none.

Check that the 7 of II7b is prepared nicely.

It is.

Next comes the opening

How do we start?

Because there's a repeated note, I can start with the National Anthem! And I'm going to add a passing note to fill the gap in the bass part.

Very good, now what goes before II7b?

I in D major – maybe in the first inversion.

The result of which is:

Which leaves but two notes to consider.

Okay, nearly there. What next?'

We have an A and a B.

Given that the key here is G major, with which chords do these notes fit? Write down all the possibilities.

The pupils' calculations should look like this:

E	**A**	C		D	F sharp	**B**
C	F sharp	**A**		**B**	D	G
A	D	F sharp		G	**B**	E
II	*V*	*VII*		*I*	*III*	*VI*

With the note A, it is easy to say what it is not – it is not VII, pupils should reserve this for Ia—VII—Ib. The most likely solution, then, will be V, which is much more common than II. The same with the note B, it is highly unlikely to be chord III, and I is stronger than VI.

This leads to a bass melody like this:

This bass-line itself is a plausible melody, moving mainly by step, and only seldom by leap. Between bass and soprano there is either contrary or oblique motion; the only similar motion is in the first full bar, where the interval of a tenth between G and B is approached from below. It's quite simple then, to fill in the alto and tenor parts.

Magical composition

Much as we would like to believe it, there is no magic in composition. 'Imagine' and *Tristan* and *Plum Blossom*, in the final analysis, are just explained by physics, are collections of waves, minutely organised by human hand. If there's magic in music, it is in the freedom possessed by every one of us to receive those organised sounds, and to generate from them in our minds meaning, power, beauty, and the feeling that we are not alone.

The magic we perceive in the works of the greatest composers and the greatest musicians is the result of their monomaniac hard work and of the luck of their birth and their circumstances. To appropriate Arthur C. Clarke, any sufficiently advanced composition is indistinguishable from magic; the greatest musicians and composers can do more, see further, imagine more, because they know more and have more musical experience than us. It's a world of possibility, an inspiring thought.

To set our pupils on the path through which they might know enough to begin to appreciate just a little of this magic – this is why we teach composition.

References

Hattie, J. & Yates, G., 2014. *Visible Learning and the Science of How We Learn*. Oxford, Oxford University Press.

Talbot, M., 2013. *The Vivaldi Compendium*. Woodbridge, Boydell Press.

Chapter 10

Performing

Working with young performers is a unique privilege. When we teachers get it right, there is nothing which is impossible for them.

This is true in every school, in every genre, and at every scale. It's true when you see the energy, commitment, and musical imagination of a hundred-strong school orchestra engaging for the first time with a Mahler symphony; it's as true when you hear the year 9 steel-pan-band master that accelerando at the end of 'Hall of the Mountain King'; and it's equally true when you hear the year 7 clarinet-group play Williams's 'Cantina Band' from *Star Wars*.

We learn our limits as we get older; some will say that this education is part of growing up. The trick with young players is to teach them that, with hard work, a little thought, and good luck, those limits are often self-imposed, that nothing is impossible.

Treat children as you would professional musicians, and they will respond in kind.

Choosing repertoire

This education starts with the choice of ensemble repertoire.

Not all music is equally satisfying to play. As an orchestral player, there is little to equal the excitement of the end of Brahms's First Symphony, or Beethoven's Ninth; the inescapable grip of the second movement of Beethoven's Seventh; the blazing choruses of Haydn's *Creation*. These moments – apogees of great musical arcs – are possible because of the music which precedes and surrounds them; these moments make the difficulties and the hard work seem worth it.

The converse is also true. When an opera company puts on a performance of Wagner's *Der Ring des Nibelungen*, it has become customary for masseurs and physiotherapists to be laid on for the string players. The music is intoxicating, great beyond measure; but it demands a price to be paid.

 DOI: 10.4324/9781003112402-10

The first thing, then, is to pick music which the pupils will enjoy playing. It's important at this moment to understand that this is not the same as picking music with which the pupils are familiar. In my day it was the theme music from *Match of the Day*; today endless themes from the Harry Potter films. Williams is a great composer, but his music is very difficult to render in its original versions, and arrangements fail to capture, if you'll forgive, its magic (I don't know enough of Barry Stoller to pass comment).

As far as possible, the original music is to be preferred to arrangements. Every composer has made myriad decisions, manipulated the musical materials at their disposal in particular ways, and the resulting work should be respected as much as possible. However skilfully done, any arrangement will always lose some of that which is essential to a work.

Young players can navigate difficult music. Indeed, it's one of the skills of ensemble playing to learn how to make a work sound good without necessarily playing everything that's in the score. Implicit in so much great music is that it is better than it can be played – that there is more musical substance and greater technical challenges than can ever be met. This is a skill which players learn through experience, and young players need to have the opportunity to build that experience.

And there's no shortage of music, certainly for the standard ensembles, and no lack of simpler music which is accessible and which is easy and enjoyable to play.

One of the great unstated truths about children is that they understand more than we sometimes think. They know, viscerally, when we are offering something half-heartedly, or when we have not done enough homework ourselves to think beyond another arrangement of music from *Pirates of the Caribbean*. And if we have taken shortcuts, given them half-measures, why should we be surprised when they do the same?

Planning rehearsals

Rehearsal time is always too short, always and everywhere. In schools the limits are that of the lunchtime, or the afterschool rumble of children's stomachs. If you lead an ensemble rehearsal, you have the duty to make the best of the time.

This is familiar territory for the teacher. Just like as in the classroom, the rehearsal room has its routines. Where possible, the room should be set and ready for work, chairs, stands, and music in place. If not, then the pupils should know their parts in furniture moving, be drilled in what chairs go where, and how many it is safe to lift at once.

Performing

Once the room is ready, pupils know to leave their cases there, that they bring to the rehearsal instruments, equipment, music, and a pencil. Ah the pencil, a talisman of good ensemble playing. The pencil, 2B soft, ideally with a rubber at its top, is a sign of the well-trained musician. The pencil is soft both in order that marking can be made clearly, and so they can be erased easily from borrowed music.

Let the pupils know in advance what they are going to rehearse and any particular difficulties they might encounter. This gives them the opportunity to prepare nasty solo moments, and for them to ask for help from their instrumental teachers. If the same information reaches their teachers, too, so much the better, as they can work ensemble preparation into lesson time. This communication with the players – usually by e-mail – is a moment to remind players what they should be doing before rehearsals, and is also an opportunity to thank them for being part of the group. Building an ensemble as a team is very important, and the small moments of communication are all part of it.

A schedule helps to keep the teacher organised, too. Reaching the concert without having prepared that difficult middle bit happens all-too-often, and a schedule is a necessary and useful discipline.

It also means that the teacher is not wasting pupils' time. If you play the triangle or the tuba, is it really necessary for you to sit through endless rehearsals with the strings and woodwind, counting rests, only for the conductor inevitably to stop just before your entry? If a teacher expects concentration and attention from their players, then what they ask should be reasonable.

Before the rehearsal

As far as possible, parts should be marked before the rehearsal. Where photocopying licences permit, pupils should have a named practice copy, as well as the part which they will use – individually or shared with a desk partner – in performance. The marking should include pedestrian instructions about beating ('in 4'), should indicate moments where the tempo might slow or become quicker (a forward-facing arrow for faster; backward for slower; an undulating line for a *ritardando*), and, for string players, bowing.

Bowing string parts in advance saves an immense amount of rehearsal time – even if the bowing needs eventually to be changed, at least the players are starting from the same agreed point. This does not mean that every director of a string ensemble need necessarily be an expert string player – although ideally they should be; it means that they should have the humility to ask for help, help from visiting music teachers, from local professional orchestral libraries (who are often hugely generous), and from the pupils themselves.

Practising your part, performing together

Pupils will do remarkable things for their ensembles. It is for a very good reason that orchestras have leaders and section leaders. Giving pupils responsibility, and teaching them as leaders what is expected of them, makes every ensemble stronger. Those chosen will necessarily be the more-experienced players (although the best players are not always the best leaders), and it is their duty both to set an example (in punctuality, conduct, and preparation), as well as to help the younger players. It is likely that they will play their instruments better than the ensemble director, and their technical help is invaluable for the newer players. And of course, to teach is to learn, and they will become better players by helping others.

If it becomes part of the ensemble culture, pupils will also commit to personal practice and to section rehearsals. Section rehearsals are of immense value. The difficulties of a piece are not evenly distributed, and in orchestral playing, there is the disparity between the wind soloists, and the collective string section. It is very helpful for wind players to have the opportunity to work through their parts in relative privacy, as solo sight-reading in public is less-than desirable. In the busy life of a school, it's easier to find time and space for a rehearsal with two or three players, than it is to call another rehearsal with the whole group.

Personal practice and rehearsal applies equally to the music teacher. To perform with a young instrumentalist is the greatest privilege and pleasure, and your contribution – most often as a pianist – needs to be good enough. There are very difficult decisions to be made here, particularly in a small department. Is it a better use of the teacher's time to practise for a single performance with one pupil, or to do a good-enough job for them, and spend that time preparing a lesson for an entire class?

Working as an ensemble pianist is one of the great unsung skills. To perform your part meticulously, whilst being totally aware of another's – that humility, generosity, and breadth of musicianship – is something really special. To discuss it goes far beyond the scope of this book. Two observations might, however, be useful.

The first is that pupils need to be trained to work with a pianist. Some of this lies in the mechanics of starting and stopping, of how to begin a piece with sufficient intention that the pianist cannot but be with them. But some of this is also in knowing what to expect from a good pianist, and expecting it to work. This next sentence sounds like nonsense, but is nonetheless true: if a player knows clearly enough what they want from a pianist, that is sufficient for a good pianist to be with them, literally and metaphorically. Teachers need to build that confidence in their pupils.

Performing

The second observation is about the nature of piano playing. Note that I have avoided the 'a' word in all of this discussion. To be a demure and too-quiet accompanist is a mistake we have all made. The great *lieder* pianist Gerald Moore asked *Am I too loud?* (1986), but did so with tongue firmly in cheek. A great ensemble pianist knows that it's the quality of sound which creates balance, that most players and singers need and enjoy a clear and rather strong bass line; know that it's possible to play quite loudly, if that dynamic is associated with clarity (to put it rather crassly: less pedal and shorter notes).

Visiting music teachers are also a wonderful resource for ensemble work. Their help in the preparation of pupils' ensemble parts combines the best of both worlds – individual instruction which will develop their pupils' techniques and musicianship, combined with an often encyclopaedic knowledge of which bits matter, of which bits will be covered, of the best ways to give the correct impression without necessarily playing all of the notes.

Better still, if time and budgets allow, to have visiting teachers take section rehearsals, and to be part of the main rehearsal. If your teacher is standing behind you in a rehearsal, score in hand and frown on face, then your motivation is guaranteed; if the teacher can immediately correct a fingering, suggest a simpler bowing, or fix a broken reed, so much the better.

Conducting

For some teachers, conducting is a great joy, for others it's a burden and a difficulty; but few can escape it at some stage in their teaching careers. It doesn't help that conducting is an activity hedged around with myth, nonsense, and ego.

For the teacher, there are two dimensions of conducting: conducting technique and score-preparation.

In its gestures, conducting is very simple; beating two is up and down; three is a triangle; four is down, left, triangle. For ensemble conducting, a baton is useful, extending the arm, and making it completely clear on what the performers' attention should be focussed. Even if you are left-handed, you should conduct with your right hand. It makes your performers' lives considerably easier.

When choosing a baton, it's a good idea to try as many as you can. The balance of bulb and stick should work for the size of your hand, and it should conventionally be as long as the distance from the inside of an individual's elbow to the tip of their middle finger.

There are many ways of holding a baton, but this is mine. It is gripped quite tightly between the pad of my thumb and the side of my curved index finger – the stick sitting where top and the second joint of the finger join. This means that my first fundamental movement is of the index finger, which is then amplified in turn by the wrist, the forearm, the elbow, and (*in extremis*) my upper arm. This focus on the index finger helps to control extraneous movement, and means that the beat (instructions to the players about tempo) comes always from the same place. This is not always true of conductors.

The gestures for two are very simple, up and down along a single vertical plane:

1 2

These diagrams are quite commonplace, but are a useful metaphor for the gesture of conducting. If you imagine that the tip of your baton is made of graphite, and that you are drawing with it on a piece of paper, secured vertically, then you should be able repeatedly to draw the pattern.

The movement starts with an upbeat (2). This begins at the bottom of the vertical plane. The precise moment of the beat comes at the very bottom, at the instant when the index finger begins to rise. With practice, this can be made very clear. The baton moves quickly at first, accelerating rapidly at the beginning of its move, and then slowing towards the top. The downbeat (1) comes when the index finger reaches the bottom of the plane and comes momentarily to a stop. The upbeat (2) is the same as the downbeat, as the index finger accelerates upwards again.

What happens at the top of the plane matters. The stick should change direction rather subtly, slowing its ascent as if being pulled back into the influence of gravity and then beginning to fall, but gradually. If the movement of the stick changes abruptly, then an additional beat is given, and the effect is of a subdivided two. It's useful to be able to subdivide a beat, of course, but to do so habitually is distracting, confusing, and impedes beautiful playing in an ensemble. There are few teacher-conductors who do not subdivide, it's one of the reasons that pupils don't watch them.

Performing

Three is essentially a right-angle triangle, extending the vertical plane of two:

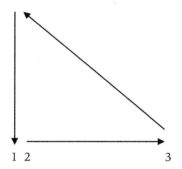

It starts with an upbeat, exactly the same upbeat which is used for a two-pattern (and for every pattern, whether three, five, or eleven). It's a move vertically upwards from the point marked '1,2' – where the beat itself falls – to the highest point on the triangle.

Gravity seemingly brings the baton down (although in reality it's controlled quite tightly by the index finger) and the down-beat is reached. This first beat (1) is marked when the descent to the bottom of the plane stops; 2 comes when the movement resumes horizontally to the right; 3 is when the movement changes from horizontal, through an angle of about 45 degrees, up again to the top of the triangle. Again, the movement of the index finger is fastest as each new beat begins, and then becomes progressively slower the further from the beat it travels.

Four adds a flat-roofed side-extension to the triangle:

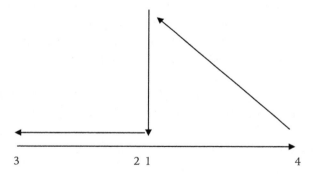

Starting with an upbeat, the first beat stops at the bottom; two is when the movement resumes to the left; three is when the movement changes from left to right; and four is when the stick begins to move upwards again at an angle of about 45 degrees.

There is much more to the gesture of conducting, of course, but these are the fundamentals upon which all else is built.

It's important to control the baton's speed of acceleration at the point of the beat. This impetus can show dynamic and attack, and it can also inhibit, showing when not to play. A beat which is gently glossed-over can prevent a player from starting in the wrong place; and an energetic beat can set chaos in train. It's worth practising bars like this:

There will be an active upbeat, a clear downbeat, then an inhibiting passive beat on the second crotchet; the note on the fourth beat is prepared by a more vigorous third, and the downbeat of the second bar should be very quiet. When a school orchestra plays in the wrong place, it's often the fault of the conductor.

Practising is the key. A conductor needs to be able to reproduce an exact gesture at a particular moment in time. Just as a violinist needs their bow to move in a particular way at a precise time, so a baton, even though it's silent, should move with analogous precision. It's embarrassing to stand in front of a mirror, silently gesturing, but, in developing the basic movements, there's really no alternative.

The basic movements are made with the stick in the right hand. The left hand should be free either to encourage dynamics, or to give cues. Beating with both hands, one mirroring the other, is a very good exercise, makes the conductor feel as if they are helping their players twice as much, but it is of very little practical use and often looks a little silly.

Players need to watch the conductor, or at least keep half and eye on them, and the conductor should encourage this by making eye contact with them as often as possible. A well-placed smile can make all the difference.

All of this means that the conductor should know the score. Thorough knowledge of a major score asks a great deal of the busy teacher, but there are some shortcuts which it's possible to take.

Preparing a score

The great conductors can imagine a full orchestral score in sound. It's possible to practise and train the aural imagination, to develop it to the extent that a new score will leap from the page. But most teachers simply do not have the time.

Fortunately, the resources available to us today mean that a teacher's knowledge of a score, whilst not perfect, can certainly be good enough to serve well both composer and children.

Performing

The first stage in the process is to mark the score in a detailed and organised way, to have a system. Taking time to annotate a score is one way of learning its intricacies, of making sure that you have at least seen every part before facing an ensemble. It can also provide a visual scheme for its performance, freeing the conductor from the score to attend to their players.

This is what a marked score, in this case, Beethoven's First Symphony, looks like:

Performing

The first thing to decide is the beating pattern and the tempo, and to write them into the score. Especially under pressure of performance, it's very good to have the reassuring reminder that yes, you are going to beat this section in 4 and not in 8.

Use coloured pens or pencils to mark the score. This helps your markings to stand out, and also allows you to invent a code for different colours. I use blue for most markings, red for the brass and percussion (who often have long rests, and always need cues thereafter), purple for dynamics, and orange for technical markings such as *pizzicato*.

The next stage is to rule thick vertical lines at the end of each phrase. Most units will be four bars long, and it's probably best not to mark phrases which are longer than this. The first two units of the Beethoven are four bars long, followed by two, two-bar units. The introduction ends with that single magical bar leading into the *Allegro*.

Next comes marking the instruments. The code used here helps to identify whether players are doubling or playing solos:

fl = two flutes

fl1 = first flute

fl2 = second flute

tr = trumpet

timp = timpani

1 = first horn

2 = second horn

I = first violins

II = second violins

Mark every entry after a rest, or where an instrument is particularly prominent. This helps to understand and learn the score, and it also reveals information important to a good performance. On the first page of the Beethoven, you can see that the first and second violins are doubled at the octave in bar 4; that the first flute and first bassoon are doubled in bar 5. The brace at the beginning of bar 9 shows that all of the strings play.

Then some technical markings. Helping string players to play *pizzicato* together is an important duty of a conductor (the best gesture for *pizzicato* is ironically quite legato – a sharp and detached gesture will, invariably, mean that the players are unable to play in unison). It's useful to mark where the pizzicato comes with a code, here, in the first three bars, a cross in a little circle (in orange ink in the original).

Decisions about bowing are made in the score and transferred to the parts. In bar 7, for instance, the string players are given a little more bow to help them both to execute the *crescendo*, and to reach the downbeat of bar 8 on a down-bow.

Dynamics are marked with circles, and crescendos are marked with hairpins in each section of the orchestra – in bar 7 there are separate markings for woodwind, horns, and strings. There are also interpretative decisions recorded here. In bar 19, the woodwind's crescendo ends with a *subito piano*, a gesture typical of Beethoven.

Finally, comes some more detailed decisions about note length. The first violins' note at the beginning of bar 13 should be quite short and light – a line after the note reminds us of this fact; the woodwind's *tenuto* chords in bar 9 should be full length – shown by an arrow ending in a vertical line.

Add strong sticky index tabs to mark the separate movements, and work out where to put tabs to make any repeats easy to execute. Use flimsy paper tabs to plan rehearsals, and to remind you what work needs to be done and where.

Please put aside the snobbery you will hear about learning scores, it comes from a different time, and applies to different people. We are teachers, and our duty as performers is not merely to the composers we serve; it is also and equally owed to our pupils, too. When performers see your marked scores, look down their noses and say, 'you should know the score so well that you don't need a score', take a deep breath, and imagine them with year 7 pupils in period 8 on Fridays. That will do the trick.

There is snobbery, too, about the use of recordings. The idea that 'real' conductors commune only with the score, occasionally turning to the piano to check a particularly complex harmony, or a difficult corner. This is nonsense. There is nothing wrong, as part of your preparations of a score, with selecting a really good recording of a work, and listening to it repeatedly, learning the sounds and the tempos and the cues from it. It's best not to conduct at the same time – if you conduct a recording you are following and not leading, you may practising becoming a bad conductor. To avoid this potential pitfall, it is better to separate out the technique of conducting from knowledge of the score.

Running the rehearsal

A good rehearsal balances playing and practice, involves as many people as possible most of the time, centres on a culture of listening and shared endeavour.

Because there is a schedule for the rehearsal, and because this lunchtime's work will be on a section of the piece which does not involve the brass, those who will not be part of it are released and are outside with their footballs. This has two effects: it means that there are not bored and disgruntled players in the rehearsal doing nothing save aching for the company of their mobile telephones; it also means that the conductor can expect full attention from everybody in the room.

Although you are a teacher working with pupils, you are also a musician working with colleagues. The balance of your duties as teacher and your status as a colleague engaged in a shared activity is an important one to strike. To all intents and purposes, gone are the days when it was possible to compel children to play or sing in a group; they need to want to be there, to know that their presence is valued, and to enjoy the adventure of working together in music. This is also a description of great teaching, of course.

A word about tuning. Young ensembles can play in tune, but have to be taught how. This seems difficult and daunting, but tuning a group is a skill like any other; it can be learnt.

Many teachers are expert instrumentalists, well-versed in ensemble-tuning; most are not. You learn to tune by paying attention to tuning in rehearsals, by helping young players to tune, and by carefully noting and learning from all the mistakes you inevitably make. If you suggest to a bassoonist that they are flat, and they return saying that they were actually sharp, then two things have happened:

you have learnt what a sharp bassoon sounds like (and that they are highly likely to be very sharp indeed in their upper registers), and the player has realised that they need to change the tuning of their note.

Electronic tuning machines or tuning apps on smartphones are available, and they can be useful. They provide another opportunity for both teacher and player to explore tuning themselves, as well as acting as a useful and fixed starting-point for tuning a group. The risk in their use is the implicit idea that tuning is absolute, that A resounds at 440Hz always and forever. It does not. Tuning is relative, whatever sounds good at the moment. Tuning is also a duty to those around you: you make adjustments for the difficulties and for the proclivities of your colleagues. By the end of a Mahler symphony, for example, the wind players will be tired, and their instruments will be very warm – accordingly the pitch will rise, just a little. And this is fine, if everyone plays a little sharper together. This common duty to each other – that if anyone puts themselves first, then the whole fails – is why ensemble playing matters in schools and in our societies.

The practicalities of tuning a chord are these: establish first the roots, then the fifths. These are the foundations of the chord, and are the easiest to get together. Then, and only then, add the thirds. It means that the teacher has to know the score well enough, and have a little confidence in transposition ('sees a C, sounds a …').

Remember that young players, particularly young wind players, have only finite stamina. A young horn- or trombone-player is only able to give their solo a couple of times in quick succession before their 'lips go'. Treat them as a finite resource.

The concert

Concerts are the final rehearsal, and you should always find opportunities for more. Which is to say that the ensemble learns a great deal in performance, and that the chance to repeat a programme, or part of a programme, is invaluable. Best of all is to repeat a programme a few months later. The marinading effect of time is a great teacher. In the heat of performance, with an audience watching, with no real chance to stop and repeat, you find the problems, find out where the ensemble needs to go next. If the next day you can rehearse, even briefly, your feedback, combined with the confidence pupils take from a successful performance, has the potential to transform the results. Record the concert, and listen objectively, adding sticky notes in the score to remind yourself. Objective listening is near-impossible, of course, but you can learn to chart a course between the Scylla of hearing only the mistakes and the Charybdis of hubris.

You will have noted in the last paragraph that these are the same components which make up great teaching – practice, assessment, and feedback. The only thing good musicians need sometimes to do is to remember that their skills, unlike so many elsewhere, transfer exactly from one domain to the other.

After the concert

The morning after a concert is always a special time. A performance changes the weather in a school, and a culture of performances changes the climate. It's really important to acknowledge the work of the pupils and staff involved. By writing a note of thanks and sending it to all concerned, you can teach your pupils that their work matters and is noticed. By doing so, you continue to build your relationship with them, and you help them to learn that they are part of something bigger than them, of a collective. You should also include some gentle feedback, marking out what's next. If it's possible, a note sent home, or at least copied to the parents, is something which matters to pupils.

Working with visiting teachers

Visiting music teachers are the heart of many music departments, invaluable and essential; without their work, these could not thrive.

At the most basic level, pupils who have instrumental lessons spend more time engaged in music every week. This is no small thing, especially as one-to-one or small-group tuition means that what they learn in those lessons is tailored more closely to the individual's needs than it can ever be, even in the best-managed classroom. But it goes far further than this; instrumental teachers, in effect, offer a separate-but-linked music curriculum running in parallel with work in the classroom. In an ideal world, the visiting teachers would know in some detail what's happening in the classroom and vice versa.

The visiting teachers' status is different in every school. Here are three: some are employed by the schools, some by music hubs and music services, others are self-employed. These eventualities create three different relationships between the music teacher and the visiting teacher. In the first, the visiting teacher will be subject to all of the school's expectations, report-writing, parents' evenings, performance management and the like. In the second, many of those functions will be taken by the teachers' employer. In the third, the success of the team relies greatly on the goodwill of the instrumental staff and on the music teacher building strong relationships with them. All three have their advantages and disadvantages: the biggest advantage of employment for the visiting teacher is that the school will afford them sick pay and access to a pension. Some may prefer this, others may not.

An annual ritual for the music teacher is to allocate new year 7 instrumental pupils to the visiting teachers. Music should be at the heart of communication between school and its new intake, an opportunity to teach the new parents and their children about the school's music, and to encourage as many as possible to try it and be part of it. It helps if you are able to offer them an incentive or two. Many schools run very successful trial-lesson and instrument-loan schemes, where pupils can have a free set of lessons on shortage instruments (tuba, bassoon, viola, horn, for example). Other schools give all of year 7 free instrumental lessons for the first year of school. Others again use the pupil premium to pay for instruments and lessons, a brilliant and effective use of funds to support disadvantaged children in both their musical and their academic development. The simplest and most basic thing every school can do is to invite the instrumental teachers into class music lessons; most visiting music teachers have a hugely-impressive *schtick*, all the better to entertain and entice potential pupils.

It's important to do your best to allocate the right pupil to the right teacher. Visiting music teachers are all different, each with their own personality, habits, and dispositions. Some will prefer more-experienced pupils, others are brilliant at the beginning. Some are fierce, some are more gentle. The chemistry between instrumental teacher and their pupil really matters, and your considered judgement of which pupil will thrive with which teacher is important.

For visiting teachers, the clue's in the name. They visit schools, often many schools (which is useful, too, as you can learn a great deal from what other institutions are doing). But as visitors, they don't always feel as if they belong anywhere. It's a common complaint that visiting teachers feel as if they are at the bottom of the food-chain. It's one of your jobs to make them welcome. Make sure that they have access to coffee, biscuits, and a lavatory, that they have pigeon-holes, that they have spaces they feel are theirs, and that in those spaces is somewhere in which music and bits can be left, safe and locked. They need access to a school e-mail address.

But there is another level in this. As a music teacher, you lead a team, and they need to feel part of this. You need to communicate clearly with them and to do it regularly. This means conversations in the corridor and over coffee, regular messages about practical things, anticipating problems they might encounter, helping them to see ways around them. Some find regular meetings helpful, but bear in mind whether or not the visiting teachers are being paid for their time. A music administrator, who can manage the department's calendar, and anticipate any difficulties with fixtures, trips, examinations, or whole-school events, is quite invaluable.

The visiting teachers will have a more complete and nuanced knowledge about pupils' development and personalities than you will, and you should listen to them. They know who's not working hard, and who's full of enthusiasm.

Performing

Armed with that knowledge, a passing conversation with the pupil can be very powerful, encouraging or congratulating. The visiting teachers are also some of the most important scouts of every school's commitment to the wellbeing of its pupils. They are often the first to notice problems or changes, and they should know that when they bring something to you it really matters, and that you will pass it on quickly to the form teachers or to the appropriate person in the safeguarding hierarchy. Visiting teachers often spot problems with reading, memory, or eyesight, can transform pupils' lives in ways far beyond the confines of music.

Visiting teachers will also be of invaluable help with school performances and public examinations. Their help with major ensembles has already been mentioned, but running smaller ensembles is just as important. For some instruments – guitar, recorder, and harp, for example – the opportunities for work in major ensembles might be distinctly limited. Visiting teachers find great fulfilment in ensemble work, and it's good to use their often tremendously impressive skills.

Visiting teachers can help pupils to thrive in public examinations, too. It's again about communication, making sure that the teachers know the syllabus requirements, the deadlines, and the expected standard.

And say thank you. These are impressive people, enthusiastically committed to their pupils, who make music better in every school. Say thank you – is a handwritten postcard too much to ask? Remember their birthdays and their children's names, communicate their importance to your colleagues and the parents. These are easy and pleasant duties, and make a vast difference to the pupils' lives.

Visiting musicians

A visit from a distinguished musician, for a master class, rehearsal, or lecture, is always special. But it's important to find the right fit of person and place. A master class sometimes puts far too much emphasis on the 'master' – it becomes a demonstration of ego and prowess, and the pupils are made to feel small. If possible, see the person at work before you arrange a visit. The best musicians have about them a tremendous humility. It's the little touches which make the class such a success – writing notes on a student's score, for instance, giving them a record of what's been said, and a template to improve their work away from the scrutiny of a public event.

Build relationships between your school and local professional groups. Good orchestras are interested in the development of new audiences and of young players, and there are both formal education departments associated with them as well as individual players who are immensely skilled and committed. A professional orchestra should be the focus and aspiration of music in your community, and good teachers make the most of them.

The young professional musician

From time-to-time you will be fortunate enough to work with a young musician so hard-working, and of such growing experience that they have the potential to become a professional musician. This is a joy as well as a significant responsibility. Such a task requires a certain humility, and a great deal of long-term planning.

The great artist develops in their own unique way, but along a single trajectory. It starts from disposition and opportunity, moves through influence and jolly hard work, and reaches a state of autonomy. By the time the young professional reaches secondary school, the disposition is quite evident, and they have probably already had the early opportunity of working with a really fine instrumental teacher.

The school music teacher has to find ways to give as much of the right kind of opportunity to them as possible. It's all-too-easy to use a fine young pianist as accompanist for the choir, rationalising the decision as a chance to work with a choir. This might well be the case, but are you sure that they might not have a better use for that lunchtime – whether practising their own repertoire, finishing homework in order to be free to practise at home, or just sitting with friends in the sunshine, away from music for a moment.

The right kind of opportunity is where the young artist has themselves some kind of agency. To teach is to learn, and by encouraging them to help others is often a catalysing experience for them. It's not appropriate for them to teach beginners, but to work with higher-level players on interpretation is very useful. There are many single-minded instrumental teachers who will only permit violinists to play one of the same seven concertos, plus a handful of technical show-pieces. In this case if it's possible, the pupil needs in school to have the opportunity to play sonatas with a pianist (again to work on interpretation), and to explore the wonders of and very different skills required by the chamber-music repertoire.

The young artist might well be a better pianist than you are, but there are still things you need to teach them. It's likely that you have a far greater understanding of how music works and of what it means, a breadth of musical knowledge which only comes with time and with experience, and some really important practical skills. Humility on the part of the teacher is important, but also confidence that you can be one of those influences.

It's a measure of the best teachers that they know when they can do no more for a student; more precisely, when the student needs a different perspective, approach, or personality. This will be true of a young artist, too. It's your job to have an overview, standing slightly apart from the relationship between pupil and their instrumental teacher, making sure that all is well. Know the teachers, and know who can develop the compelling musicianship, and who can develop the perfect technique seemingly all-important in modern musical careers. There might be times when you need to speak, to suggest a different way forward.

You need to monitor work in school, too. Most musicians are hugely capable academic students – the skills they learn as an instrumentalist (attention, practice) are those which generate in them scholarly success, too – but they are practising their instruments for many hours each week. There are times, a major competition for example, when the school might need to be a little more tolerant about dead-lines; and it's your job then to be the musician's advocate.

There is one more conversation you should have. Before you is a clever, hard-working, and altogether impressive young person. You need to be sure that music is what they need to do, that the difficult and sometimes thankless career for which they are preparing themselves is absolutely necessary to who they are. There are easier and sometimes more lucrative ways to live, and shooting for the highest echelons of music is always a gamble.

Partnership work

Let's get the name right, first: working with other schools is partnership work, not 'outreach'. The latter is debilitating, all participants gain from partnerships.

If yours is a school lucky enough to have the time and resources to help, part-nerships have the potential to bear the most extraordinary fruit.

Let me tell two stories. The first happens on Fridays. Friday afternoons at King Edward's are a time without lessons. Pupils and staff pursue their own interests, in activities ranging from birdwatching, through coding, to historical reenactment. The musical contribution is Concert Party. A small group of pupils visits a differ-ent primary school each week, and works with the entire school. The pupils play their pieces, talk about their instruments, answer questions, and sometimes play musical games with the school. The primary children hear live music, of good quality; they learn something too. They learn something about instruments and music, and, more importantly, learn what's possible for them with a few years of hard work and practice. The King Edward's pupils learn to perform and present under sometimes quite unfamiliar circumstances. They practise communicating with large groups, and they practise the skills of performance. This is very simple partnership and it works very well.

The second tale is much more involved. The orchestra at King Edward's is of 60 years standing at the time of writing, large and ambitious. It's shared with King Edward VI High School for Girls. Our partners in this second story of partnership were seven primary schools throughout our city; our aim was to develop the teaching of composition in each. The project addressed a specific need: that often music was taught in primary schools by non-specialists, expert teachers who were much less confident in music, and particularly in composition. It was called 'Exploring music through stories' and it used fairy-tales from around the world to teach composition.

In two workshops, primary school teachers as well as our pupils were trained in the teaching of composition by a primary specialist. A set of teaching materials – a short book really – recordings, and videos were prepared and issued. The primary specialist visited the schools individually, and pupils went too, supporting and offering their expertise to the class teachers, and teaching themselves.

The final event was an afternoon performance at King Edward's. Pupils from the primary schools performed their final pieces for each other and for our symphony orchestra, and the orchestra played to them the 1919 suite from *The Firebird*, with live drawing and narration from a children's illustrator. A second children's performance was given in the evening, which gave the orchestra an opportunity to develop by performing twice in a day, and the younger members of the schools' communities a chance to hear a remarkable piece.

This was the best kind of partnership work. Both parties learnt from each other, and both gained from the experience. It was a brilliant opportunity for all participants, memorable and inspiring; but, most-of-all, it developed the skills of 14 teachers, and equipped them with a new set of curriculum materials in music, and with the confidence necessary to use them. The pupils of King Edward's learnt more about composition, and became better musicians by working in different schools, and this music teacher became a better teacher by practising his explanations of composition, and by testing his skills in a very different environment.

If partnership work is new to the school, the place to start is with the people you know. There is a diversity of skills and enthusiasms in every school, but in one of them, in a school near you, there will be someone who is a great musician, around whom your projects can be planned, and from whom you and your pupils can learn an immense amount. It's highly recommended.

A unique privilege?

Working with young performers is a unique privilege and when we teachers get it right, there is little which they cannot achieve. It's a really special part of being a music teacher, one of ways in which we are different.

But does it make this, our job, the best in the world?

Chapter 11

The best job in the world?

I'm in my office and there are mince pies waiting. It's a quiet moment, at the end of a long term, that precious lull between Christmas Concerts and the Carol Service. It's odd to be working by the illumination of fairy-lights. The lights in question are old and dubious both in taste and safety; but we've never had the heart to throw them away, secretly treasuring their strangeness and the memories associated with them. They're Rosebud to our Kane; Proust's Madeleine.

In the library next door, a sixth-former and a year 9 are talking earnestly about last week's university interviews; the older boy explaining to the younger what he was asked, and why he thought that the extract he had to discuss was a piece by Takemitsu. Knowing him, it probably was.

In the corridor, younger pupils are crowding excitedly around a notice-board, looking for their own faces in photographs of the concerts. There were almost 500 performers last weekend, it's not easy. Other pupils are in a practice room, trying to work out 9sus4. One thinks he knows – he doesn't – and vocally takes the lead.

Visiting teachers hurry by, not-quite-late for their break-time lessons, their need for coffee steamily satisfied. Floating in the air these fumes mingle with the pupils' excitement from last night – the bitter-sweet tang of a performance over, the next one still too far away, and freeze-dried coffee.

In the technology-room, another teacher is checking his presentation for the next lesson, about to bring together the strands of the term's teaching, practising one last time those things which have not quite yet been learnt by the pupils. It's the last segment of the new course we've built; not-quite new in every particular, but presenting things in a different and more-considered order, and with a new and very clean set of slides for each lesson. We're quite pleased with it, but know that there are a few things we will need to change before we put it away, ready for next year.

DOI: 10.4324/9781003112402-11

And so, as I inhale my own coffee, watch quietly, I think about all the things it means to be a music teacher. A portrait of master-teacher Pablo Casals should preside over the scene, but does not.

Is this, then, the best job in the world? The answer comes quickly, decisively, and truthfully: quite probably.

Acknowledgements

So many people have been part of this project, over so many years; it's impossible to mention them all. But a few people's particular contributions need to be acknowledged, the huge debt of gratitude I owe stated formally.

Geoff Barton, himself a remarkable teacher, was there at the very beginning, suggesting that a book might be the place for these ideas.

Mark Paine, Howard Griffin, Nick Heppel, Margaret Cookhorn, and Michelle Sanders – all far better teachers than I could ever be – contributed ideas, encouragement, and inspiration.

Keith Farr, Jason King, and Gill Sparrow taught me about the world of primary education, and so much more.

Liz Green and Debbie Lovatt helped to make the book stronger in structure and content.

Jurgita Dean and Tilly Clark kept me in order – an unenviable task.

The Instrumental Teachers of King Edward's School, for making the impossible possible most days, and for doing so with a smile constantly in place.

My own teachers, Mr. Young, Mr. Taylor, Mr. Longstaff, Martin Roscoe, Charles Mackerras, and Roger Norrington; Robert Pascall, who taught me about the writing and the thinking game; and my parents, for giving me the chance to become a musician and my first example of what a great teacher does.

Paul Griffiths for his example and the use of his archive.

And to the boys of King Edward's School and the girls of King Edward VI High School, for the unique education they continue to afford me.

My thanks to Molly Selby and Annamarie Kino at Routledge, for all their patience, expertise, and encouragement. Also to Meeta Singh and the team at KnowledgeWorks Global Ltd.

And to Louise, finally, to whom this book is dedicated, without whom nothing would be possible, always and forever.

Index

Index

Printed in Great Britain
by Amazon

21970150R00143